SPORT, SPACE AND THE CITY

SPORT, SPACE AND THE CITY

John Bale

London and New York

For F.T.B.

First published 1993
by Routledge
11 New Fetter Lane, London EC4P 4EE

Simultaneously published in the USA and Canada
by Routledge
a division of Routledge, Chapman and Hall Inc.
29 West 35th Street, New York, NY 10001

© 1993 John Bale

Typeset in 10/12pt September by Leaper & Gard, Bristol
Printed and bound in Great Britain by
Biddles Ltd, Guildford and King's Lynn

British Library Cataloguing in Publication Data
A catalogue reference for this book is available from the British Library

ISBN 0–415–08098–3

Library of Congress Cataloging in Publication Data
has been applied for

ISBN 0–415–08098–3

In the adult's world, play often has to yield to necessity. There is still time for play, but under restrained circumstances and with a sort of lid placed on the élan of imagination.

Yi-Fu Tuan, *Dominance and Affection*

The social spaces of distraction and display become as vital to urban culture as the spaces of working and living.

David Harvey, *Consciousness and the Urban Experience*

CONTENTS

CONTENTS

FIGURES

TABLES

ACKNOWLEDGEMENTS

I am glad to acknowledge the following who have made their work available for reproduction in this book: the editor of *Mappemonde* for Figure 2.5; Christian Bromberger for Figures 4.1 and 7.5; The Sports Council, The Lobb Partnership and YRM Anthony Hunt Associates for Figure 2.8; The Sports Council for Figure 3.1a; Applied Science Publications for Figure 3.1b; the editor of *When Saturday Comes* and Paul Johnson for Figure 3.3; Margaret Roberts for Figure 4.6; Shirespeed Ltd for Figure 4.7; The Atlanta Falcons for Figure 4.8; Roger Peabody for Figures 4.10 and 5.10b; the Sir Norman Chester Centre for Football Research for Figures 4.10b, 5.9 and 7.3; Rick Everitt, editor of *Voice of The Valley*, for Figure 4.12; Bert Moorhouse for Table 4.2; the editor of the *Illinois Business Review* for Table 4.3; Colin Mason for Figures 5.4 and 5.12; Michael Grayson and the University of London Library for Figure 5.8; Brian Goodey and the editor of *Arquitetura Urbanismo* for Figure 5.11; and the Balsam Corporation, USA and Ed. Milner for Figure 7.4. I have tried to trace all copyright holders and apologize in advance for any unintended omission or neglect. I will be happy to add the appropriate acknowledgement in any subsequent edition of this book.

I am also pleased to take this opportunity to thank several people who directly or indirectly contributed to the writing of this book. The stimulus for starting work on it came from a paper on 'Football and topophilia' which I presented at a colloquium on 'Football and its Publics' at the European University Institute in Florence in 1989. For the invitation to attend that meeting I must sincerely thank Pierre Lanfranchi who opened more intellectual, academic, social, gastronomic, and vacational doors than he could have possibly realized. I would like to thank Henning Eichberg, not only for reading and commenting on a version of the text, but for being a regular source of ideas over the last few years and for contributing greatly to the stimulating times I had at Gerlev and Fønsborg. I was also helped at an early stage of this project by the encouraging observations of Bert Moorhouse and Dick Holt and I am appreciative of the helpful comments on various versions of the text from Steve Redhead, Paul Nixon, Andrew Ward, and Colin Mason. That the names of the people mentioned above are notionally attached to almost half-a-dozen different scholarly 'disciplines' just goes to show how permeable the boundaries between academic subjects have thankfully become.

An unusual debt for a book of this kind must go to several undergraduate as well as postgraduate students from a number of universities who were generous in discussing their dissertations with me and subsequently allowing me to borrow freely from them. I must especially thank, therefore, David Humphrys, Richard Hill, Roger Peabody, Andrew Moncrieff, Eddie Lowe, Rich Callaway, Philip Eardley, and Steve Cooper. I must also thank Maralyn Beech and Andrew Lawrence of the Keele University Geography Department for their photographic and cartographic expertise. Last, but far from least, I would like to thank my wife Ruth for her help over the years and her tolerance of my enthusiasm not only for writing about sport and geography but also, very occasionally, watching live football while undertaking fieldwork in the cultural landscapes of Gresty Road, Vale Park and the Victoria Ground. In acknowledging the help of all the above I must also acknowledge that any errors of fact or judgement are my own.

John Bale, Keele
October 1991

1

INTRODUCTION
Sport, football and the city

North American newspapers rarely pay any attention to British football but on Sunday, 16 April 1989 readers of *The Dallas Morning News* (and, no doubt, many other American papers) opened their 28-page sports section to discover a one and a half page report of a match played the previous day in far-away England. The result of the match was not important. The headlines told a story which was transmitted all over the world from the northern city of Sheffield: *'England's bloody shame: overzealous soccer fans, old stadiums a tragic mix'*. It was, of course, a report of the Hillsborough disaster at which ninety-five spectators died and which is widely regarded as Britain's worst-ever sports disaster. Yet Hillsborough was perceived by many as one of Britain's best football grounds on virtually every criterion which could be used to define the quality of such a facility. A little over a year later during the televising of the 1990 World Cup, British viewers were exposed to the splendours of some of the grand Italian stadiums. In contrast to the best Britain could offer, the San Siro Stadium in Milan and the Stadio Olympico in Rome seemed part of another sporting culture. The same reaction is likely to be felt in 1994 when the World Cup is hosted by the USA in spectacular arenas like the Los Angeles Coliseum or even those of top-flight college football teams, facilities already viewed in British living rooms during transmissions of gridiron football games. The same televiewers may have pondered the implications of the report of Lord Justice Taylor, commissioned by central government following the Hillsborough tragedy (Taylor 1990). From the despair of Hillsborough to the joy of *Mondiale '90*; it would be difficult to conceive of a greater clash of images.

The disaster at Sheffield, preceded by those at Bradford and Heysel, placed sport on new journalistic and political agendas. Sport was no longer simply the subject of the sports pages; it was no longer the concern of just the Minister for Sport. Professional sport had always been a serious business but it now became viewed, literally, as a matter of life and death.

This book is about British football ('soccer') and the urban milieux in which it is found. Hillsborough brought the state of the British football environment to the attention of the world while the World Cup brought the state of the world football environment to the attention of the nation. For many, the sport remains, as Pelé described it, *The Beautiful Game*; it is also, as James Walvin termed it, *The People's Game*, but the 1990s sees the British football industry in a state of disarray. It is not only the decaying fabric of the sport's facilities which causes concern; its basic organization is frequently questioned. On the one hand the Liverpools and Arsenals of this world achieve elite status in a premier league, and a Euro-League is widely regarded as an inevitable outcome of the next few years. On the other hand the minnows of the Fourth Division struggle for survival in an increasingly cut-throat world. The rich clubs get richer and the poor get poorer, seemingly locked in respective spirals of success and failure, so that the First Division of the Football League has, during the course of this century, increasingly assumed a 'southern' look with many of the traditional clubs in the northern hotbeds of the sport having either slipped into the minor divisions or out of the League all together (Bale 1989a: 97–101).

These football sites are, in many ways, marginal places – not only often at the geographical and economic margins of the country but also at the margins of the cultural system, frequently in stigmatized or derogatory places where a 'disdained social activity' undertaken by participants, a sizeable proportion of whom are labelled as 'deviant', occurs in shabby stadiums on a bi-weekly basis. Football is an element of 'low culture', a rugged leisure pursuit in contrast to the high culture (for example, opera and ballet) of the privileged (Shields 1991: 3, 230–1). As a result of their economic marginality clubs are talking more and more about ground sharing and relocation, usually meaning suburbanization in synthetic stadium complexes. The Taylor Report, commissioned by the Thatcher government, proposed all-seater stadiums for the football environments of the future (Taylor 1990). The sport faces several decades of change, the nature of which is not yet clear.

The focal points of the UK football industry are the ninety-three Football League and thirty-eight Scottish League stadiums, or grounds as they are more frequently called in Britain. The word 'park' is sometimes used by managers and TV commentators as a nostalgic euphemism for what may, in the future (and in other countries), be a large plastic carpet. Although barely mentioned by the chronicler of English architecture Nikolaus Pevsner in his monumental work *The Buildings of England*, and despite the many criticisms made of them, these structures can be truly called the folk cathedrals of modern Britain. It is in the stadium that modern urban rituals take place; it is the floodlights of the stadium, not the spire of the cathedral, that more often than not act as urban landmarks and points of reference; and as I shall show, more than one sociologist has seen in the football stadium and its rituals many of the characteristics of religion.

The football pitch also seems to assume a peculiar significance as an almost universal referent for a unit of size. The American observer of the urban scene, Grady Clay, has shrewdly noted how it is the football pitch which provides 'a universal yardstick for describing complex environments', a 'unit of psycho-geographic size and shape' (Clay 1988). When I want to describe how large a particular site is, I'll probably use the football pitch as my spatial parameter. I do not draw such a spatial unit from boxing, badminton or bowls; I have internalized it from the game of football.

The sport is obviously important. Despite the many changes that have taken place in football it remains the most popular participant sport in the world. In countries like the USA, which had traditionally been felt to have filled all its available 'sports space' (Markovits 1988), the sport is growing in popularity and there are now more college soccer teams than in gridiron football. Spectator visits in 1989/90 totalled over 19 million in England and Wales and over 4 million in Scotland, and despite the dramatic post-war decline in attendance (in 1948/9 attendances were more than twice the current figure) it remains far and away the nation's most popular spectator sport.

Recent years have witnessed a proliferation of serious books on football (the result, no doubt, of the sport's many 'problems') to complement the ubiquitous reminiscences, or the invariably ghosted autobiographies, of the stars. In Britain, such so-called 'serious' writing has been undertaken mainly by historians such as James Walvin (1975, 1986), Tony Mason (1980), Bill Murray (1984), Wray Vamplew (1989), and Richard Holt (1989), but also by economists such as Peter Bird (1982) and Peter Sloane (1980) and, perhaps most notably, by sociologists spearheaded by Eric Dunning and his associates at Leicester University (see Dunning *et al.* 1989, Williams *et al.* 1989c, Murphy *et al.* 1990, and Williams and Wagg 1991). Ian Taylor (1971a, 1971b, 1990), Bert Moorhouse (1984), John Clarke (1978) and Steve Wagg (1984) have also made noteworthy sociological contributions. For social scientists –

and there have been more than those named above[1] – the catalyst for much of their work has been the widely reported (and even more widely perceived) 'football hooligan problem'. More recently the literature on ground safety has been fuelled by the aforementioned tragedies at Bradford, Heysel and Hillsborough.[2] Various aspects of the football environment – in its broadest sense – have also become increasingly viewed by undergraduate and postgraduate students as legitimate subjects for dissertations and research and I have used material from such sources in parts of this book.

It is, perhaps, surprising that American academics have also been attracted to the game which Britain gave to the world. The two most graphic examples, apart from Janet Lever's work on football in Brazil (Lever 1983), are those of Stephen Tischler (1981) and Charles Korr (1986) but Allen Guttmann, a polymath scholar who has reviewed the broad field of sports studies in highly readable form, is also attracted to the peculiarities of British football.[3] On mainland Europe the sport has also attracted the interest of scholars from a variety of disciplines. German scholars such as Henning Eichberg, the French anthropologist Christian Bromberger, and Danish educationalist Ove Korsgaard have much to say that is relevant to the British football scene.[4] I name these three simply because I have found their studies to be of immediate relevance to my own; much more work published in French, Italian and German remains to be explored and brought to the attention of students of sport in the English-speaking world.

In addition to the writings of academic outsiders, the 1980s saw the publication of a rich literature providing the 'insider's' view of the game. Alongside the magisterial studies of Europe's football grounds by journalist Simon Inglis (1987, 1990), there is now a vast literature spawned by the somewhat anarchic football fanzine movement. Given the wide variety of formats assumed by this family of publications, it is not yet proven that fanzines represent the authentic voice of the typical fan or whether they are merely outlets for frustrated middle-class amateur journalists who happen to love football; but they undoubtedly represent the best available source of insiders' feelings and views. A definitive history and interpretation of the genre has yet to be written and the total number of such fanzines published in Britain is uncertain, partly because many of these publications are both fugitive and ephemeral; but it certainly exceeds 300 and attracts a readership estimated at over one million.[5] In this book I include both the 'outsider-academic' and 'insider-fan' as sources of information, adding my own original findings and interpretations.

4

But what else is there to be said about the national sport? A peculiar and paradoxical omission from the literature on the state of Britain's most popular sport – and, indeed, sport in general – is one which adopts a more explicitly *geographical* perspective.[6] The omission is peculiar and paradoxical because geography, like sports, involves the analysis of space and place. Although I do not want to labour the distinctive contribution of any single 'discipline', I believe that a rather more geographical approach adds to our knowledge, not just of British football but of what it means to people, hence aiding an interpretation of the problems the sport will face during its immediate future. In this book, therefore, I try to go beyond the descriptions of Britain's football grounds, so magnificently achieved by Inglis, and I certainly do not wish to add to the hypotheses about, and descriptions of, football hooliganism. Instead, I focus on two basic themes: first, what the stadium as a focus for football *means* to different groups in the city and, second, the implications of such meanings for the future shape of the British game. These two themes require an interpretation of the sites (and sights) of British football grounds, their changing forms of spatial organization, their impact – both positive and negative – on the urban environment and the pressures which exist to force them to new locations, often beyond the cities which they have traditionally represented. I recognize that the changes taking place in football are rationalistic and modernist tendencies which have been felt in many areas of culture apart from sports.

Although this book is about football in Britain, I have chosen to include material from overseas where it helps both to inform, and provide a contrast with, the British situation. Far more studies of the impact of sport on the city, for example, have emerged from the USA than from Europe. Likewise, the conceptual bases of much of the book's contents originate from the ideas of a number of social and cultural geographers based in North America who have studied the affection which people have for particular places and environments, the growing rationalization of the cultural landscape, the negative impacts of various facilities on urban residents, and the local activism of interest groups who perceive their quality of life to be threatened. These are, I suppose, best described as 'humanist' and 'welfare-liberal' philosophies of human geography, though I do also allude to the radical critique. I do not apologize for a plurality of approaches.

Cultural-geographical writings barely mention sports but the ideas and concepts which have emerged from welfare, humanistic and radical geography find ready application in, and relevance to, the increasingly rationalized landscapes of sport. So too do the ideas of thinkers from the broader field of cultural studies. As part of his avoidance of 'totalizing' concepts or 'grand theory' in cultural studies Michel Foucault noted that 'it may be wise not to take as a whole the rationalization of society or of culture, but to analyse such a process in several fields, each with reference to a fundamental experience' (Foucault 1982). This book is certainly concerned with the study of the rationalization of *one* field of popular culture, that of British *professional* football (not, I stress, football *per se*), its landscapes, and the experiences of various groups involved in it, and though there are parallels in North American and other European sports I would not want to universalize from the ideas and examples in the pages which follow.

This book is essentially made up of three parts. One deals with football at the scale of intra-stadium space, another with intra-urban space, and the third with the sport's locational dynamic. The chapter which follows is concerned with the changes which have occurred in the shape and layout of the spaces in which football has been played during the past few hundred years, in the course of the sport's transition from a rough and ready folk-game to its present status as part of the entertainment industry. I try to show how developments – if developments they be – in the spatial organization of the stadium reflect broader tendencies towards confinement, control, surveillance and territorialization in society at large. In Chapter 3, however, I go on to show how the tendency towards 'sameness', or 'placelessness' in stadium design can result in unexpected and paradoxical reactions from the very people for whom 'progress' and 'safety' are provided.

At its pinnacle football extends beyond the ritual and is undoubtedly a form of spectacle – indeed, a form of 'heroic consumption' (Ley and Olds 1988) – and it could be argued that even at more modest levels the very existence of spectators encourages the spectacular (Stone 1971). Although not as spectacular as the Olympic Games, it is difficult to deny that the World Cup, the FA Cup Final, and even some local derbies, possess the qualities which differentiate spectacle from ritual, that is 'the sheer scale and intensity of it all mock the puny efforts of the television camera to capture it in two dimensional images' (MacAloon 1984). But the ritual or spectacle is one which is perceived differently by various groups in society. Some view it with love and others with hate, hence its fractured and contested character. In Chapter 4, therefore, I explore what the stadium means to some people for whom football assumes an almost religious significance. I illustrate how the stadium can not only generate a love of place, a sense of place-loyalty, place-bonding and other kinds of localism, but also how some stadiums have become what amount to sacred places, worthy, perhaps, of future protection and preservation like other revered monuments and buildings of yesteryear. In addition to those fans who gain non-monetary benefits from football there are also those for whom the game provides revenue and income and these are also considered in this chapter. When sources of income or affection are threatened, a relatively passive attitude towards the stadium can become converted into one of political activism which in the context of the British football industry has proved remarkably successful against the forces for change. Examples of such active involvement in defending a much-loved place are included in Chapter 4.

Chapter 5 is concerned with the more negative aspects of football in the urban environment. It is the crowds, the noise, the congestion and the hooliganism which form the stereotypical picture of the urban football environment. I want to show that this stereotype is only partially accurate and that the general public has an exaggerated view of what can be, nevertheless, a very real problem for the people who live in proximity to football grounds. Whereas in Chapter 4 I describe examples of activism in support of a much-loved stadium, in this chapter I show how passive prejudice against football can likewise be converted into activism when the sport's spillovers are perceived as likely to create intolerable annoyance.

Whereas the early chapters are concerned with the stadium itself as an increasingly rationalized landscape, later ones focus on the quest to establish stadiums in more rational locations. The much-debated question of ground relocation forms a major part of Chapter 6. A large number of moves have already taken place in the British game, most of them during the late nineteenth century. I explore the nature of, and motives behind, some of these moves and compare them with the kinds of forces which are today trying to push soccer to the suburbs. I conclude that the future of British football will not lie in the post-Hillsborough prescriptions produced by applying the logic of economic rationality but in the outcomes of *contested* scenarios between the forces of mass cultural conservatism who wish to see football remain in its long-cherished locations and those of advocates of modernist (or, perhaps, post-modernist) football in peri-urban leisure complexes. But I again emphasize the significance of human agency and 'community' in the confrontation with capital in all this.

The tendencies towards modernization and rationalization which are currently appearing in the British football landscape have probably been pushed furthest in North America and, to a lesser extent, in parts of mainland Europe. Indeed, the US model of professional team sports is one to which some people believe the UK should aspire. Throughout the book, therefore, I refer to the American experience of stadium development and franchise location and also comment on such changes in several European countries, where appropriate. The book concludes with some interpretations of sport as carceral space and the prospects and alternative scenarios for British football.

In most of the chapters which follow I try to include the views of football's 'insiders'. Although I do attend games myself and watch far more football on television than is good for me, I cannot call myself a hard-core fan; I cannot even say that football is my favourite sport. But seasons of standing on the terraces at Ninian Park several decades ago have not dampened my fascination for football. As a relative 'outsider', therefore, I have tended to rely on discussions with true fans for some of my information, while also using the aforementioned fanzines as another source of data and information in addition to the more conventional sources.

To the best of my ability I have tried to take a broad approach to my subject and not be too constrained by the bounds of any single discipline. As this book is, however, concerned with environment, landscape and location, I suppose it is a modest contribution to the geography of sport;[7] but to confine myself to disciplinary boundaries would produce as incomplete a picture as if a game of football was viewed simply as twenty-two people kicking a ball around a field.

2

THE CHANGING SHAPE OF THE STADIUM

It is in the *football* stadium, more, I would argue, than in other sports grounds, that the largest crowds are most often found in the modern city. Other crowd events such as rock concerts, the Olympic Games, coronations, royal weddings, papal visits or international fairs and conventions are irregular occurrences. Football matches, because of their regular and serialized nature, are also different from pre-twentieth-century crowd-generating events which have been 'seen by historians . . . as isolated and melodramatic interventions in urban life' (Harrison 1988). Spectator sports are central features of modern urban society and it is the stadium which is the prime twentieth-century container of the urban crowd.

In this chapter I want to describe the ways in which the 'containers' in which football is played have gradually changed over time and have come to increasingly reflect broader aspects of modern society. My basic theme is that the confined spaces of football are the manifestations of modernizing and rationalistic trends which have been taking place since the seventeenth century, trends which have aimed to improve and make more efficient the comfort, control and discipline of crowds. An awareness of the changes which have occurred in the milieu of football serves to contextualize the strength of feeling which football fans have towards 'their' home ground and hence towards the potential relocation of stadiums, subjects considered in more detail in later chapters. The changes in the stadium also show how human beings demonstrate their own preferences, and convert such preferences into activism.

Most football which is played today takes place outside the confines of the stadium on sportsgrounds and playing fields up and down the country. But such games do not take place in unconfined spaces; they occur within prescribed spatial parameters or legalized territories,[1] the extent of which is laid down by authorities or bureaucracies who write

9

and administer the rule books. In the case of Association Football the laws of the game state that the playing area shall be at least 100 but not more than 130 yards long and at least 50 and no more than 100 yards wide. The spaces on which inter-village games are played are therefore essentially the same as the spaces within which the games of the World Cup take place. It is in the surrounding ensemble of landscape elements – the stands, terraces, advertising hoardings, floodlights, etc. – that the environmental differences between the elite and the grass-roots game are found (Raitz 1987, 1988).

It is also in this ensemble that the most interesting, exciting or spectacular aspects of the football event might be found. There is often nothing particularly spectacular about a defensively played-out 0–0 draw, or even a victory which has been the outcome of an untidy, unskilful or scrappy game. The scenes within the ground, the crowds and their banners, the singing and the chanting, played out against the backdrop of the stadium or its surrounding cityscape really are often the most spectacular parts of the event and the significance of the changing nature of this ensemble will form the basis of this chapter.

At one time, however, all football was played outside stadiums and before the mid-nineteenth century (generally) lacked any standardized spatial limits. This is not to say that no sport-like activities had ever possessed demarcated or confined sites. Far from it; it has been suggested by Henning Eichberg that ancient stone labyrinths could have been used for sport-like activities (Eichberg 1989a), while the stadiums of Roman times, evidenced in the British landscape at Caerleon and Chester, for example, almost certainly housed such events as well as providing sites for military training.

The evolution of the sports landscape has hardly been linear and progressive and a cycle of 'green waves' and 'stages of immurement' has taken place in the development of sports. In the sixteenth century a number of courtly (both in a social and spatial sense) games like tennis, equestrianism and fencing were practised, isolated from commoners, behind the walls of stately homes (Eichberg 1982, 1986). Later, body cultural activities moved out of doors. The masses most frequently engaged in sport-like activities in the open air and in unconfined spaces but also took part in some events which were carried out in specially constructed sites and enclosed spaces, the cockpit being the most obvious example. Football possesses both 'open' and 'closed' components in its overall environment and Eichberg (1990a) has suggested that its success as a popular sport at the turn of the century can be attributed in part to its open green field on the one hand and its enclosure on the other which permitted the different social classes, each with their own spatial preferences, to feel at home.

Football took less than 100 years to change from a folk-game, played in public spaces used for a large number of other activities, to an industry confined to specialized private sites and played at specified times. Broadly speaking, the changing football environment can be described by fleshing-out a four-stage model shown as Figure 2.1. The model is what sociologists call an 'ideal-type'; that is, it is not meant to exactly represent four distinct phases of stadium development but four hypothetical norms – a simplification of the real world but nevertheless an aid to understanding it. It is possible that the model could be applied to football in both Europe and the Americas and, indeed, to other sports. Each stage of the model, which in reality overlapped with one another, is a reflection of not just developments in sports but of changes in the broader society within which sports and games are firmly embedded.

In elaborating on Figure 2.1 two dimensions will be stressed. The first is that the changing shape of the arena, in little more than a century, has shifted from open space (stages 1 and 2) to enclosed-commodified (stage 3) and technological space (stage 4). The second dimension is the extent of spatial confinement of participants, principally the spectators. Whereas in stage 1 there is really very little spatial distinction between players and spectators, by stage 4 we have arrived at what Michel Foucault called an 'enclosed segmented space . . . in which the individuals are inserted in a fixed place' (Foucault 1979).[2] Indeed, in interpreting the stadium's evolution I am struck by the analogies with Foucault's description of the history of the prison. In *Discipline and Punish* Foucault describes the transformation of punishment from an 'event' which occurred in public spaces where spectators were integral to the activity, to the apparatus of the prison where punishment is spatially confined and ultimately subjected to sophisticated forms of surveillance. These situations are analogous to the stages shown in Figure 2.1. Central to my analogy – and I stress that it is an analogy, not an homology – is the power relationship between 'professionals' (that is, prison authorities/football authorities) and their 'clients' (prisoners/football supporters) and I will return to this analogy during the course of this book.

FOLK-GAME FOOTBALL

My four-stage model of the evolution of the modern football stadium starts with the antecedents of what is today the world's most popular

STAGES	ENVIRONMENT
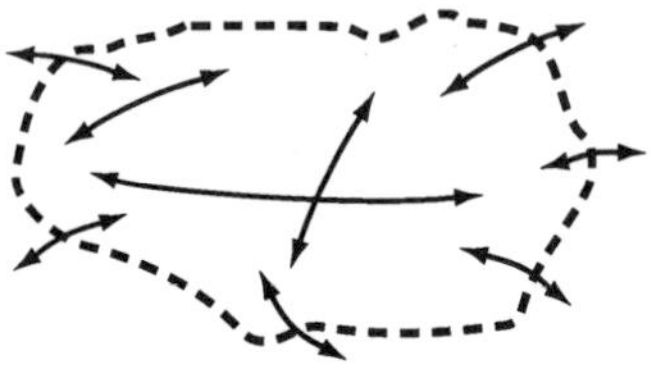	PERMEABLE BOUNDARIES WEAK RULES OF EXCLUSION No spatial limits; uneven terrain; spatial interaction between 'players' and 'spectators'; diversified land use.
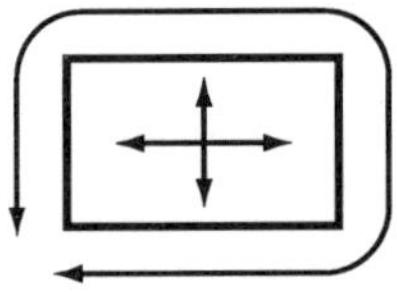	ENCLOSURE Limits of pitch defined; players segregated from spectators.
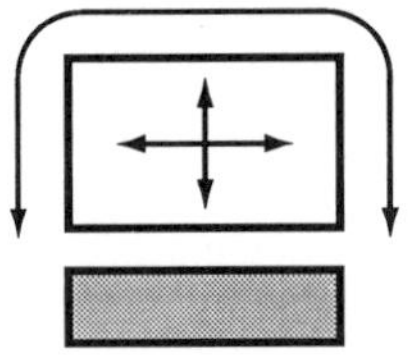	PARTITIONING Embankments, terraces,grandstands; payment for entry; segregation of spectators by social class; start of segregation within crowd; specialized land use.
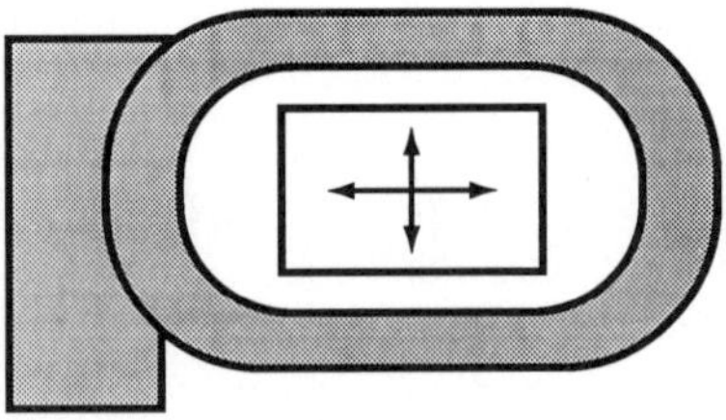	SURVEILLANCE Enclosed ground; synthetic pitch and concrete bowl; TV replay screen; total segregation within crowd; panopticism; diversified land use. RULES OF EXCLUSION STRONG IMPERMEABLE BOUNDARIES

Figure 2.1 A four-stage model of the evolution of the modern stadium. Lines refer to possible freedoms of movement of participants (that is, players and spectators)

sport. Modern sports, with their distinctive characteristics of bureau-
cratic organization (that is, governing bodies), quantification, precision,
record keeping (look at any copy of *Rothman's Football Yearbook* and
other such statistical compendiums to see what I mean), and competition (for example, Leagues, Cup competitions) (Guttmann 1979)[3] are
only one form of a large number of activities which Scandinavian sports
scientists call 'body culture' or 'movement culture' (Eichberg 1989b, see
also Korsgaard 1989), forms of which have been practised from time
immemorial. Movement cultures may be play-like, dance-like or sport-
like; many are based on cultural norms other than our own, often more
egalitarian and co-operative and less individualistic and competitive
than the modern sports played in Britain, other European countries and
the Americas; some are choreographed while others are more serendipi-
tous. A family of such movement-cultures has been called the folk-game
family, of which pre-modern football was a member.

Football in medieval and pre-modern Europe was much more a form
of play and carnival than of seriousness and sport. Its fun-like character
was reflected in the landscapes in which it was played. No specialized
sites existed for football; it was played, not simply *in* places usually used
for other activities, but also *while* other activities were going on. The
sixteenth- and seventeenth-century marketplace and street, for example,
were environments not simply for transportation and movement but
also for a wide range of other activities, including play. Hogarth's *Night*
showed the street as an untidy place, work and play being spatially
intertwined. The street was a meeting place and a market place, a place
for refuse and for refuge, a place for washing and eating; it was also a
place for entertainment and playing, with street football being one of
the things that was played.

Folk-football was also played on commons and fields. The games
were frequently played between villages and towns – not simply in the
sense that villages and towns competed against each other but also,
literally, *between* each other – in a spatial sense. The first team to get
the ball from one village to another was often the winner. There were no
fixed bounds on the territory in which the game was played, no spatial
separation existed between players and spectators and spatial interaction between them was common. Indeed, it was often difficult to tell
who was playing and who was spectating; it was certainly corporal
recreation. As with the medieval carnival, there was a tendency for folk
football (which, along with other games, often featured at street carnivals and festivals) to 'not acknowledge any distinction between actors
and spectators' (Bakhtin 1968: 5–8). Furthermore, players 'represented'

their teams on the basis of ascription, not achievement; to be a member of a place was enough to represent it (Dunning and Sheard 1979: Ch. 1).

The bifurcation between players and spectators appears to have commenced during the sixteenth century though inevitably there were antecedents in some parts of Europe (Guttmann 1979)[4] while, as I show later, a lack of strict demarcation between players and spectators continued well into the nineteenth century in other areas. Because there were no standard rules the precise nature of football varied from place to place. In some places it was street football in towns; in rural areas it was played on meadows and commons, the game often continuing through rivers and streams. In some places youngsters watched their elders; in others everybody seemed to take part. While laughter and fun were central to the carnivalistic and Rabelaisian folk-games of medieval Europe they were also rough-and-tumble affairs with relatively high levels of violence and injuries; such games live on in 'museumized' form in the Shrove Tuesday game at Ashbourne and in Florentine *calcio* in the Piazza Santa Croce (see Figure 2.2).

Figure 2.2 The Piazza Santa Croce in Florence, home of *calcio* and a typical urban millieu of pre-modern street football. The game is now performed annually in the piazza in museumized form

THE CODIFICATION OF FOOTBALL

During the late eighteenth and nineteenth centuries society at large experienced a growing rationalization and geographic confinement, such space-consciousness accompanying a growing time-consciousness among the population, associated with the rise of capitalism. An increasing division of labour was accompanied by an increasing division of space and of time. There was a time for work and a time for play; there were also to be specific places where various activities, previously found in streets and on commons, could now be undertaken in the emerging 'carceral city'.

The codification and resulting confinement of football can, therefore, be interpreted as part of a broader socio-economic tendency towards territoriality. I interpret this word, not in the sense employed by ethologist Konrad Lorenz (1967) (and later, in a football context by Desmond Morris (1981)) – that is, an almost instinctive defence of territory – but in the sense used by American geographer Robert David Sack who views territoriality as the *control* of space or territory, seeing it as 'a primary geographical expression of social power' (Sack 1986: 5)[5] acting as a physical restraint on movement and spatial organization. He defines territoriality as 'the attempt by an individual or group to affect, influence, or control people, phenomena, and relationships, by delimiting and asserting control over a geographic area' (Sack 1986). An act of territoriality means that people have been removed from, or possess restricted access to, one kind of place and that specially prescribed spaces have been provided for particular activities. What is more, territoriality creates the idea of a space to be filled and emptied at particular times.

Let me now relate this concept of territoriality to the game of football. The growth of commerce from the seventeenth century onwards led to growing restrictions on public access to spaces like commons, streets and squares. The street, as I noted earlier, was, in pre-modern times, a place to play as well as work, a place of entertainment as much as travel. The appropriation of the street and square and the enclosure of the commons reflected the increased territorial partitioning which could produce, in turn, increased specialization and division of labour of activities. It should be added that it could also provide improved surveillance. Foucault (1967) called the seventeenth century the start of 'the great confinement', but it was most evident in the world of sport two centuries later.

By the mid-nineteenth century pressure to play inter-regional rather

15

than simply local, games of football led to pressures to impose a standardized set of rules on the game. Such attempts dated from 1815 when Eton College, an elite private school, formulated the earliest known set of rules. In the decades which followed, other such schools followed suit. It appears that these rules only had local applicability and it was not until 1863 when the Football Association was formed in London by upper-class Englishmen that association football as we know it was formally started. Strictly speaking, a unified set of rules did not emerge since Rugby was to go its own way.

The rules of sports invariably include the spatial limits within which they can be played. It is this essential spatiality which serves to distinguish sport from play or recreation, neither of which *require* specialized, geographically delimited areas. Geographer Philip Wagner (1981) has elaborated on this theme in these words:

> What is commonly called 'sport' ... stands out clearly from all other recreational activity, and even from work, by virtue of an essentially geographic attribute, its time–space specificity. It likewise is distinguished by the eminently spatial formulation of its drama.[6]

In the case of football, successive refinements to the first set of rules were added towards the end of the nineteenth century which were to increasingly confine the spatial extent of play. In 1875 the cross bar was added to the two goal posts, defining the vertical extent of the goal. But before touchlines were introduced, spectators sometimes encroached on to the pitch to the extent that only about 30 metres of playing space was left. As a result, players mingled with spectators for the ball, often dodging and fighting with those who had come to watch (Marples 1954: 163). Clearly, the inexact division of space between the players and the spectators was a residual of the folk-game tradition and the crucial rule which was to bring this to an end was enacted in 1882 when the touchline, formally demarcating the players' territory from that of the audience, was introduced. Significantly, the boundary line in cricket was part of the MCC's revised code of laws two years later and the dead-ball line in rugby was introduced in 1891 (Bale 1988).[7] Sports places were becoming composed of straight lines rather than of irregular shapes as a geometric tradition (a sporting analogue of the landscape garden, perhaps) was enforced (Eichberg 1985, 1993).

The demands for rule-boundedness coincided with the need for special sites for the game as the streets and commons were appropriated for vehicles and farming respectively. The appropriation and enclosure of the commons from the eighteenth century onwards obviously had an effect on the countryfolk's sports as well as on their livelihoods. But this is not to say that resistance to the confinement of football space was totally abortive. It has been recorded that in 1768, for example, a football riot was associated with the successful defiance of an attempt to ban football during the enclosure of Holland Fen in Lincolnshire, such games also being popular ways of affirming traditional communal rights on enclosed land with riots often accompanying the symbolic game (Holmes 1985: 171). Likewise, successful actions were taken to prevent bans on street football where opposition to the game resulted from its inconvenience in public thoroughfares and the negative effect it had on business. Resistance was particularly successful in Ashbourne where nineteenth-century attempts to clear it from the street were unsuccessful (Malcolmson 1979). Generally, however, the forces of law and order prevailed and although informal street football continued into the 1940s it all but disappeared with the rapid growth in car ownership and the triumph of autopolis in the 1950s and 1960s.

The kinds of places at which football was being played in the late nineteenth century varied considerably. Often games were on open ground behind public houses; games were also played on the municipal recreation grounds which were springing up in the growing urban areas of Victorian England. But the football stadium as a specialized territory was only to emerge with the commodification of football, the subject to which I now turn.

FOOTBALL AS A COMMODITY: FOOTBALL ENCLOSED

Henri Lefebvre has argued that a major characteristic of the development of capitalism was the increased commodification of space – the need to make space pay its way[8] – and football was no exception in this respect. The game played in open space with a chalk line demarcating the playing area on land normally used for other activities became, at a certain level of skill and entertainment, attractive enough for someone, somewhere, to charge admission to watch the game. Football became 'paying consumption rather than participating recreation and could be more easily confined to particular locations and precise time slots' (Thrift 1981: 56). The moment spectating became an integral part of the activity, football moved closer to popular theatre and spectacle, away from play and towards display,[9] with spectators increasingly becoming a necessary part of the action.

Football became a commodity and football grounds became spaces, not simply where football could be played but which could be filled, emptied, and partitioned. As Allen Guttmann has noted, 'one facet of specialization was the separation of roles that put increasingly skillful players on the field and increasingly unpracticed spectators on the side-lines' (Guttmann 1988: 83). In this sense, football (and other sports) simply reflected the processes of economic, social, and spatial specialization which were taking place in society at large. Football places (that is, pitches) were emerging just as transport arteries (roads) were being given over to traffic rather than to the earlier, more varied activities. In the city land-use zones were developing around an incipient Garden City movement and the separation of spaces was likewise occurring in the home, the factory, the school, the hospital, and the prison.

The selling of a game of football to a paying public begs the question of what was being paid for. 'Mere entertainment' might be one way of looking at it but Alain Ehrenberg (1980: 46) has suggested that the stadium 'was a temple of hygiene symbolizing the vigour of the people'. Implicit in such a comment is that the stadium was performing an edu-cational role – a school for the people – providing a physical-educative function including the inculcation of the ideal of fair play and the example of sporting role models. An educational role for the stadium was certainly one which would have been welcomed by Pierre de Coubertin, founder of the modern Olympics. For him the 'ideal specta-tor at a sports event is a resting sportsman who is interrupting his own exercise to follow the movements of a comrade more skilled or better trained than himself' (quoted in Wimmer 1975: 215). But it did not take long for the sport to become more analogous to the circus than to the schoolroom.

I have been unable to trace the first recorded payment made to obtain entry to a football match. James Walvin records that Aston Villa took gate money in 1874, their 'takings' being 5s. 2d. (Walvin 1975). In order to restrict entry to matches, the pitches (the touchline had yet to be introduced) would have had to be initially roped and subsequently fenced off from neighbouring land, with specified points of entry. Tony Mason (1980), in his superb history of football's early years, records that in 1879 clubs were charging between 2d. and 6d. for admission and even in 1888 games could still be seen for this kind of entry fee though cup ties and internationals cost a shilling or more.

From the 1880s a further stage of spatial separation in football was introduced. With simply a roped or fenced off field there was nothing to prevent the mixing of social classes. With the development of grand-

18

stands, preceded by pavilions, social segregation based on differential payment of entry money could be enforced. Cricket had started charging for entry to matches as early as 1744 (Bale 1988) and cricket clubs often formed football clubs or rented their pavilions and fields to outside clubs. Those which could afford to do so now obtained a modest form of protection against the winter elements by paying to watch from a pavilion. So that people could obtain a better view of the game, sloping banks of earth, sometimes made up of rubbish, were constructed around grounds. Many grounds, sponsored by companies, required space for entertaining and comfort, and grandstands were built halfway along the touchline, invariably on the western side of the ground to avoid the glare of late afternoon autumnal and winter sunshine. The modern football stadium was beginning to take shape.

Improved facilities attracted growing crowds and growing crowds needed improved facilities. With the enclosure of open spaces and the improved policing of cities, the football ground became the main container of crowds. Tony Mason (1980) notes that from the late 1870s attendances at a sample of forty-six football matches ranged from 700 to 20,000. Crowds in excess of 10,000 grew rapidly in the 1880s; whereas only ten such attendance figures existed for the years 1878–81, the respective number for 1882–5 was thirty. In the 1890s the crowds were larger, the Sheffield Wednesday v. Sheffield United derby of 1896 attracting 30,000 (Mason 1980). Whereas the average size of First Division gates for the season 1888/9 was 4,600, Wray Vamplew (1989) records that for 1913/14 it had risen to 23,100, while the average crowd for the FA Cup Final for the period 1905–14 was 79,300. Photographs of the crowds at some of the turn of the century games often show vast banks of cloth-capped spectators without the slightest sign of protection from the elements.

Simon Inglis, in his epic study of the football grounds of Britain, shows how the landscape of the football ground was changing in the early years of the twentieth century. The architectural genius of Scotsman Archibald Leitch (1866–1939) was evident in a number of grounds such as Ibrox, Hampden, Stamford Bridge, Villa Park and Old Trafford (to name a few) where his impressive grandstands were erected (Inglis 1987). Perhaps his major contributions were the full-length, two-tier (or double-decker) stands of the inter-war period, the 'familiar white balcony, criss-crossed with steel framing' being typical of his style (Inglis 1987). Grandstands obviously made viewing more comfortable but by adopting such structures clubs also aimed to increase revenue. In 1906 representatives of the Birmingham club claimed that a new stand would raise income by £3,000 per year (Vamplew 1989).

The 1920s and 1930s were the 'golden age' of British football and, as I shall show in Chapter 6, this was a period of relative locational stability in the geography of the British football stadium and clubs appeared settled in their existing sites. As a result, the landscapes of their stadiums changed incrementally and willy-nilly. With additional stands and terraces, stadiums became investments, not to be left lightly for pastures new. Nicholas Fishwick, in his work on football in the inter-war period, records how average First Division gates had risen to over 25,000 for 1927/8, over 30,500 for 1938/9, and over 40,000 for 1949/50 (Fishwick 1989: 49). In the famous 1923 FA Cup Final at the brand new Wembley Stadium, it has been estimated that 200,000 were inside the stadium, though how many actually saw the game is uncertain.

By the late 1920s the English football ground (rarely actually called a stadium) seemed to be developing differently from its counterpart in other parts of Europe where it was often designed as a multi-sport facility with running track and adjacent tennis courts and gymnasiums. British grounds were mainly private facilities, often surrounded by terraced houses, whereas in Germany and elsewhere in Europe the football ground was emerging as part of a municipally-owned sports complex of complementary land uses. The German observer of British sport, Rudolf Kircher, noted there was nothing in England (Wembley excepted) that could match the magnificence of the stadium at Frankfurt which was to be superseded in the 1930s by the technical wonder of the Berlin Olympic Stadium (see Figure 2.3). Such continental facilities were designed as part of an urban sports zone for use by all sports participants, not simply footballers and football spectators. By the mid-1930s many cities and towns in Western Europe possessed their 'sports parks' but Kircher believed that 'it has never occurred to the English mind that the state, town council or anyone else, could provide them with a sports ground offering everything their hearts desired, from swimming bath to football' (Kircher 1928). This was not to deny the excellence of some of the professional football grounds (such as Highbury or Villa Park), but the absence of any integration of the grounds into broader complexes resulted, thought Kircher, from the fact that 'the mass of Englishmen [sic] are modest in their demands' (Kircher 1928). But football, with its dominantly blue-collar clientele, would have nested rather incongruously with the tennis club set from the suburbs and the social heterogeneity of British sport was therefore reflected in its geographical arrangement in the city. This is not to say that the enclosure and artificialization of the sports environment was not opposed by some groups

Figure 2.3 The Berlin Olympic Stadium, completed in 1936, would still be capable of hosting a modern Olympic Games. Its rather brutal bowl, originally planned to hold 250,000 as part of Nazi megalomania, is today the home of Hertha Berlin FC. Note the substantial open space around the ground

in Germany at the time. As late as 1933 those who defended a form of romantic nationalism were critics of the rational, competitive, quantitative and achievement orientation of sport. They argued that society should renounce the 'concrete stadium, … stopwatch, manicured lawns' in favour of 'the simple meadow, free nature', essentially an anti-English view which saw professional and competitive sports as alien to the German *volk* (Guttmann 1979: 88).

Segregation by social class, or at least by ability to pay, had become fully established by the First World War. In the inter-war years virtually nothing changed in this respect; those who could afford them had seats but the majority stood, some undercover but many exposed to the elements. They braved wind, rain, sleet and snow on cold December afternoons, the pall of smoke from the ubiquitous Woodbines pervading a damp and dank atmosphere. Children, or more accurately, young boys, did not have an enclosure to themselves but were often good-heartedly passed down to the front of the terraces in order to get a decent view of the game. They would meet up with their fathers when the match had finished.

If spatial segregation on the basis of cash had been commonplace from the turn of the century, segregation on the basis of team affiliation was essentially a post-war phenomenon, notably a product of the 1960s. Traditionally, there had been scope for supporters to move from end to end at half-time, basically in order to get a better view of any goals their team might score. In other words, there was considerable spatial freedom on the terraces and confinement was on the basis of economics rather than enforcement. In the period up to the late 1950s such unrestrained movement rarely produced any crowd trouble. Confrontations and fights between opposing supporters were the exception and verbal abuse was basically directed against the actions of players, linesmen or referee. Pitch invasions, though theoretically possible, rarely took place. If spectators did venture on to the pitch in the late 1940s and early 1950s it was to congratulate players at the end of the game; the term 'pitch invasion' would carry all the wrong connotations. Indeed, Ian Taylor has suggested that invasions of the pitch did not occur during this period because the ground was still seen as 'belonging' to the fans; it was not yet viewed as having been appropriated by the dispassionate middle-class 'consumer' of football (Taylor 1971a).[10]

It was on foreign fields that stadium-based football violence was perceived to be a problem. In his book *Football*, B. W. H. Hill was able to state that 'the violent partisanship of the crowd ... makes playing on foreign soil an unnerving experience' and it was foreign grounds that were being 'wired in so that spectators are kept at a distance' (Hill 1961). Eleven years later George W. Keaton, in *The Football Revolution*, looked with scorn on the 'South American expedient of erecting iron grilles, or ... the Italian method of building a moat and iron fence' (Keaton 1972: 85), not anticipating that such methods of containment were soon to be widespread among British grounds. Although by the early 1970s football hooliganism was being highlighted by the Press, penning people in cages was still viewed by many as suitable only for those of 'Latin temperament'!

Spatial separation on the basis of both affiliation and income has continued to the present day. Such territorialization seems to have occurred in three stages which can be summarized as follows.

The 'football ends'

It was noted earlier that the pre-1960s tradition was for young fans to change ends at half-time. In the mid-1960s football became characterized by more assertive singing and chanting, the popular press's identification of 'football gangs' inside stadiums, and the staking out of gangs' territorial claims on the terraces behind the goals. The behaviour of such gangs deterred other spectators, and home gangs increasingly watched the game from a fixed location. The absence of any physical constraints on movement, however, allowed visiting groups of young supporters to try to 'take' the opposing 'end'. The stadium had become a sort of forum for local geopolitics with rival gangs engaging in end-to-end warfare.

The socio-spatial composition of the football end was more complicated than it may appear on the surface. The terraces, which may superficially appear to be an undifferentiated mass of humanity do, in fact, possess many informal territorial niches which have been carved out of the overall crowd. In *Knuckle Sandwich*, David Robins and Phil Cohen describe how the physical layout of Highbury's North Bank terrace assists in the construction of its social geography, the terrace being a reduced mirror image of the city region:

> It happens that the top section of the stand is divided by a corridor. Below it stands the locals, the Highbury, the Essex Road, the Packington, as well as the other 'London Boys', the Burnt Oak, the Hackney, even a few non-conformists from the East End, where West Ham hold sway. Above the corridor, at the back of the terrace . . . are gathered the ex-urbans and provincials; from Borehamwood to Swindon, from Basildon and Kidderminster to Uxbridge and Elstree. It's as if, for these youngsters, the space they share on the North Bank is a way of magically retrieving the sense of group solidarity and identification that once went along with living in a traditional working-class neighbourhood.
>
> (Robins and Cohen 1978: 137)

Peter Marsh and his associates have identified underlying patterns in the terraces at the much smaller Manor Ground, home of Oxford United (Marsh *et al.* 1978: 61–3). The composition of the crowd on the London Road end terraces was found to involve seven groups, the socio-spatial patterning of which is shown in Figure 2.4. According to the Oxford researchers, the 'most striking thing about such groupings is that they provide for *careers* on the football terraces' (Marsh *et al.* 1978: 63), fans aspiring to pass through the hierarchy, but within an ordered and rule-bounded framework.

Apart from the interesting reference to the work in *Knuckle Sandwich* previously cited, the way in which the micro-geography of the stadium

23

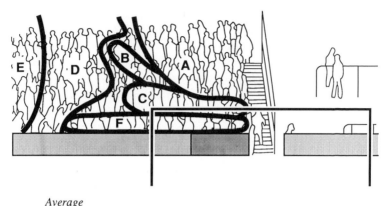

	Average age	
A	15.1	Aggro; easily identifiable; flags, banners; noisy.
B	16.5	Criminal records.
C	18.7	No flags; unremarkable dress style.
D/E		Much less homogeneous; older; some females.
F	10	'Novices'

Figure 2.4 The socio-spatial structure of the 'end' behind the London Road goal at Oxford United
Source: After Marsh *et al.* (1978).

mirrors the geography of the city has remained relatively unexplored in Britain. Detailed studies undertaken by Christian Bromberger at the stadium of Olympique Marseilles FC in France, however, reveal astonishing similarities between stadium-space and urban-space. As Bromberger and his associates comment,

> broken down by residential origin, the public in the stadium presents a faithful copy of the spatial structure of the city. The different districts are represented in proportion to their respective demographic importance. ... The distribution of spectators in the stadium does not reflect the simple mechanisms of segregation by price of ticket ... [and] ... although the prices are very similar, the east and west sides, and the north and south ends form clearly distinguished sociological universes.
>
> (Bromberger *et al.* 1991: 21)[11]

Spectators living in the north, mainly working class, and those from the south – the upwardly mobile – occupy respective ends of the stadium (see Figure 2.5); if they have been upwardly mobile and moved resi-

24

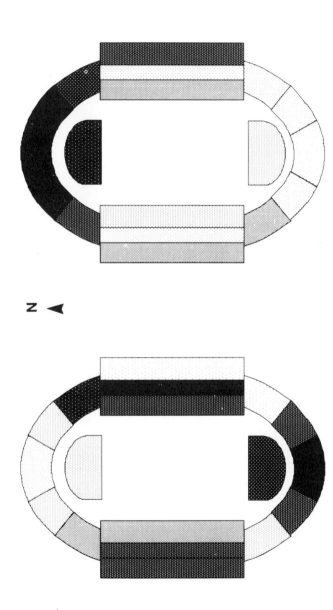

Figure 2.5 The stadium as a map of the city: the case of Olympique Marseilles FC. Maps show the distribution of spectators coming from the southern (left) and northern (right) parts of the city respectively. The darker the shading, the greater the number of spectators from the respective areas

Source: After Bromberger (1989a).

dences from one to the other it is reflected in their stadium location also. Black fans have a black quarter of the stadium as they have a black quarter of the city; even fans of particular players are concentrated in particular parts of the stadium. Whether such patterns exist in other countries, including Britain, remains to be seen. In the late 1960s and early 1970s opposing ends *were* taken in some cases. But the over-reporting of such incidents by the mass media meant that, despite Keaton's 1972 comments, the late 1960s press was averring that in terms of crowd behaviour the British fans were actually *worse* than the Latins.

'Pens' and 'boxes'

In Britain the growth of inter-end rivalries led to enforced segregation of fans, first by the 'thin, blue line' of the police and later by physical barriers and 'pens'. This latter development was stimulated by the growth of skinhead gangs during the late 1960s and the increasingly successful 'taking' of ends by visiting supporters. It was perceived that physical restraint was required. In October 1970 the FA advised all League clubs that more stringent methods of confinement should be introduced. In 1974 the Stretford End at Old Trafford, Manchester, witnessed the erection of a metal barrier to segregate supporters, something that was to become 1970s and 1980s football *zeitgeist*. Segregation of rival fans at a ground like Old Trafford was achieved at a cost of over £100,000. An additional form of confinement was provided by the more widespread adoption than hitherto of perimeter fencing to prevent pitch invasions at many stadiums. In the mid-1980s Chelsea's ground at Stamford Bridge witnessed the installation of an *electrified* fence, though this controversial anti-hooligan device was dismantled before ever being used (Dunning *et al.* 1989; note also Eichberg 1988: 35).

Today, visiting fans are not simply segregated from their 'opponents' within the stadium, they are isolated from their point of arrival in the town – at the railway station or bus terminus – and 'herded' by police to their 'pens'. At the end of the game they are made to remain in their pens until the home crowd has dispersed and then herded back to their point of departure, often under video-surveillance.

As the more lumpen elements of football's fandom were being constrained in their pens (visiting fans often having to endure appalling viewing and sanitary conditions as the contents of many current fanzines make clear), the more socially and economically desirable groups of spectators were being increasingly distanced from grass-roots support by the installation of more comfortable, but also more expensive forms of segregated accommodation. First established at Old Trafford, the special glass-fronted 'boxes' for the small number of more discerning, often corporate spectators who wished to combine watching football with business entertaining in relatively lavish surroundings, became a feature of the more wealthy grounds of the late 1960s. They are now common among First and Second Division clubs. At Tottenham Hotspur's White Hart Lane executive boxes were built on the most popular side of the ground, resulting in the demolition of the popular 'Shelf' terrace, despite protests from fans and the local council (Shaw 1989). The conversion of a terrace into boxes may half the capacity but double the revenue; though obviously catering for a very small minority of the overall crowd, boxes are leased at several thousands of pounds per season. John Clarke feels that there are two important implications of such physical changes in the stadium's development:

> First, the image of the spectator as someone who can only be tempted to watch the game if it offers standards of physical and social comfort which he would expect elsewhere. Second, it implies a particular way of watching the game. Seated, dispassionately critical, the new spectator waits to be entertained. The show is something out there, not something of which he is part. In the gaps in the entertainment, he expects to be provided for with food and drink, music and spectacular demonstrations.
>
> (Clarke 1978: 47)

Chas Critcher (1979) sees the introduction of luxury boxes as identifying a new kind of spectator; 'no impassioned troublemaker he – no physical involvement, chanting or swearing in these new stands'. With 'whisky in hand', he is the recipient of 'instant entertainment'. Meanwhile, the community of local fans is relegated to insanitary, alcohol-free 'pens'. The provision for visitors is even worse.

Surveillance and seating

Despite these measures considerable concern about violent behaviour inside grounds continued into the mid and late 1980s. The response was for all league clubs to install Football-Trust-funded closed-circuit television equipment in all Football League grounds which could be used to identify troublemakers. This panopticism brought the stadium into line with the long-standing traditions of the asylum, clinic, and prison. In Foucault's words, the spectator, like 'the inmate must never know

27

whether he is being looked at at any moment; but he must be sure that
he may always be so' (Foucault 1979). Where people had to be
contained, efficient surveillance was a necessity (see Figure 2.6).

The Lang Committee of 1969 had thought such forms of surveillance
to 'be of value in the general subject of crowd control' (Lang 1969).
Video equipment was also widely employed by the police in their moni-
toring of herded crowds between stadium and station. In the infamous
Luton case, away fans were banned under the club's membership
scheme with computer-coded cards forming the basis for entry (and
'surveillance') and police costs plummeted. Whereas in 1985/6 charges
for police attendance at Luton matches was £285 per 1,000 attendance,
the respective figure for 1987/8 was £201. These figures should be

Figure 2.6 Closed-circuit TV surveillance is now a pervasive feature of all
Football League grounds in Britain. It seeks to produce, through knowledge of
individuals' behaviour, both power and 'docile bodies'

contrasted with those of £170 and £207 for Division I as a whole (Williams *et al.* 1989a).

The result of such measures of containment and surveillance was that by the late 1980s crowd violence inside grounds had been virtually eradicated. But it had never been as serious as the media suggested. In the 1975/6 season, for example, the 122 arrests of 15–20-year-olds at Manchester United matches amounted to only 0.03 per cent of that age group attending (Marsh 1977). In 1977 a Survey of Scottish football showed that of nearly 4 million spectator visits in 1976 to Scottish games, 1,079 people were apprehended for a variety of crimes or offences. This figure amounted to:

- 4 per match;
- 0.28 arrests per 1,000 spectators;
- 1.13 per cent of all breaches of the peace and assaults committed in Scotland that year;
- 7.32 breaches of the peace and assaults were committed by 100,000 spectators every hour, a figure comparing very favourably with the number of such arrests in leisure activities on Saturday nights;
- the football-related apprehensions, mainly for petty offences, was about one-thirteenth the number of arrests for drunken driving.

(Scottish Education Department 1977)

In 1988 arrests inside Scottish grounds amounted to 0.017 per cent of the attendance figures, a statistic not very different from that for England (*The Guardian*, 17 January 1989: 14).

Given such low figures, which pre-date the most serious forms of containment, the measures used to control spectators seem draconian in the extreme. It has been suggested by some observers that the severity of the measures may have resulted, in part at least, from a 'moral panic'. This is the result of what Stanley Cohen (1987) has called 'deviancy amplification' in which the initial perception of deviant (in this case hooligan) behaviour is exaggerated by the mass media which produces stereotypes of the football hooligan. The resulting self-fulfilling prophecy leads to increased hooliganism, a polarization of attitudes and confirmation of the stereotype. I will return to the question of moral panic in Chapter 4 when I explore the reaction to 'hooligan' behaviour outside the stadium, but the argument seems applicable to reactions of the authorities both inside and outside grounds.

It must be added, however, that the low arrest figures do understate the anti-social behaviour of fans inside the stadium. Verbal violence has far from abated and is probably on the increase. In the highly gendered space of the stadium, sexist language (for example, 'get your tits out for the lads') is endemic. Racial abuse (for example, 'black bastard') is fuelled, to a limited extent and only in certain grounds, by associations with the National Front, but everywhere the localism and nationalism which are inherent in team sports encourages an 'us' against 'them' mentality. David Canter's research showed that for supporters of each of ten British football clubs surveyed at least 15 per cent of respondents thought that 'there are a lot of racist shouts and chants', while in the cases of Celtic and Chelsea the respective figures were an exceptionally high 66 per cent and 45 per cent (Canter et al. 1989). A substantial proportion of the remaining spectators may have become desensitized to it, thus failing to recognize it. In summary, violence – both physical and verbal – inside the ground has never been as small as the arrest figures alone suggest but never nearly as great as is widely assumed.

By 1988 a survey of police officers with responsibility for policing football matches in England and Wales indicated that for only 8.9 per cent of grounds had hooliganism been increasing in recent years inside the grounds (Sir Norman Chester Centre for Football Research 1989a: 27). Whereas the annually infamous clash between the members of the 'Old Firm', Rangers and Celtic, in 1980 resulted in 219 arrests, the equivalent game in 1983 led to only 38, with a substantially reduced number of police (Scottish Education Department 1977). Only about six arrests *and* ejections were taking place in the average Football League game in the late 1980s; even in Division I the figure averaged only about twelve (Football Trust 1988).

A further tendency from the end of the war to the present day has been for a greater proportion of the game's spectatorship to be accommodated in seats rather than standing on the terraces. This has been a response to declining League attendances from a post-war peak of over 41 million in 1948/9 to around 16.5 million in 1985/6 – a post-war low. Since then attendances have risen slightly to around 18.5 million.

Seats were a response to not simply the perceived demand for greater comfort but also to the view that they would restrain the violent tendencies of the 1970s and lead to safer stadiums and, in Foucault's terms, 'docile bodies'. A numbered seat meant that 'each individual has his own place; and each place its individual' (Foucault 1979: 143). Seating represented a move towards the Americanization of the football stadium, some characteristics of which are discussed later (see pp. 32–6), and widespread implementation of all seater stadiums would mean an end to the patterns shown in Figures 2.4 and 2.5. Collectivities of fans would give way to numbered individuals.

The first all-seater ground in Britain was Aberdeen's Pittodrie Stadium (in 1978), though as Bert Moorhouse has cynically observed, seating at Aberdeen often means sitting on a plank of wood nailed to another plank of wood, often encrusted in moss and exposed to the elements (Moorhouse 1990: 8). This was followed by another Scottish club, Clydebank and, in England in 1981, by Coventry City. If all-seater accommodation was adopted by each of the 92 Football League clubs, total ground capacity would be reduced by just over 2 million to under 1.5 million (*Rothman's Football Yearbook*, 1989–1990). In the case of Coventry, the all-seater experiment proved abortive, in contrast to the success at Pittodrie; I describe the response of Coventry's fans in a later section (see pp. 49–50).

More recently the so-called 'family enclosure' has emerged as an attempt to attract a new kind of consumer, attending games in family units. This innovation has met with some success in certain places (notably Watford) but is derided by hard-core traditionalists as evidence of the further bourgeoisification of the game. The family enclosure can, however, also be interpreted according to Foucault's all-pervasive panopticism. As with the hierarchical 'family' of supervisors in nineteenth-century prisons, the family seated together as a group of 'docile bodies' replaces the fear of continual visual inspection by the 'anti-institutional and natural weapon' of the family, perhaps the ultimate in the art of power relations (Foucault 1979: 293–5, Philo 1989: 265).[12]

THE TECHNOLOGIZING OF THE STADIUM

In most US and in many European stadiums it has been normal for several decades for the great majority of – in many cases all – spectators to sit rather than stand. The British stadium of the future will, likewise, be an all-seater, high-tech, concrete theatre. Surveillance will be by sophisticated video equipment and closed-circuit television. Each and every spectator will be identifiable by the number of the seat which he or she is occupying. In Foucault's words again, we will have arrived at 'a compact model of the disciplinary mechanism' (Foucault 1979: 197). Surveillance will provide knowledge; knowledge will provide power.

One of the first technological innovations to change the nature of the spectating experience was the widespread use of floodlighting at football matches, which, while commonly used at friendly games and cup competitions in the early 1950s, was not 'legalized' by the Football League until 1956. Ian Taylor saw floodlighting as the start of the transformation of 'grounds' into 'stadia' (Taylor 1971b), a semantic distinction rich in symbolism, for much the same reasons (that is, image upgrading) as American 'poolrooms' were rebaptized 'billiard lounges' (Polsky 1985: 3). In the United States the use of the word 'stadium' to replace terms like 'park', 'field', or 'ground' seems to have been adopted after the construction of the Yankee Stadium in New York City in 1923 (Reiss 1978). Interestingly, the great bowl which was built in the same year in the north London suburbs was likewise termed Wembley *Stadium* but the term 'ground' has been difficult to remove from the British fan's vocabulary. In any case, Wembley was never *just* a football ground.

The spatial and environmental changes which accompanied the stadium's image-upgrading were, with the advent of floodlighting, to be paralleled by a temporal change; 'the night frontier could now be crossed and new "regions" of [football] time could be colonized' (Parkes and Thrift 1980: 323). The conflicting claims of other Saturday afternoon forms of leisure were reduced. Once evening games had become acceptable to the sport's bureaucracy, they became very difficult to stop, given the investment in floodlighting. Saturday afternoons were no longer the only time that football was played and midweek matches became commonplace. Although the number of spectators attending matches was declining, the number of times football could be (and was) played was increasing.

Innovations in construction technology have made the high-tech stadium essentially a sports saucer, likely to have been designed by a computer. Structures with 'complex curves such as domed stadiums ... probably would not have been started were it not for computers because the calculation of stresses and bar-bending structures ... would have been too time consuming and costly' (Relph 1987: 123–4). The technology already exists to produce domed stadiums with retractable roofs and flexible pitch and seating arrangements (see Figure 2.7). Compared with the incrementally developed architecture of the traditional English stadium the sports saucer possesses few landscape elements; at its worst, the overall ensemble tends to be one of unrelieved sterile concrete. Because of such limited variety within the ensemble of the high-tech stadium the need for interest and arousal of spectators might need to be manipulated by installing electronic scoreboards and musical interludes. According to the somewhat sinister prognostications of environmental psychologist, Albert Mehrabian (1970), 'there seems to be much potential for use of electronic music to manipulate and reinforce crowd feelings' – rousing pieces at half time, pieces carrying apprehension just before a penalty is taken, and 'aggressive tunes played during high scoring periods by the home team'.

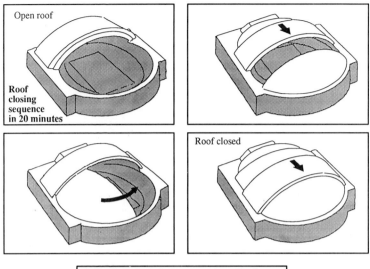

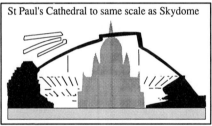

Figure 2.7 The Toronto Skydome

The giant television screens in the stadiums of the future will relay action to spectators unable to witness it as a result of being spatially distanced from the action, or because they feel the 'need' for an instant replay. In an era when people experience television from cradle to grave, televised sport may not necessarily be seen as an impoverished form of spectatorship. Australian sociologist John Goldlust argues that today the

> defining power of television as an authoritative interpreter of the sporting experience has successfully inverted the social validity of this assumption. The view of the sporting experience, mediated by television has established itself as the primary experience. The giant video screen is there to attract people to the stadium event

and to ensure that by attending they will not be deprived of the 'television experience'.

(Goldlust 1987: 174)

In these stadiums the preferred seats will be those giving the best view of the video screen. Safety and surveillance having been satisfied by seating, the stadium will have become more than a theatre; it will have become a huge television studio. One interpretation is that the spectators in the stadium will have become simply pieces of scenery for television coverage (Penz 1990: 164).

Technology will have imposed itself on the techno-stadium in other ways. Although such stadiums are only on the drawing-board stage in the UK, they already exist in North America (see pp. 35–6). A 1989 proposal for a London dome, costing between £400 and £500 million, describes the stadium, with its seating capacity electronically altered to suit different-sized audiences and different sports as 'an air-conditioned "mini-city" with shops, a 650-seat restaurant, a 350-seat bar, 161 private boxes for corporate entertaining and the world's largest video screen' (*The Sunday Times*, 10 December 1989: B7). This comes close to being a description of the Toronto Skydome (see Figure 2.7).

If the terraces and stands have changed during the course of the century the fields of play of the overwhelming majority of League clubs have remained physically the same. Grass remains the surface on which most games are played; four clubs – Preston, Oldham, Luton, and Queen's Park Rangers – innovated with plastic in the 1980s but all have now returned to grass following the 'banning' of plastic by the Football League. But there is always the possibility of improved technology producing synthetic surfaces which possess the playing characteristics and unpredictability of grass but the durability of astroturf. The playing surfaces in the aforementioned 'domes' may be plastic or grass but, like their roofs, they could be retractable, a 'roll-in, roll-out' field being used in order to satisfy purists who dislike plastic pitches. Structural engineering possesses the technology for such plans to be converted into reality if the money is put up-front.

FUTURESCAPE?

If the concrete bowl represents the apogee of modernist sports architecture, the sports dome is rapidly becoming the leitmotiv of post-modernism. In North America the sports dome has become a symbol of urban vibrancy with the mayor of New Orleans, Moon Landrieu, being quoted

34

as saying that the 'Superdome is an exercise in optimism. A statement of faith. It is the very building of it that is important, not how much it is used or its economics'.[13] In San Antonio, Texas, the local residents approved the building of the 'Alamo Dome' in 1989 even though no professional sports outfit existed to occupy it. It will be used for trade shows and conventions until a sports tenant is found (Baade and Dye 1990).

The costs of domed structures, often erected to out-boost a neighbouring or rival city, typify an excess of urban monumentalism. The New Orleans Superdome (at 1989 costs) involved construction costs of over $374 million – nearly $5,000 per seat. A crucial variable in the cost calculus, however, is the precise structure of the stadium roof, and the per-seat cost of the Superdome with an air-supported roof was around $1,500. The 1989 cost of air-supported Teflon roofs ranged from 23 to 64 per cent of the cost of structures with rigid roofs (see Table 2.1). Lack of durability and energy inefficiency are cited as problems associated with flexible roof domes. Whether these disadvantages would be enough to favour the construction of rigid-roof stadiums seems unlikely, however (Baade and Dye 1990).

Table 2.1 Alternative roof structures and costs of domed stadiums in the United States

Stadium	Construction cost in 1989 ($m)	Cost per seat in 1989 ($)	Roof structure	Year completed
Superdome (New Orleans)	374	4,890	Steel	1975
Kingdome (Seattle)	158	2,420	Reinforced concrete	1976
Astrodome (Houston)	136	2,580	Steel	1965
Silverdome (Detroit)	108	1,350	Air support	1975
Hoosier Dome (Indianapolis)	92	1,530	Air support	1984
Metrodome (Minneapolis)	87	1,390	Air support	1982

Source: Baade and Dye 1990: 4.

The roof of most domed stadiums is fixed and, as noted in Table 2.1, may be made of various substances; however, in the case of the Toronto Skydome, widely regarded as the state of the art in stadium design, the roof is retractable, being pulled in and out depending on the prevailing weather conditions or the precise use to which the stadium is to be put. In the case of the Skydome

> the 9,000 ton roof covers eight acres, spans 700 ft. and is made of steel tubes covered with PVC. It can be opened and closed in 20 minutes. Safety precautions include pressurised airpipes in strategic locations to blow out smoke from a fire. The exits and ramps are positioned, so that, in theory, 70,000 can be evacuated in about 12 minutes.
>
> (*The Sunday Times*, 10 December 1989: B7)

Such technological developments are not restricted to mega-stadiums. It will be crucial for the future of many clubs that if they occupy new stadiums such facilities will need to be *flexible*, accommodating modest crowds in some seasons but being able to adjust to newer demands should promotion to higher divisions take place and induce larger crowds to attend home games. In Britain it has been suggested that the 'stadium for the nineties' should be able to cater not only for current needs with modest initial financial outlays but also at the same time provide 'a flexible masterplan allowing future expansion in stages to suit the club's progress' (Sports Council 1991). Phased development of car parks, private boxes and various other entertainment facilities would take place with the final stage being a fully covered stadium with facilities matching the best in the world (see Figure 2.8).

Because climate is more easily controlled in a domed or covered stadium, such facilities may attract near-capacity crowds more frequently than open-air stadiums. Furthermore, they can be more easily used for non-sporting events such as conventions, concerts, and exhibitions. In a sense, therefore, such stadiums reveal the contradictions of such developments. They are undoubtedly modern but in so far as they permit a return to a dual use of space they are post-modern. The presence of a carefully tended grass surface makes the football stadium a form of monoculture or sportscape, given over solely to the cultivation of football. Unlike the environments of folk-football and early football, the traditional stadium can be used for little else (see Chapter 6). The football pitch of the future, be it plastic or retractable, is no longer just a football pitch, however; it can be a site for festivals, rock concerts, playforms of various kinds, and a wide variety of other sports. On the other

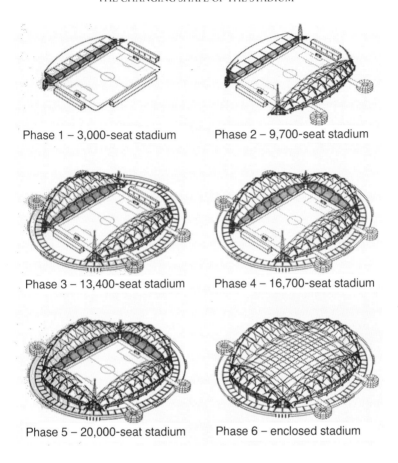

Phase 1 – 3,000-seat stadium   Phase 2 – 9,700-seat stadium

Phase 3 – 13,400-seat stadium   Phase 4 – 16,700-seat stadium

Phase 5 – 20,000-seat stadium   Phase 6 – enclosed stadium

Figure 2.8 Flexibility in design will characterize the post-modern stadium
Source: Sports Council (1991).

hand, unless post-modern architectural forms are employed, as at Lord's Cricket Ground in London, the Stadio Luigi Ferraris in Genoa, or as at non-league football club, Dorchester Town, the visual appeal of the stadium could be as sterile as the 'placeless' concrete bowls so disliked by fans and players alike (see Chapter 3).

CONCLUSION

The confinement of football seems to have resulted from three inter-related factors. First, the increase in commercial activity in the seventeenth and eighteenth centuries contributed to the spatial separation of sports from other land uses which led to sports themselves being commercialized. Second, the growing achievement orientation of football during the nineteenth century meant that it was necessary to standardize the spatial parameters of the sport in order to make serious competition meaningful. Third, the most recent confinement has been introduced with a view towards improving the safety and control of spectators, though such measures could be also related to the sport's commercial imperatives.

Initially, a limitation on playing space, then an exact spatial definition of the pitch with, today, enforced segregation of spectators both from players and other spectators, the story of the stadium has indeed been one of 'great confinement' and illustrates the extension of surveillance strategies into the public space of leisure and sport. Whereas the intra-stadium space of the early twentieth century included a number of 'permeable boundaries', in the modern stadium the boundaries between various groups (players/spectators, home/away fans, rich/poor fans) tend to be 'impermeable'. With the ever-present video surveillance the football ground is in many ways a model of 'panopticized society' and, in addition, there is a hierarchical or concentric circle of 'social guardians' with the fan being surrounded by stewards, police, and then magistrates – further exemplification of Foucault's 'bio-politics' (Foucault 1979, Hewitt 1983). The enclosures and boundaries between various stadium spaces might also be interpreted as defining what Lefebvre calls a 'scene (where something takes place) and an obscene area to which everything that cannot or may not happen on the scene is relegated' (Lefebvre 1991: 36). For 'scene' read the field of play; for 'obscene' read the fans.

Increasingly, an outdoor activity with a strong element of laughter and play has come closer to a choreographed form of what is, in extreme cases, indoor theatre, though until the element of uncertainty in sport is removed it will never be fully analogous to a scripted play. I should also be careful in drawing analogies with the theatre because, while there are obvious parallels, football does not possess the 'critical distance' which theatre now has (but has not always had) between its (middle class) audience with its ritualized, polite applause, and the actors. Football has shouting, chanting and pitch invasions, and the 'critical distance' between fans and players will need to be increased before it becomes more like theatre (Bourdieu 1986, Shields 1991: 96). Clearly, some sports (for example, track and field athletics or 'traditional' English cricket) are more 'theatrical' than others in this respect.

This is not to deny, however, that in becoming 'sportified' a reduction occurred in football's sense of fun, being replaced by an increase in seriousness. And in the transition from play to display the 'ownership' of the stadium has shifted from community to capital, the controlling interests being increasingly distanced – both socially and geographically – from the locality in which the club is found.

Well-defined spatial boundaries characterize modernity and, as Eduardo Archetti has noted,

> the stadium full of spectators silently watching the performance and not taking part in the drama, who consequently cannot change the result, comes to be the ideal image of modern sport.... The ideal of modernity is built on the clear separation between representation and performance, between players and spectators, between activity and passivity.[14]

I have shown that since the eighteenth century football has been regularly subjected to forms of territorialization or spatial confinement, with the game moving from being a form of corporal, to one of carceral, recreation. In this way a division between not only the players and the spectators but also between the 'respectable' and the 'hardcore' fans was *created* (Redhead 1991a: 483). But in this chapter I have tried to show not simply how football has moved closer to Archetti's hypothetical 'ideal' but how such tendencies have been resisted.

Just as some of the traditional privileges of the 'lower classes' had been redefined as 'criminal' with the enclosure of the commons and the appropriation of the streets, so too the traditional spatial behaviour of many football fans became increasingly 'criminalized' during the postwar period. But just as some of the commoners of seventeenth-century Holland Fen were able to rebel successfully against the modernizing tendencies in the legal struggles against early folk-football, and just as some Coventry fans successfully opposed the all-seater stadium, I shall try to show in more detail in Chapter 4 how modern supporters are far from marginal figures and have been able to successfully convert an affection for the stadium into successful political activism when their space is threatened. But before doing so I want to review the paradox of progress – the fact that 'improvements' in the environment of football have been accompanied by dissatisfaction from fans.

3

THE PARADOX OF MODERN STADIUM LANDSCAPES

In *Rational Landscapes and Humanistic Geography*, the geographer Edward Relph notes that

> it is paradoxical that while analytic and rational methods of ... planning have been demonstrably beneficial, for they have helped to improve living standards and to increase material well-being, they have also resulted in the creation of landscapes which are frequently judged to be inhumane or dehumanising.
>
> (Relph 1981: 64)

He goes on to note that the dehumanized landscape is paradoxical because it is the result of 'too much rationalism and an excess of humanism' (Relph 1981), and then proceeds to describe such inhumane landscapes, citing examples such as international airports, fast food restaurants, some suburbs and shopping malls. Such places are often described as 'inauthentic', 'placeless', or 'disneyfied' (Relph 1981). The concrete-bowl model of the football stadium could also be interpreted as an example from the world of sports.

Relph's interpretation has been criticized by some as being too academic, romantic, or elitist. For example, John Eyles notes that what is authentic and meaningful to Relph seems shaped by middle- and ruling-class creations, that the mass of people simply have inauthentic experiences in inauthentic, 'placeless' places (Eyles 1985: 73, 1989), and by implication, no sense of place. In the case of the football stadium, however, it is neither the dominant classes nor academics who have negatively criticized the increasing placelessness during the stadium's evolution; indeed, the most vocal critics have invariably been the fans themselves. In this way 'traditional' football grounds, generating as they do intense identification between people and place, are, for fans, examples of authentic places, given the intense sentiment and attachment generated by them (see Chapter 4). This chapter is therefore concerned with examining the reactions of fans to the changes which I described in the previous chapter.

There can be little doubt that the tendencies towards modernism in stadium design and location can be interpreted as manifestations of placelessness and that the characteristics of placelessness suggested by Relph can be applied to the football environment. They are (a) the *standardized values* inherent in internationalized, globally televised, synthetic entertainment; (b) the *gigantism* reflected in the 'formlessness and lack of human scale' (Relph 1981: 119) of proposed mega-stadiums; (c) *uniformity of design* in international styles of stadium architecture; (d) the stadium as part of an *entertainment district*, resulting from its purpose of attracting outsiders ('other-directedness'); and (e) the tendency towards both *futurism* in some cases and *museumization* in others. Placelessness as a philosophy is also implied in the tendency towards 'place destruction' or topocide – that is, in a football context, the redevelopment of sites occupied by much-loved stadiums by expropriation or development. It could be argued, of course, that fans could come to love the new stadiums just as they have developed a sense of place for the old. But the new stadium *will* be different from the old and the strength of feeling expressed towards demolition, relocation, and ground sharing shows clearly how a sense of place is associated with the traditional British ground.

The football stadium of the future, as described towards the end of the previous chapter, will be a landscape which is safe, comfortable, and convenient. These will be undeniable gains but they will undoubtedly lead to dissatisfaction among football's most sincere fans. As Hargreaves has put it, 'the rationalization of spectator sports has had counter-productive effects in relation to audience satisfaction' (Hargreaves 1987: 157). I want to explore the paradox of the modern football landscape by applying the ideas of Relph, who argues that 'progress', as reflected in the urban landscape, is often associated with 'a manifestation of rationalism pushed to its limits and already turning against itself, becoming restricting rather than enlightening' (Relph 1981: 211). Relph feels that little exists in the modern landscape of concrete and glass

> that has not been been conceived in terms of efficiency or improved material conditions. But there is almost nothing in them that can happen spontaneously, autonomously or accidentally, or which expresses human emotions and feeling. If this absence

diminishes the quality of our lives it does so sadly, quietly, unob-
trusively, rather than with some overt, brutal denial.

(Relph 1981: 104)

I want to consider several aspects of the modern stadium which, while
demonstrating technical progress, engender dissatisfaction in players
and spectators alike and can be interpreted as exemplars of the paradox
of scientific humanism to which Relph alludes. Each of these can be
examined briefly in turn.

THE LANDSCAPE ENSEMBLE

Geographer Karl Raitz has argued that gratification from the sport
experience is enhanced if the sport landscape within which the action
takes place possesses a number of varied elements, contributing to an
overall landscape ensemble. He would argue that there is simply more to
enjoy in landscapes with a variety of elements than in those where the
elements are few in number; Gay Meadow, a tree-girt ground at Shrewsbury (see pp. 73–4), would be at one end and the concrete sports
saucer at the other end of a 'place'–'placeless' spectrum (Raitz 1987).
The same point, favouring 'scenery' to blandness, was emphatically
made by the founder of the modern Olympics, Baron Pierre de Coubertin, and subsequently in non-sports contexts by psychologists and architects. In 1917 de Coubertin forcefully stated that the entire Olympic
complex should be an 'imposing and worthy ensemble' and that 'the
first thing to be taken into account in consideration when staging a
sports festival is the scenery. Before actors appear, the scenery strikes
the eye of the spectator'.[1] Erik Maaløe has demonstrated quantitatively
that people find designs with a degree of variation in them more fasci-
nating than those that are predictable (Maaløe 1973: 135–47), and
students of architectural form have stressed that pleasure increases with
an increase in complexity, though it is stressed that complexity 'over-
load' can lead to aversion (Smith 1979: 60–1).

For many fans, the various landscape elements may offer a rich
combination of stimulating and gratifying sensations and emotions
(Raitz 1987), typified, for example, by a view of his or her city, a much-
loved stand, even a particular corner of the ground. In the case of West
Ham United's ground, for example, the 'most famous sacrifice to "progress"' was Boleyn Castle, first built in 1544 and a local landmark of
sentimental value to local residents and supporters. At the same ground,
the 'chicken run', a drab, wet (even if covered!) bank 'where the wits

seemed loudest and crudest' was torn down in 1968. Despite its lack of creature comforts, it was the sentimental home of many old supporters (Korr 1986: 212). Take such landscape elements away and surround the pitch with a concrete bowl and the potential for gratification is reduced. The grounds become anonymous, the aesthetic experience reduced.

As I noted earlier, these kinds of comments may sound academic, nostalgic, and elitist. But although I am not suggesting that all fans consciously go through a process of evaluating their fottball environments, a large number of comments, carried in fanzines in particular, attest to the preference for the traditional English ground. In his amazing and anarchic book, *Sing When You're Winning*, Steve Redhead quotes from the 1970s fanzine *Foul* in these, perhaps extreme, terms: 'football is not about covered stadiums, padded seats, ice cream and women and kids. It's about hitching, getting pissed, shouting, standing ...' (Redhead 1986: 49). A letter to *Foul* attacked the vision of society's dominant groups whose

> Utopia is a spotless concrete bowl lined with thousands of little blue plastic seats, lots of clean toilets, a restaurant, a sports complex, piped muzak, and 22 clean-cut, goal hungry young zombies ... on a plasti-grass pitch. ... Bollocks to their visions! It is on those cold, forbidding terraces that you find the central nervous system of football from which adrenalin rises and the life-blood flows.
>
> (Redhead 1986: 49–50)

A decade later fanzine editors were echoing these sentiments. In *Off the Ball* it was noted that

> in promoting itself as just another arm of the wider entertainments industry, ignoring the special excitement, atmosphere, passion and comradeship that is football's heritage and most marketable asset, the game is reduced to ritzy-glitzy hype, heavily commercialised with forced and ordered excitement. This sanitised soccer becomes, to the hamburger culture society, just another thing to do – last week the cinema, this week football, next week the theme park.
>
> (Beauchampe 1986: 6)

The newer stadiums in Europe and the USA have also produced the paradox that the optimal viewing distance for the average spectator has been exceeded by placing a running track between the pitch and the crowd. It has been estimated that the ideal limit for viewing football is about 90 metres from the centre circle or 150 metres to the furthest corner flag. In the traditional English ground the optimal viewing circle encloses the majority of the spectators, but in newer stadiums, including the Aztec Stadium in Mexico City, most fans are simply too far away from the action to enjoy the small detail and hence a greater sense of involvement. At Wembley, one of Britain's most modern stadiums even though built in the 1920s, nearly one-fifth of the spectators are beyond the maximum viewing circle (Inglis 1987). The most recent 'improvements' at Wembley have been severely criticized because of the poor visibility which has been the end product of such 'developments'.

There is much in what Desmond Morris says about the traditional English ground:

> To the English soccer fanatic modern stadia in South America and continental Europe are too impersonal, the pitches too remote, and the all-seating facilities too controlled. The Englishman [sic] prefers to feel he is breathing down the neck of the player making a throw-in on the touch line, and to immerse himself in the crowded frenzy of standing body-to-body on the terraces. The oddity of the shape of the differing grandstands gives him a sense of *special location* and provides each ground with its own characteristics. (Emphasis added.)

(Morris 1981: 42)

Simon Inglis, in defence of the traditional British football ground, stated that 'the traditional atmosphere is still highly regarded. Would we really want to see our local teams perform in soulless concrete bowls that look much like any other concrete bowl?' (Inglis 1987: 7). The erosion of the unselfconsciously and incrementally developed place which is the typical British ground, and its replacement by a modern football space (or in Raitz's terms, a shift from a complex to a simple landscape ensemble, creating not a sense of place but a sense of placelessness), is viewed sadly by fans, despite the progress implied by such developments.

FLOODLIGHTING

On the face of it floodlighting might appear to be a benign development but, using the place–placelessness spectrum, it can be interpreted more critically. Simon Inglis notes that in football, unlike theatre or cinema where eyes are focused on the screen all the time and where all else is in darkness, the landscape elements of the stadium are as much a part of the event as the match itself (Inglis 1990: 7). Describing the first floodlit

44

Football League game in 1956, however, *The Times* correspondent noted enthusiastically that there was 'a *dramatic, theatrical* quality about it' (emphasis added) (Inglis 1987). What floodlighting did was to accelerate the tendency, already well under way, to bring football closer to theatre. It did this particularly by highlighting the action on the field and obliterating, through the darkened background, any architectural details or elements of the landscape which could, incidentally, provide distraction or additional gratification for spectators. If the number of visual elements is reduced, it can be argued that the potential for enjoyment is also reduced. By focusing solely on the game, the urban context within which it is played was visually eliminated. As with the case of the anonymous concrete bowl, 'the temporal and historical associations that say "Here is a place connected to a landscape that grew out of a particular process" are severed' (Neilson 1986: 39–47). The place (in daylight) becomes a non-place (in darkness). If places and their appearances do matter to people, the elements which make them places are temporarily eroded during floodlit games.

THE PLASTIC PITCH

Pioneered and widely used in the USA, the plastic pitch has often been viewed as the saviour of British football. Though currently out of favour with the sport's administrators, it is always possible that the synthetic pitch will make a comeback with the inevitable 'advances' which will occur in fibre technology. Whereas a grass pitch can just about withstand a season's fixtures (that is, 21 home League games plus cup and reserve matches totalling, at most, around 50 games), Luton's plastic carpet took over 200 matches in seven months (Sports Council 1986). Community involvement, non-footballing activities, and reduced maintenance make plastic an attractive proposition, despite high initial costs.

Although there has been progress in pitch construction, 'astroturf' and similar, but improved, surfaces tend to be disliked by professional players and fans alike. Inglis (1987) succinctly notes that 'if every surface was perfect, football would become soft and clinical'. The relative predictability of the bounce of the ball on plastic pitches is illustrated in Figure 3.1a which shows how the rebound height, as a proportion of the height from which the ball is dropped (3 metres) varied less on QPR's 1982 plastic pitch than on natural grass. This pitch, and other artificial surfaces, records higher than average bounces than does natural grass. Artificial football surfaces also record reduced rolling resistance, the ball moving faster over synthetic pitches and

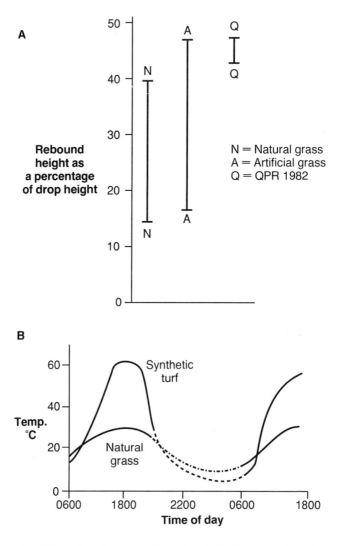

Figure 3.1 Effects of pitch composition: (a) on ball rebound height and (b) on surface temperatures during a 36-hour period
Source: (a) Sports Council (1986), and (b) Tipp and Watson (1982: 282).

making control more difficult (Sports Council 1986). In addition to these disadvantages, synthetic pitches create other problems. Sliding tackles produce more frequent abrasions and painful 'astro-burns' which are inevitable on such surfaces. Plastic pitches also have the effect of increasing player discomfort by having, on average, summer temperatures 4°C higher than those on grass. As solar radiation increases, the synthetic carpet, helped by the layer underneath which acts as an excellent thermal insulant, becomes significantly hotter than natural grass (see Figure 3.1b) (Tipp and Watson 1982). So while appearing to represent progress, innovations in pitch development can, at the same time, produce dissatisfaction for those who play.

THE ALL-SEATER STADIUM

Pioneered in the context of British football at Pittodrie (see p. 31), the all-seater stadium was recommended by the Taylor Report to be an essential element of all British grounds. Introduced to produce greater comfort on the one hand and to reduce hooliganism on the other, spectator attitudes to these more comfortable – and more expensive – forms of accommodation are ambivalent.

Seating provides the spectator with a place of containment; the terrace, on the other hand, provides less constraint and the potential for dialogue and interaction with other members of a group. There is a greater sense of camaraderie and group cohesion. Seating may be more comfortable but it is arguable whether it is more enjoyable; indeed, many would argue whether it is, in fact, more comfortable. Baron Pierre de Coubertin, in his writings on the layout of the stadium, argued along similar lines. In his view, the optimal number of spectators, even for an Olympic Games, was about 10,000 – more than the seasonal average of most Football League clubs but less than those of the super clubs. De Coubertin opposed the grandstand, feeling that 'an attempt should be made to avoid those tiresome overcrowded gradins whose general effect is of a heavy figure with geometrical edges, displeasing to the eye and calculated to clash with everything about it'. By contrast, 'terraces make it possible to avoid this drawback. The spectators are free to move about in them'.[2]

The penning, the fences, the boxes, and the seats can certainly be interpreted as the outcome of 100 years of territorialization of football space. An interesting interpretation of this territoriality is presented by David Sibley who argues that the compartmentalization of space into socially homogeneous areas (that is, away fans' terrace, home fans' terrace, seats, boxes) reinforces 'boundaries between social groups and gives people a stake in a particular territory encouraging conservatism' (Sibley 1981: 45). The fanzine columnist put it differently but with equal emphasis when he noted that 'the sectoring of grounds for home and away fans, family enclosures, executive boxes etc. only serves to isolate different sets of fans, further substantiating the idea of first and second class supporters' (Beauchampe 1986: 6). A sense of territory is therefore subtly imposed *within* the stadium and place to place differences at the micro-scale are emphasized; people come to 'know their place' metaphorically and literally. In all-seater stadiums place-specificity reaches its extreme form with people becoming numbers. A further unintended consequence of seating is that some of society's disadvantaged groups already subject to abuse at football matches – that is, women and ethnic minorities – may be less safe than in existing grounds. They will be unable to form groups and the chance of black fans sitting next to racists or women next to sexists will be increased in the all-seater stadium.[3]

Following the Taylor Report in early 1990 there was widespread criticism about the insistence on all-seater stadiums in Great Britain. One of the nation's newest stadiums, that at Scunthorpe, was seen by Steve Beauchampe as a 'production line stadium, like a Ford; good quality, compact, functional and characterless' (Beauchampe 1989: 5–6). Similar comments have been applied to other new stadiums – at Walsall ('a classic example of boredom' notes Inglis[4] – see Figure 3.2), and at non-League locations such as Yeovil and Weymouth. Such styles – 'as welcoming as a DIY superstore' according to iconoclastic sportswriter Frank Keating (1990) – are not inevitable, however. A new ground for non-League Dorchester Town has used imaginative approaches to ground design – 'fun, odd and quirky' according to Inglis[5] (see Figure 7.6).

But many fans do prefer to stand to watch games, and could quite easily continue to do so even if seats were installed. A MORI poll conducted in late 1989 found that most fans who usually stand to watch games wanted to continue doing so, the majority being greatest in the Third and Fourth Divisions where crowds are admittedly smaller (*The Guardian*, 17 January 1989: 14). According to David Canter's research, about 20 per cent of fans appear not to care whether they sit or stand, but whereas 32 per cent prefer to sit the respective figure for those who prefer standing was 44 per cent (Canter *et al.* 1989). A survey of Northampton Town fans undertaken by a local fanzine revealed that should the 'Cobblers' move to a new site only 20 per cent would prefer

Figure 3.2 'Container architecture' typified by Walsall's new (1990) Bacton Stadium, located among industrial and retail (but not residential) land use

an all-seater stadium while 21 per cent felt that they would be less likely to attend matches if an all-seater stadium were developed.[6] In a survey of members of the Football Supporters Association it was shown that 69.3 per cent would oppose seating at their own ground, 15.6 per cent claiming that they would not watch their club in an all-seater ground (Sir Norman Chester Centre for Football Research 1989b), while, if readers of Millwall's fanzine *The Lion Roars* are typical, 93 per cent of fans believe that they should have 'the right to stand'.[7]

Despite having introduced the all-seater stadium to England, Coventry City found that fans complained forcefully enough for the club to reintroduce terraces. At Pittodrie, however, where 100 per cent 'seating' was introduced in 1978, a survey of supporters in 1983 showed that 85 per cent felt that spectator accommodation should be all-seater. This contrasted with respective figures of 48 per cent for spectators at Ibrox, which retained some terracing, and only 38 per cent at Hibernian's Easter Road ground which was mainly terracing. The implication is that people come to accept seating. Indeed, only 15 per cent of the Pittodrie spectators felt that accommodation should be a mixture of seating and standing compared with respective figures of 52 and 62 per cent for the other two clubs (Centre for Leisure Research 1984).[8] But as the Coventry example shows, seats are certainly not always welcome, especially in the short term. And as with children in school classrooms, fans cannot be *made* to sit down (in fact in Italian games they have been observed to stand in seated accommodation during the game, only to sit down before the match and at half-time). What the terrace–seating dichotomy illustrates is that more comfortable forms of accommodation may not make the football experience more enjoyable. It seems more than reasonable, moreover, that some terracing be retained in new or modified stadiums; it is not intrinsically dangerous and many fans prefer it.

CONTAINMENT AND DANGER

I have stressed that one of the characteristics of the twentieth-century stadium has been the tendency towards spatial segregation and enclosure. From many visiting fans' points of view, 'greater segregation generally means that the opportunities to mingle with the more peaceful natives are very few and far between' and tend to be restricted to pre- and post-match meetings in 'safe' pubs (Wadmore 1988). The intention of the increased confinement of fans has been, in addition, to control and to provide greater crowd safety. Yet paradoxically, it has been in the late twentieth century that the most serious disasters have occurred, the Heysel and Hillsborough deaths resulting from the very fences and walls which were constructed with safety in mind. The Football Supporters Association (FSA) survey, alluded to above (see p. 49), revealed that 76.8 per cent of fans interviewed disagreed with the view that grounds should be all-seater for purposes of safety, while only 34.3 per cent agreed that in an emergency they would feel safer in seats than on the terraces (Sir Norman Chester Centre for Football Research 1989b).

Dissatisfaction with the modern stadium is not just voiced by British football fans. The paradox of progress can also be illustrated by examples from other countries and from other sports. A few years ago US baseball fans were asked by *The Ballparks Bulletin* to rate their favourite parks and to comment on them. The best and worst five, as perceived by fans, are listed in Table 3.1. It is obvious that the newest stadiums are not highly rated, their comfort and glitz failing to compensate for their lack of tradition and sense of nostalgia. The top five were built in the 1930s or earlier, truly historic by US standards! One long-term baseball fan wrote that a 'good ballpark must have real grass, be exclusively used for baseball, have box seats close enough so you can hear the players, and have cold beer not frozen margaritas' (Douglas 1987).

Others voice discontent about the ultra-modern milieu of the domed

Table 3.1 Best and worst baseball stadiums as rated by fans

1 **Fenway Park** (Boston). *The Green Monster, the closeness, the real grass – it has it all.*	22 **Three Rivers Stadium** (Pittsburgh). *There's always a good seat because nobody's there.*
2 **Wrigley Field** (Chicago). *A tough-to-beat neighborhood.*	23 **Veterans Stadium** (Philadelphia). *Haven't I seen this park somewhere before?*
3 **Tiger Stadium** (Detroit). *Great place to see a game because you're on top of the action.*	24 **Olympic Stadium** (Montreal). *Love Montreal, but give me Jarry Park anyday.*
4 **Comiskey Park** (Chicago). *Wish it weren't on the endangered species list.*	25 **HHH Metrodome** (Minneapolis). *Even football games look bad here.*
5 **Yankee Stadium** (New York). *Renovation scrubbed away a lot of history.*	26 **Kingdome** (Seattle). *You bring the dynamite and I'll bring the caps.*

Source: Douglas (1987: 36).

stadium complex. Consider the views of English professor and erstwhile footballer with the University of Notre Dame and Kansas City Chiefs, Michael Oriard:

> in domed stadiums which bring the game indoors as television does, posh theater seats try to duplicate the comfort of the living room. Elaborate electronic scoreboards lead cheers, provide statistics, and sometimes even run replays of the previous downs – as do announcers on TV. The packaging of professional football is increasingly transforming heroes into mere celebrities and moving the game away from sport to spectacle, from mythic contest in which the true fan is involved to sensory overload which is viewed from the outside.
>
> (Oriard 1981: 38)

Oriard recalls his experiences as a player during games at some of America's most modern stadiums. He described 'the seeming lack of air in the semi-domed stadium in Dallas [which] impressed on me a sense of unnatural stillness that was eerie as well as stifling. But playing in the Astrodome produced my ultimate non-experience' (Oriard 1976). Baseball pitcher, Howie Reed, former player with the Montreal Expos far preferred the old Jarry Park to those 'big sterile stadiums in the States'. At Jarry 'intimacy was an asset ... the best place in the world to play baseball' (quoted in Michener 1976: 432). In Hamburg in Germany, a new suburban development was constructed but attracted modest crowds, people disliking its isolation, its difficulty of access by public transport, and its impersonal character. The inner-city stadium in the working-class area of St Pauli, however, remained in favour and continued to attract fans. Comments such as these compare favourably with those made about 'developments' in British football.

The modern-day stadium with its internal segregation and its surveillance and security is indeed an efficient form of containment of crowds and the future stadium is likely to typify the 'container architecture' (see Figure 3.2) already exemplified by indoor sports halls and leisure centres. Indeed, an American observer has noted that the 'guards, barbed-wire fences and escape tunnels which are deemed necessary in some places to protect players and officials from those they have come to entertain reminds those on the other side of the Atlantic of a security system more suitable to *a prison*' (Ahrens 1980: 80), reinforcing the point I made earlier (see p. 11) about the way Foucault's history of the prison seems analogous to the history of the stadium. Indeed, the French radical observer of sports, Jean-Marie Brohm has gone so far as to suggest that 'sport is perhaps the social practice which *best exemplifies* the "disciplinary society"', analysed by Foucault (Brohm 1978: 18n.). In many respects, as Alain Ehrenberg (1980) has pointed out, the stadium today is similar to a fortress. Like a fort the exterior walls of the stadium must be strong enough to keep out invading hordes and caricatures of the modern stadium depict it as a heavily defended bastion (see Figure 3.3). Indeed, during times of civil strife stadiums (after *de jure* prisons) are probably the most secure bastions in the urban area, and in Ireland and in Chile stadiums *have* been used to intern prisoners (Eichberg 1988: 32, 35). In such situations the stadium–prison analogy is replaced by homology. Sports space, notably the stadium, also provides excellent facilities for militaristic activities additional to internment. Eichberg (1991b: 258) notes the significance of the sports ground for paramilitary political displays and rituals. As I will show later, a ground can project an image of a landscape of fear. As a result, the modern football stadium can be interpreted as the antithesis of play and freedom; instead, it has become a symbol of control and constraint, a landscape which shares much in common with other modern landscapes – 'subtly but tightly controlled by invisible overseers despite the open appearance of fantastic freedoms of choice' (Soja 1989: 246).

Figure 3.3 Fortress football

Source: When Saturday Comes, no. 25, 1989: 10–11.

CONCLUSION

This chapter has shown that changes in the architecture of the stadium imposed by an ideology of rational recreation and passive spectatorship have not been without reaction from football's fandom. In this way I have tried to show that the attitudes and actions of society's 'dominant groups' have been contested by the fans upon whom they were imposed. On the one hand, the modern stadium typifies what Eichberg would call the 'ecology of achievement sport' (Eichberg 1988: 24–38). It is space which has been broken down into a number of segments, it is fortified, it is a modern example of Foucault's 'panopticism', and it increasingly consumes more and more land with its car-parking and associated facilities. But the changing human landscape of the stadium may also illustrate the blurring of polarities more reminiscent of the post-modern. Along with high-tech surveillance equipment we have the increasingly *less* serious forms of behaviour by fans and, through the synthetic surface, the potential for multi-purpose land use – as in the vernacular, pre-modern game. I will return to these ambiguous aspects of the modern stadium in Chapter 7.

Despite attempts by supporters to claim back the game and inject into it a new sense of fun, it cannot be denied that for many people the stadium and its vicinity do conjure up images of annoyance, nuisance and fear. I will explore such negative spillovers from the stadium in Chapter 5 but before doing so will deal in the next chapter with the rather more positive attitudes and experiences which many people have towards football.

4

FOOTBALL, THE STADIUM AND A SENSE OF PLACE

Having considered the evolution of the stadium and its choreography, I now want to turn to what the stadium means to those who periodically occupy it and posess allegience to the team that plays in it. In this chapter I will emphasize people's positive attitudes towards the stadium while in the chapter which follows I will concentrate on the negative attitudes possessed by urban residents, not only fans but also those who might be termed 'the silent majority'. Attitudes towards football are far from uniform and the viewpoints of non-fans are all-too-rarely articulated and reported. While this chapter considers what are often regarded as 'positive' attributes of the 'people's game' it must be stressed that while some people regard the stadium as a religious shrine, others view it as a source of nuisance, annoyance, and stress.

The significance of the stadium in providing football fans with a 'sense of place' cannot be fully appreciated without an awareness of the popular significance of football itself and for this reason I want to start this chapter with an overview of the social-bonding function of modern representational sport in general and of football in particular. I then go on to identify different ways in which the stadium is held in affection by fans. An awareness of such feelings and their sources aids an understanding of some of the problems inherent in the (post-Hillsborough) scenarios for the brave new world of British football.

FOOTBALL AND COLLECTIVE IDENTIFICATION

Sport in its modern form, and archetypically football in its modern form, provides what is arguably the major focus for collective identification in modern Britain and in much of the rest of the world. In the USA, football, baseball, and basketball perform a similar function. How else can such diverse (and to outsiders, nondescript) towns as Crewe,

Scunthorpe, Torquay, or Carlisle regularly project themselves via the national media and, at the same time, find a focus which unites the towns' various residents? Only football can do this. For most weekends of the year the towns' place names are projected via radio and television to millions of people across the nation, hence providing a free source of advertising. Places are hardly regarded as real places (cities are certainly not viewed as real cities) without a Football League team, and centres like Milton Keynes, which, on the basis of size and location are worthy claimants to a league club, have for several years striven to attract one. Even the civic worthies of a place like High Wycombe, situated success-fully in the southern Silicon Strip, have felt that the town would benefit from the possession of a Football League club.

Of course, the more successful a club, the more media attention it receives. Clubs like Liverpool, Manchester United, and Arsenal receive much more national press and television coverage, and hence more image projection, than their more humble Fourth Division colleagues. But football does not serve only to project a place to people who would otherwise never hear its name mentioned; it also provides a potent medium for collective identification with a place.

An American sociologist, James Coleman, noted that most places 'have few common goals. They fight no wars, seldom engage in community rallies, are rarely faced with such crises as floods or tor-nadoes that can engender a communal spirit' (Coleman 1961). Team sports events do provide that communal spirit. Football is an example of a civic ritual which is made more attractive than other civic rituals because it possesses a serialized character; that is, it has a strong element of succession about it with its seasons and its regular and predictable fixtures. Indeed, it has been suggested that such periodic and regular events provide a 'sense of stability to urban space, including a sense of place' (Parkes and Thrift 1980: 109). At football matches places unite in support of 'their team', a form of unity seldom experi-enced in other contexts. It has been suggested that it is the sports stadium that is the 'legitimate successor of the agora or forum; it is where we demonstrate local loyalties – loudly as the Greeks would have done' (Jackson 1984: 20). Charles Korr, an American professor of history and a devotee and chronicler of West Ham United, suggests (perhaps with more than a hint of hyperbole) that 'even people who know little about football talk about "our club", "our lads" or what "we" did on Saturday. The phrases carry a sense of common interest and an almost proprietory [sic] view of the club' (Korr 1986: 19). As well as providing a source for intense localism, the football ground is also, according to Chas Critcher (1979), 'the established venue for the exploration and expression' of a masculine working-class identity and 'in the absence of alternatives it is likely to remain so'.

Collective identification, especially when coupled with success, makes people feel better and engenders a sense of place pride (see Figure 4.1). 'Local pride' emerged as the most frequently cited reason for supporting a football club – exceeding the influences of family and peers – in a survey of fanzine readers in the early 1990s (Curren and Redmond 1991: 8). In Britain this was classically illustrated some years ago by the surprise FA Cup Final victory of Sunderland over the favourites Leeds United. After the event, researchers from Birmingham University descended on Sunderland to elicit people's 'self-image' following the Cup success. They noted that

> there is now something to identify with in being from Sunderland: everybody in the country knows they won the cup, more of them might know where Sunderland is – Sunderland has been 'put back on the map'.
>
> (Derrick and McRory 1973: 15)

Figure 4.1 'Naples, open your eyes and look at the sky; it's the only thing which is bigger than you. Thanks lads!' One of the many banners in the 'Spanish quarter' of Naples commemorating Napoli's Italian championship victory in 1987
Source: Bromberger (1988: 150).

Being put 'back' on the map reflects the 'marginal' status of many football towns which often fail to feature in the mental maps of even some professional players, managers, and supporters. It is not surprising, therefore, that following Sunderland's Cup success one resident noted that 'a not particularly glamorous town feels more proud of itself after a win of this sort', while another stated that 'before the Cup people wondered where Sunderland was: now we're back on the map again' (Derrick and McRory 1973).

A rather less benign view of the collective identification engendered by football is one where the football–city nexus is interpreted in terms of power and hegemony. Contrary to superficial impressions, it is argued that through major team sports the concept of community is promoted at the expense of economic or social class. Team sports can be viewed as promoting allegiance to place rather than allegiance to class. The emphasis on inter-place competition is obvious to any casual observer of inter-terrace chanting at any Football League game. Newcastle oppose Sunderland; Crewe oppose Chester; Manchester United oppose Manchester City; Bristol Rovers oppose Bristol City; Stoke oppose Port Vale – not just on the field of 'play' but also on the terraces. Indeed, John Pratt and Mick Salter (1984) believe that it isn't so much 'the actual playing team which is supported but the name of the home town or city and the supporters as loyal and worthy representatives of it'. Opposition between clubs (representing places), runs the hegemonic argument, brings similar groups of working-class people into conflict and hence serves to obfuscate class tension, replacing it with place tension. In this way the modern football ritual differes from tribal ritual; according to Levi-Strauss the former ends with a winner and a loser (that is, it disjoins) whereas the latter works towards 'equality' between the contestants (that is, it conjoins) (Levi-Strauss 1966).[1]

The radical view of football outlined above sees the sport as ideologically conservative in that it diverts class consciousness towards place consciousness and hence preserves the *status quo* view of society. Taken further, radicals argue that team sports such as football negate the basis for revolution which Karl Marx predicted would be based on those very class divisions. Attention was diverted from revolution by the 'people's game' and the existing power elite could hence be sustained. Indeed, football could be viewed as actually bringing the classes together in support of 'their team', additionally acting (and continuing to act) as a source of social control.[2]

This interpretation may be persuasive and I accept that watching football can divert people from more socially pressing tasks. But I find it flawed on at least two counts. First of all it assumes that political activism and watching (or playing) football are mutually exclusive. This is clearly incorrect; even the most fervent revolutionary might want to relax occasionally.

My second objection to the hegemony argument is that it ignores the fact that the majority of the population is simply not interested in football, though I do accept that other kinds of mass culture can serve to divert people from more pressing and socially relevant tasks. In the 1988/9 season the number of fan visits to English League games was 18,464,192 but the number of fans who actually went to a game was obviously much lower than that. According to a mid-1970s survey, 19.6 per cent of the adult population had paid to watch a match at some time during the 1974 season, though the figure rose to 26 per cent in Scotland and fell to about 15 per cent in Wales (IPC 1975: 12). Of course, the percentage of the population which watches football has fallen since then and the number which watches it regularly has always been smaller. Even if the number watching the sport on television and reading about it in the newspapers is taken into account, it is almost certainly less than the number of people whose prime interest lies elsewhere.

Research into football and social control in Scotland by Roy Hay showed that attendances at Scottish League games in the late 1970s accounted for less than 2 per cent of the total population – a population often projected as being besotted with football (Allen 1968: 193). This figure obviously varies considerably between different places. For Aberdeen and Glasgow, for example, it was suggested that a respective figure of about 7 per cent would be more appropriate. Such a statistic has been shown to apply to certain places in England. At Carlisle, for example, one estimate placed the proportion watching football at over 10 per cent while at the other end of the spectrum the figure fell well below the national average (Rivett 1975).[3] Hay's comments for Scotland apply equally to the rest of Britain:

> If we are talking about social control through spectator involvement, then we are discussing less than 10% of the population of the locality concerned, probably 5 per cent; while if whole national units are taken, then the proportion falls to 1–2 per cent.
>
> (Hay 1981: 244)

It needs to be stated, however, that most of those attending football matches are men, mainly between the ages of 16 and 45. The proportion of this particular group which watches live football will obviously be greater. An extreme example, perhaps, is provided by a survey of secondary school students in Liverpool which revealed that 65 per cent attended 'regularly' or 'occasionally', while for boys it rose to 84 per cent (Sir Norman Chester Centre for Football Research 1987a: 13). It is clear, therefore, that in some places football does provide a consuming interest for a large proportion of certain groups of the population.

If attendance is biased in terms of age and gender it is worth speculating whether it is also biased over intra-urban space. Some examples of stadium–distance relationships are discussed later in this chapter (see, for example, Figure 4.9), but in a very general sense the well-known geographic effect of distance imposing a 'friction' on movement ('distance-decay') might be expected to apply in football, as it does in many other things. Given the traditional working-class support for British football it might also be expected that it is the working-class parts of the city that provide a disproportionate contribution to football's fandom. I am not aware of any British studies which have actually analysed the degree of congruence between the social class of fans and the social geography of the city – that is, whether some areas of the city are over-represented and others under-represented in the geography of club support. It seems likely that they are but this is not necessarily the case elsewhere in Europe where, in many cases, football is a more socially heterogeneous sport that in Britain. In Marseilles the stadium is not only a reduced mirror image of the city in terms of the geographic distribution of fans on the terraces (see Figure 2.4), but also the relative numbers of fans from particular parts of the city are reflected in the proportions from those parts which visit Olympique Marseille. Hence, for example, whereas 29.9 per cent of the population of Marseilles live in the northern quarters of the town, the respective figure for those inside the stadium from the identical area is 29.3 per cent (Bromberger *et al.* 1987). The relationship between the percentage of the total urban population from each of the seventeen administrative areas of Marseilles and the percentage of the fans of Olympique Marseilles (L'OM) from each area is shown in Figure 4.2.

It is often not simply distance from the stadium or social class that determines the support for a club. Family traditions and religion are often cited as crucial. The relationship between religion and club allegiance is most starkly illustrated, perhaps, in Belfast where in the Clonard area 98 per cent of the population is Catholic, 73 per cent support the traditional Glasgow Catholic club, Celtic, while none support the local (Protestant) team, Linfield. In the Shankill area, on the other hand, where only 1 per cent is Catholic, none support Celtic while 74 per cent

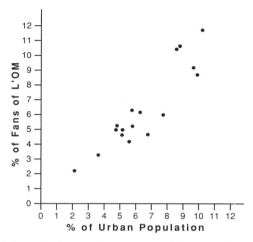

Figure 4.2 As each urban zone's percentage of the Marseilles population increases, so does each zone's share of the fandom of Olympique Marseilles
Source: Bromberger *et al.* (1987: 31).

support Linfield (Boal 1970). A similar, if less dramatic, effect is present in Glasgow (Catholic Celtic and Protestant Rangers) and Liverpool (Protestant Everton and Catholic Liverpool).

A point to emphasize at this stage is that there has been an undoubted reduction in the degree of spatial circumstances of most football clubs' support. If a 'community' does still support a club it often embraces a wider geographical area than that in the immediate vicinity of the club's home stadium.

It is widely felt that the idea of a strongly place-based community has been a casualty of modernization and that a transition has taken place whereby a reduction in the friction of distance has produced a 'non-place urban realm' in which if a community exists at all it is an example of what Melvin Webber (1963) called a 'community without propinquity' – arguably in the case of British football a working-class example of what is usually thought of as a middle-class phenomenon – a community made up of a network of people oriented to a nodal point (in this case the stadium). Although the bulk of support may come from the club's home town or borough, the proportion which lives close to the stadium has certainly declined over time, especially in the case of certain embourgeoisified 'super clubs'. Such changes may be attributed in part to the changing population geography of the city (see p. 146) but they are likely also to result from the emergence of the more discriminating spectator. It has been suggested that over 50 per cent of Liverpool's fans travel over 50 km to home games (Hill 1989: 97), while Manchester United's supporters are found nation-wide (see Figure 4.3). The role of television in reducing fan attachment to place – or, more precisely, relocating such attachment in space – cannot be underestimated. TV coverage of football is highly selective and Manchester United and Liverpool can be supported from all parts of the country from living rooms where fans can wear red shirts and display their football icons without ever visiting the town in which their adopted club is found. If allegiance to a professional sports team is regarded as a kind of 'reconstruction' of some former *Gemeinschaft* then the spatial dimensions of some football 'communities' are extremely large!

A late 1980s survey of 1,500 school students mainly in their early teens revealed that four teams accounted for two-thirds of respondents' support, with 34 per cent supporting Liverpool and 17 per cent Manchester United. Over 60 per cent supported three clubs in the

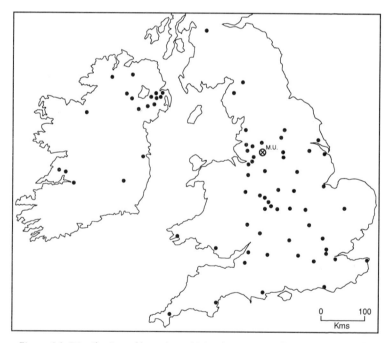

Figure 4.3 Distribution of branches of Manchester United's supporters' clubs
Source: Manchester United Official Yearbook, 1990.

north-west of England, despite that fact that less than 20 per cent of respondents came from that region (Institute for Advanced Studies 1987). Many fans support a club outside the region in which they live – certainly not their local club in the traditional sense.

The changing pattern of support over time can be illustrated by two contrasting examples. Charlton Athletic typify a relatively modest club, located in the south-east London borough of Greenwich, having fluctuated between the First and Third Division of the League in recent years. In 1971 the shares of its supporter-club membership which came from the suburban counties of Kent and Surrey were respectively 37.5 and 2.5 per cent; in 1990 the equivalent statistics were 44 and 5 per cent.[4] In the case of some of the north-west's super clubs, data for the year 1951 indicated that about two-fifths of the total number of spectators in Lancashire watched Liverpool, Everton, or the two premier Manchester clubs. By 1971 the proportion had risen to two-thirds (Rivett 1975).[5] This tendency was reflected in other parts of society with the decline of the corner shop and the local cinema, each giving way to a smaller number of large outlets and satisfying the economic rationality of the discriminating consumer. In the case of football it was partly a spatial manifestation of the abolition of the maximum wage for players in 1961 which meant that clubs in large cities could capitalize on their market potential, buy better players, and attract fans from a wider geographical catchment. In doing so the traditional provincialism of the game started being eroded. The growth of widespread car ownership and the development of the motorway network also helped the consumer of football to bypass the small clubs in favour of the bigger operators. Those for whom the club provides a source of affection are, therefore, often spread over a relatively large area; those suffering football nuisances – a subject covered in the next chapter – tend to be more spatially concentrated around the ground.

The widening spatial catchment of support for some football clubs has led a number of observers, notably those from the fanzine scene, to distinguish between 'true' and 'pseudo' fans. The former are those who travel to support their club through thick and thin, irrespective of their current form and sometimes locked into a 'support your local loser' syndrome. The latter, sometimes called 'glory hunters', will change their allegiance according to the degree of success a particular club is achieving. They will follow their club vicariously, making contact with it through television, magazines and newspapers. Such fans are not experiencing the sport-place bond in the way the 'true fan' does. Television creates 'new communities' separated from their *raison d'être* by considerable distances – often hundreds, even thousands, of miles. To be with other people at a football match is a very different thing from watching the same football match (Meyrowitz 1985: 143–5).

Football *per se* may constitute one of many forms of social control but its significance has probably been overstated. This is not to deny that it may well remain the main form of collective identification in which status may still be found simply by being ascribed to a particular place in an era when status is more usually obtained from acts requiring achievement. I must stress, however, that for a small number of people – the true fans – football and the stadiums within which it is played are of immense significance. For them the sport does unquestionably con-tribute to their quality of life. What is more, though small in number, dedicated supporters can exert a surprising amount of political muscle. It is to this affection for, and activism in support of, the stadium that I now want to turn.

FOOTBALL AND TOPOPHILIA

The American geographer Yi-Fu Tuan uses the term 'topophilia' to describe 'all the human being's affective ties with the material environ-ment' and, in the present context, the situations where football 'couples sentiment with place' (Tuan 1974: 113). While it is not the strongest of human emotions, place attachment or a love of place is regarded by many as certainly contributing to the quality of life (Eyles 1985). Another geographer, Edward Relph, has likewise argued that 'land-scapes matter. They are not just incidental visual backgrounds to other social concerns but are part of our being that enter directly into the qual-ity of our lives by providing countless small pleasures' (Relph 1989a: 151). For some people the stadium may be a modern example of what Relph called an 'authentic place'; that is, one for which 'affection does not result from fad or fashion but is felt in an unselfconscious way' (Relph 1976: 66).

I believe that for a small number of people, whose influence I will show to have been quite disproportionate to their numbers, the football stadium provides a potent source of topophilia in a number of ways. The stadium may create a sense of place because of its quasi-religious connotations, its 'homely' character or its scenery. In the future it may come to be loved and enjoyed as part of our heritage. And some people enjoy the stadium because it contributes to their earnings. I will deal with each of these sources of the stadium's satisfaction in the sections which follow.

The stadium as a sacred place

Next to Goodison Park, home of Everton FC, St Luke's church nestles uneasily in the corner of the football stadium (see Figure 4.4). It is almost a relict feature of the urban landscape, today dominated by the steel structure which is Goodison Park. The alarming juxtaposition of what might once have been termed 'the sacred and the profane' reflects, in fact, the changing 'religious' allegience of a substantal proportion of the public. Rather than worshipping at the altar of Christ, Everton's masses have preferred the terraces of Goodison. The modern religious icons are the billboards and hoardings around the ground.

It is not just grand grounds like Goodison which receive religious-like devotion from fans. Consider the view of a Chester City fan to that club's humble and rather nondescript former Sealand Road ground:

> Sealand Road has been part of my life for 30 years; it's more than a football ground, it's a way of life not just to me but to thousands of people alive and dead whose life has revolved around a match at The Stadium. It's more than bricks and mortar, it's almost something spiritual.[6]

Figure 4.4 The sacred and the profane? Or different kinds of sacred space? St Luke's Church and Goodison Park (home of Everton), Liverpool

Following the closure of Sealand Road and the (temporary) relocation of Chester City's home games to Macclesfield (see Chapter 6), the ground itself was felt to have 'died' and a graffitist asked that it be left to 'rest in peace' (see Figure 4.5).

A number of football clubs were, of course, founded by churches and chapels, part of the drive towards 'muscular Christianity' of mid and late nineteenth-century England. But the game itself has often been viewed as a 'surrogate' religion (Coles 1975) and it has been argued that if sport performs the same human and social functions as 'real' religions it should be analysed if it were one (von Kortzfleisch 1970; see also Korsgaard 1990). Football certainly shares many similarities with religion; each seeks perfection, each is built on discipline, they involve an integration of the mind and spirit, and they have established rituals

Figure 4.5 The death of a football ground is likened by some to the death of a friend. Sealand Road, Chester, is left to 'rest in peace'

and symbols related to people, places, and procedures. Football, like the Church, possesses ceremonial and a liturgy – that is, the game itself and an enclosed space consecrated to a cult. American sociologist Jay Coakley (1987) feels that a difference between sport and religion is that sport is competitive and individualistic whereas religions are communal and non-competitive, but I am not so sure. In sport communities do exist on both the field of play and on the terraces with (like the Church) an integrated crowd which – to an extent at least – cuts across different social classes (Edgell and Jary 1973: 224–5).[7] It has been suggested that 'the paradigms offered by the sociology of religion may be usefully employed in the analysis of a phenomenon which at the moment claims more than its fair share of journalistic misconception and sensationalism' (Coles 1975). An interpretation of the stadium, in the eyes of many fans, as a sacred place certainly aids an understanding of the strength of resistance to locational change in football, something I deal with in Chapter 6.

Following the deaths of ninety-five fans, mainly Liverpool supporters, resulting from crushing on the Hillsborough terraces, Ian Taylor highlighted the religious character of British football in highly personal terms:

> The 'reconstruction' and decoration of the goalmouths at Hillsborough and Anfield with flowers, wreaths, and other memorabilia of soccer, including apparently, scarves of the Juventus club, on Saturday evening and Sunday morning 16 April, by supporters of all three clubs, was nothing if not a mass popular religious rite.
>
> (Taylor 1989: 91)[8]

The people of Sheffield (the city in which Hillsborough is located) responded to the tragedy in a highly religious way in the days following the horrendous events in the stadium. The entrances through which crowds had surged on that sad Saturday were covered with scarves and flowers, turning the gates into a much-bedecked shrine (see Figure 4.6). The goalmouth at Anfield had developed a similar appearance, with mourners filing slowly past the goal as if in a cemetery. Across the road from the Hillsborough turnstiles through which hundreds of fans were channelled, residents of the city of Sheffield have erected a small memorial to those who died, a lovingly tended symbol to remind us of the Hillsborough tragedy.

The popular sanctification bestowed upon some football grounds does, in some cases, go to the extent of treating them as actual cemeteries. Also at Anfield, fans have had their ashes scattered over the ground or over the Kop terrace. The legendary Bill ('Football's not a matter of

67

Figure 4.6 Hillsborough Stadium, Sheffield, the day after the 1989 disaster
(Photo by courtesy of Margaret Roberts)

life or death; it's more important than that') Shankly is one of them,
while a former stadium cat is buried under one of the goal lines. Anfield
is not unique as a football ground doubling as a final resting place.

Within the stadium particular parts, not necessarily (indeed, invariably not) having the best view of the game, come to possess sacred
qualities for those who regularly congregate there in the same place each
week. In Britain different parts of the terracing become revered spaces
for different groups of fans. Even in somewhat soulless stadiums such as
that in Munich, certain fans show allegiance to the 'south curve'; in
Milan, where Milan and Inter play in a shared stadium, the fans from
the former occupy the south curve while those from the latter take up
space on the north; the Florence 'ultras' show allegiance to the 'Fiesole
curve', while in Stoke-on-Trent it's the Boothen End where spaces are
carved up by various groups of fans. Such places create what David
Seamon rather grandly calls 'place ballets' – the bringing of people
together and hence fostering a collective entity, enhancing the quality of
life (Seamon 1979: 64–5).[9] About one-quarter of male respondents to a
questionnaire survey of readers of Britain's leading fanzine had watched
games from the same vantage point for over ten years, a figure rising to
nearer one-third in lower divison clubs (Curren and Redmond 1991:
17–18).[10] Thus, while a stadium may appear placeless, its interior may

be 'closely differentiated into places by the personalisation' of particular areas, 'by association with local events and the development of local myths . . . all of which give a genuineness and authenticity to somewhere quite inauthentically created' (Relph 1976: 71).

Football also has its tangible, quasi-religious icons in the vernacular landscape. Examples include the Shankly Gate, again at Anfield, with its latter-day psalm 'You'll Never Walk Alone' dominating its wrought-iron archway through which fans enter as if entering a church; the famous 'Cottage' at Fulham; Villa Park's magnificent facade; the clock-stand at Highbury, and the concourse at Old Trafford. In the middle of Hanley shopping centre in Stoke-on-Trent is a statue of Sir Stanley Matthews, a modern secular saint. Matthews is perhaps the best example in Britain of a genuine local folk-hero, known (and not simply through the presence of his present-day statue) to virtually every resident of the Potteries.

In a Midlands cemetery stands another reminder of football's quasi-religious significance. If soccer had saints then the grave of former young genius of Manchester United, Duncan Edwards, who was killed in the tragic Munich air crash of 1958, would be football's equivalent of Lourdes. Arthur Hopcraft, in *The Football Man* written in 1968, described it in these words:

> His grave in Dudley cemetery is elaborate. The headstone has an ingrained picture of him in football kit holding a ball above his head for a throw-in. An inscription reads 'A Day of Memory sad to recall. Without farewell, He left us All'. There are three flower stands and one is in the shape of a football.
>
> (Hopcraft 1968: 72)

A recent book on British football in the inter-war period finishes by averring that the 'football grounds of England were the Labour Party at prayer' (Fishwick 1989: 150). Such a claim might overstate the proportion of the working class that show any interest in the sport, but an awareness of its undoubted religious character aids an appreciation of the devotion which some people show towards it. From a topophilic perspective few would deny that Tuan's recognition of a 'sacred place' as being one possessing 'overpowering significance' (Tuan 1974: 99) must undoubtedly apply to the football stadium.

The stadium as home

Tuan comments that 'familiarity breeds affection when it does not breed

contempt' (Tuan 1977: 144–5), and many football fans possess bonds
with their stadium that can be likened to ties with home. The home
ground, like the home town 'may be plain, lacking in architectural
distinction and historical glamour, yet we resent an outsider's criticism
of it. Its ugliness does not matter ...' (Bennett 1988). The closure of
Charlton Athletic's ground at The Valley elicited this response from a
long-term fan of the club:

> Is it just because I am a Charlton fan through and through that I
> regard the Valley as something special? Sometimes the size and
> old-fashioned nature of the stands (apart from the South Stand)
> make it unique. It's not a palace, but I prefer homes to palaces.
>
> (Everitt 1989)

Following the announcement of a proposed return to The Valley from
their alien Selhurst Park site, where Charlton Athletic FC had been
involved in an unhappy ground sharing scheme with Crystal Palace, the
Charlton fanzine, Voice of the Valley, was able to announce 'We're
going Home!' (Everitt 1989).[11] For some, the ground is more than the
club, and the fanzine editorialized in these words:

> We know that there are people who argue that they support the
> team and not the ground, but they miss the point. The two cannot
> be separated without compromising the club's identity. Do that
> and you lose the deep emotional hold that even today football
> clubs exert over their supporters. ... Now the soul of Charlton
> Athletic will be renewed.
>
> (Everitt 1989)

Although such sentiments will not be held by all fans, and certainly not
by the more discriminating among them, it does seem that for some,
'home' is not a few kilometres away or next door. It is the ground for
which they have developed a profound sense of topophilia. A 25-km
move to Milton Keynes was, in Luton's case, viewed as 'tearing the club
from its most loyal supporters' (Williams et al. 1989a). In the case of
Millwall FC, the club's directors expressed a preference for their
cramped, 79-year-old stadium at The Den, rather than occupy a new,
purpose-built stadium 400 metres away (though they subsequently
relented). In the 1970s a study revealed that 'Chelsea' would simply not
be 'Chelsea' if it relocated a few kilometres away at Wormwood Scrubs
within the same borough (Bishop and Booth 1974). The extremely
ardent, and continuing, campaign to return Bristol Rovers to the city
which bears its name, following a move to neighbouring Bath, further

indicates the sense in which stadiums generate affection and a sense of place.

The memory of home recalls familiar sensory experiences and the football ground is no exception. Tuan notes how odour 'has the power to evoke vivid, emotionally charged memories of past events and scenes' (Tuan 1974: 10). One football fan told me that whenever he smelt cigarettes being smoked in the open air he was immediately reminded of his times on the terraces of Easter Road, home of Hibernian FC. A long-term Derby County supporter recalls with great affection the 'smell-scape' of the Baseball Ground:

> When all is said and done about Derby, and you've forgotten all the players and all the matches, I think the one memory I have of Derby, or at least the Baseball Ground, which I'm sure no other club ever had, is the smell. For me the magic is just coming down to that ground. You just swing in from Dairyhouse Road and into Cambridge Street and it gets you straight away – that drifting, acrid odour coming out of the foundry. . . . Football grew up with that sort of smell. Saturday afternoons for working men who'd been at heavy industry until one o'clock, and Derby County encapsulates all the strong points. It's got its own foundry as well as its own stands. Even as a kid, if I went on me bike down to that end of the town – not on match days – and happened to smell that smell, that was a football smell, that was Derby County's smell, and I can smell it to this day, you know.[12]

If the stadium is a symbolic home to fans it produces similar sentiments in players. Players generally prefer home games because their team is likely to secure more wins, both scoring more and conceding fewer goals when playing at home. This widely observable outcome is known as the 'home field advantage' and has been shown to exist in a number of sports in a wide variety of countries.[13] It has been suggested by Torsten Malmberg that 'it is difficult to find another explanation for this than that of territoriality' (Malmberg 1980).[14] I will contest this simplistic explanation later, but initially will provide evidence of the widespread existence of the home advantage in British football.

Table 4.1 shows how for fifteen levels of British football, ranging from Division I of the Football League to the Vauxhall Opel League, a consistent pattern is found of clubs securing more wins and scoring more goals when playing at home than away. The ratio of goals scored home/away tends to be greater for the Football League (average of 1.49 for all divisions) than in arguably the most minor of the leagues

Table 4.1 The home advantage in British football, 1988–9

League	Goals: Home/Away	Ratio	Wins: Home/Away	Ratio
English League: Div. 1	583/424	1.37	157/111	1.41
Div. 2	884/581	1.52	261/128	2.04
Div. 3	902/593	1.52	268/138	1.94
Div. 4	899/599	1.50	267/124	2.15
Scottish Premier Div.	231/191	1.21	82/ 44	1.86
Div. 1	417/342	1.22	118/ 68	1.73
Div. 2	413/354	1.17	119/ 68	1.75
GM Vauxhall Conference	670/556	1.20	181/141	1.28
HFS Loans Premier Div.	737/583	1.26	204/145	1.41
Div. 1	850/608	1.40	223/135	1.65
Vauxhall/Opel Premier	676/560	1.21	189/148	1.28
Div. 1	629/541	1.16	178/151	1.18
Welsh League Nat. Div.	438/391	1.12	109/104	1.05
Premier Div.	519/403	1.29	135/100	1.35
Div. 1	519/466	1.11	138/102	1.35

Source: Rothman's Football Yearbook, 1989–90, London, Queen Anne Press, 1989.

examined, the Welsh League (1.17). The respective ratios for wins at home and away are 1.90 for the English leagues and 1.25 for the Welsh. The averages for the Scottish and five English non-league clubs lies in between these two extremes though the data from one season's games are no firm basis for any inter-league generalization about the home advantage.

Territoriality and a sense of place may well contribute to the home advantage but mathematician Richard Pollard (1987) has argued that several other factors may need to be taken into account. For example, the distance that an away team has travelled for a fixture may produce varying degrees of tiredness, the referee may be biased in favour of the home team, and different tactics may be employed by visiting teams. And in crucial matches, where the crowd's expectations and pressure to win are unusually high, a home-field disdvantage might exist, excessive expectations interfering with the execution of skilled performances by players (Baumeister and Steinhilber 1984).

In part, however, the home advantage exists because of the familiarity players have with their own ground and the support they receive from their spectators. The significance of familiarity is supported by the effect of plastic pitches on home performances; for the three clubs with plastic in England in 1988/9 the home goals ratio was 2.32 and the home wins ratio 3.44 – much higher than the average for any of the leagues shown in Table 4.1. Just as plastic pitches enhance the home advantage, the futuristic domed stadium appears to do so even more. Evidence from the United States suggests that 'the fortunes of a [football] team can be enhanced by the building of dome' to the extent of 1.5 to 2 points per game (Zeller and Jurkovac 1989).

The stadium as scenic space

In the previous chapter I referred to the idea of a variety of landscape elements contributing to the overall stadium landscape ensemble. The greater the variety within the ensemble, the greater the potential for gratification from the sport experience. I now want to return to this idea and suggest that the scenic elements of the football stadium provide a source of topophilia for many fans.

Over time, places develop a character that transcends the behaviour of particular people (for example, footballers) at one point in time (Harrison 1988) and come to possess a symbolism that the architect had never intended. But the love of the stadium is not based on any conscious awareness of any merits of design. Instead it possesses what Edward Relph calls an 'authentic sense of place [which] is above all that of being inside and belonging to your place both as an individual and as a member of a community, and to know this without reflecting on it' (Relph 1976: 65). Such authenticity is threatened with the development of the sanitized, safe, concrete but 'placeless' stadium which will possess fewer landscape elements and simply less scenery for the spectator to absorb and enjoy. It will be similar to many others of its kind. The introduction of the concrete bowl is also likely to sever the visual connection between the stadium and the town. In aspiring to a rational, universal space, claims Brian Neilson (1986), 'sports saucers' succeed only in 'defining a non-place, rather an anti-place, hostile to the bounds imposed by locale and history'.

Despite the dominantly negative characteristics attributed to the British football stadium many can be regarded as scenic. Gay Meadow, the quaintly named ground of Shrewsbury Town, is scenic not simply because of its famous wrought-iron Victorian turnstile, but also because the visual link between ground and city is not broken. Surrounded by trees, on the banks of the River Severn, the ground conjures a surprisingly rustic image in contrast to football's traditional industrial, Lowry-esque connotations. In Simon Inglis's words, 'grounds like those at

Chester and Cambridge do not reflect at all the towns they are in. Gay Meadow not only reflects the town of Shrewsbury but is an inescapable part of it' (Inglis 1987). The various elements seen from inside the stadium include 'a lovely old half-time scoreboard', 'a thick range of trees along the river bank', and 'Laura's Tower on the hill, a small red, sandstone tower standing out above the trees, built in the castle grounds in 1790 by Thomas Telford' (Inglis 1987).

Gay Meadow is exceptional in its scenic quality but grounds elsewhere, because of their uniqueness, attract favourable comment. Charlton's ground at The Valley received the attention of a *Guardian* leader writer in 1985 who described it thus:

> There's a sense of history in the higgledy-piggledy mix of spare acres, 50 year old stands and the goals that Sam Bartram once defended. When the sun shines, it's one of the most endearing grounds in the land; when a storm crackles over the Thames, you watch the Twilight of the Gods from a natural balcony.[15]

While not quite the view of the Fiesole Hills from the seats of the Stadio Communale in Florence, the environments of grounds like The Valley or Gay Meadow, each in their different ways, undoubtedly provide a sense of place through their various scenic qualities, just as the older baseball stadiums are preferred to the newer ones in North America (see Table 3.1). The incremental growth of the British football stadium with spectators being close to the game and without having the *cordon sanitaire* of the running track – common in many countries – makes the stadium a place of character, even if it has all too often been relatively uncared for.

It is not only the permanent architectural features, however 'ordinary', that provide a sense of place but also some of the more ephemeral elements of the stadium's landscape ensemble. The mockery, facetiousness and fun of the terrace banter, music, gestures, grafitti, emblems, and banners with their varied inscriptions; all are part and parcel of the overall stadium experience – an experience which often spills out of the stadium into the streets and districts surrounding it. Such iconography may reach its apogee in France and Italy where mock burials with imitation coffins and caskets are paraded as a form of mockery to poke fun at the defeat or decline of rival teams (Bromberger 1988).

The stadium as heritage?

Although Relph tends to deride tourist places because of their 'other directedness', that is, places directed towards outsiders (Relph 1976:

93), it has been suggested that tourism is, almost by definition, a pleasure trip (Jakle 1987: 9–10). Several football stadiums have achieved
the status of places to be enjoyed through the perspective of the tourist
or visitor rather than the fan. The ground provdies pleasure to a clientele
distanced from the intense affection of the fan. In the tourist office in
central Liverpool the visitor is invited to enjoy a 'Soccer City' weekend
(see Figure 4.7). The Merseyside Tourist Board classifies Liverpool FC
as a 'category 1' tourist attraction – that is, being unique to Merseyside
or being capable of attracting national and international visitors in its
own right. 'They compete favourably with similar attractions anywhere
in the world'.[16] And elsewhere in the world the tourist's itinerary will
often include the Berlin Olympic Stadium; Olympiapark in Munich
(including the futuristic stadium), today the home of Bayern Munich;
and, of course, the 1896 Olympic stadium in Athens. In Britain guided
tours take place around Wembley Stadium, Anfield, and Old Trafford,
the latter also having its impressive football museum. In Pittsburgh the
Three Rivers Stadium is only twenty years old but is nevertheless
mentioned in the tourist publicity and included in one of the 'Grey Line'
tour itineraries. The Skydome in Toronto is even newer but is likewise a
tourist attraction.

Such pleasurable experiences, based on what are (at least presented
as) much-loved places, will no doubt increase if the suggestions of David
Canter and his associates were implemented. They aver that 'football
heritage' is a potent source of education about the game and suggest
that 'this can be achieved by means of exhibitions, trails, audio visual
aid shows, theatre, interpretive panels, events, leaflets and bookings at
heritage [football] sites' (Canter et al. 1989). This may not be as bizarre
as it first sounds. The potential certainly exists for 'football trails'
around some of the northern towns in the hotbeds of football culture:
Middlesbrough's ground is already on that town's tourist schedule as
visitors enjoy a Tees Valley tour of the 'Valley at Work' (Halsall 1991).
Given the unlikely sources of much existing 'heritage', football may,
after all, be a potential source of marketable images and a candidate for
museumization, given the voracity of the heritage industry.

The status of the stadium as a heritage site may well enhance local
people's pride in their football ground but no precedent exists for giving
an old stadium preservation status. Even the 1908 Olympic Stadium at
the White City in London fell prey to the developer's bulldozer. In other
parts of Europe, however, it is unlikely that certain famous stadiums,
such as the ivy-clad, gothic, Stockholm Olympic Stadium or the 1936
Berlin Olympic stadium, each quite different architecturally and aesthet-

LIVERPOOL & EVERTON

THE
FOOTBALL CAPITAL OF
THE WORLD

Soccer City Weekends are run by Shirespeed Ltd
who are fully bonded members of ABTA

Figure 4.7 Soccer City Weekends in Liverpool. Football projected as part of a
tourist's itinerary

ically, could ever remain anything but monuments to sport. In Florence, the Stadio Communale, designed by Pier Luigi Nervi, dedicated to a local Fascist martyr and completed in 1932, is a listed monument.

ECONOMIC BENEFITS

So far I have described the benefits that football brings to the city's population in humanistic and 'psychic' terms. Yet it cannot be denied that in varying degrees, but rarely quantified by research, hard economic benefits do result from having a football club in an urban area. And just because benefits may be economic rather than psychological, it does not mean that they fail to provide a source of topophilia.

It may be a symptom of the widely held view that British football is not run with profits primarily in mind that, to the best of my knowledge, no economic impact study has ever been undertaken of a British football club. This contrasts starkly with several such studies which have been undertaken in the United States into both the costs and benefits to a community of attracting a professional sports outfit and the economic impact of an existing sports franchise on the city in which it is located.

But even in the United States the income created by commercial sports organizations is not large when considered as part of total income. Roger Noll, doyen of American sports economists, has noted that in the US the

> total revenue of all teams in the five major team sports – baseball, basketball, football, [ice] hockey and soccer [Noll was writing in 1982] is less than half the revenue of such mundane endeavors as the manufacture of cardboard boxes or the canning of fruit and vegetables. Professional team sports have revenues ranging approximately from those of a large gas station to those of a department store or large supermarket.
>
> (Noll 1982: 348)

Data for Cook County, Illinois, in which is much of Chicago (including fifty-four commercial sports establishments), showed that in 1982 sports events accounted for only 1.26 per cent of services income and 0.24 per cent of Cook County's personal income (Baade and Dye 1988a). Nevertheless, the overall expenditure generated by just one sports team can appear large when stated in absolute terms. Another study, of the impact of the Atlanta Falcons on the city of Atlanta, Georgia, showed that over the period of seventeen years of the Falcons' presence in Atlanta the $291 million spent by the Falcons and by out-of-town fans attending their games stimulated $640.6 million in revenues and incomes to businesses, households, and local government (Schaffer and Davidson 1985).

Respective figures for the football impact on British cities would be much smaller, partly because of the fact that in the US a visit to a sports event is also a visit to the city, much more being spent than in the UK on food and drink, overnight accommodation, shopping and entertainment (see Figure 4.8). It is important, therefore, that US evidence should not be applied to the UK situation. The kind of data illustrated in US studies of the expenditure induced by professional team sports would be more likely in Britain in the event of a continental-scale league where the spatial extent of fandom was large and fans treated games as part of weekend in a city.

A better example, to which the typical British experience might be compared, is highlighted by a study of the economic impact of football on the French city of Rennes which found that the total direct impact on the city was in excess of 5 million francs in 1985/6 (Nys 1990). The club itself also spends money in the local area, hence benefiting the local economy. In the Rennes study it was found that only 24 per cent of expenditures made by the local club (not a member of the French First Division) went directly into the local economy. Such percentages will depend, however, on the size of the urban area and how it is geographically defined, and a figure of over 60 per cent might be more typical of many UK clubs. The typical total annual average expenditure of an average UK Football League club is about £1 million.

Although the most obvious forms of spending on football might be viewed as (a) that spent by the club on players and other costs of 'production' (see Table 4.2), and (b) that which passes hands at the turnstiles, there are a large number of other indirect transactions which would not take place were it not for the presence of a football club. It is these that I now wish to consider and in doing so map out the geographical extent of a club's economic impact.

Let me start by considering the positive economic effects of football on perhaps the most local of beneficiaries, namely, retailers whose shops are close to the stadium. For such shopkeepers football creates what economists call positive externalities, or as I prefer, positive spillovers.[17] Spillovers are benefits (or costs, which I deal with in the next chapter) that originate from a source external to the recipient; put another way, benefits spill over from a football ground and shopkeepers may obtain advantages just because they happen to be nearby. It is the football that generates the crowds that pass their shops, not the shops *per se*.

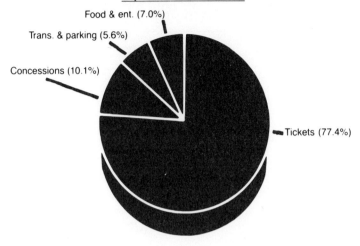

Expenditures of local fans

Food & ent. (7.0%)

Trans. & parking (5.6%)

Concessions (10.1%)

Tickets (77.4%)

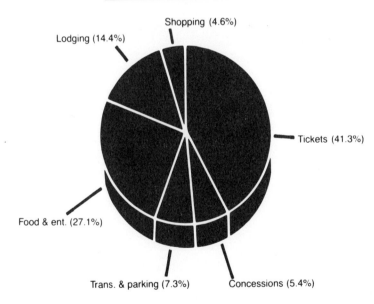

Expenditures of out-of-town fans

Shopping (4.6%)

Lodging (14.4%)

Tickets (41.3%)

Food & ent. (27.1%)

Trans. & parking (7.3%)

Concessions (5.4%)

Figure 4.8 The nature of expenditures in Atlanta by local and out-of-town fans
of the Atlanta Falcons, 1984
Source: Schaffer and Davidson (1985: 15).

Table 4.2   Extracts from recent balance sheets of Rangers FC and East Stirlingshire FC

| | Rangers: | |
	1987	1988
Turnover:	£ 4,193,175	£ 6,600,812
of which:		
– football activities:	£ 3,072,862	£ 4,356,987
– commercial activities:	£ 1,120,313	£ 2,243,825
Trading Profit:	£ 555,075	£ 1,489,387
Exceptional Items:	−£ 2,278,146	−£ 3,147,573
(transfer fees)		
Loss Before Tax:	£ 1,723,071	£ 1,658,186
Extra Income:		£ 586,350
Loss For Year:	£ 1,723,071	£ 1,071,836
Loss Carried Forward:	£ 3,150,483	£ 4,222,319
Tangible Fixed Assets:	£11,776,263	£23,354,874
(mainly stadium)		

| | East Stirlingshire: | |
	1987	1988
Total Income:	£55,637	£67,968.34
of which:		
Net Gate Receipts:	£ 8,670	£11,673.51
Pools Copyright Fee:	£25,340	£30,005
Donations and Sundry:	£12,871	£14,885.98
Bank Interest:	£ 6	£ 3.85
Net Transfer Fees:	£ 8,750	£11,400
Outgoings:	£55,252	£66,180.96
Profit for Year:	£ 285	£ 1,787.38
Loss Carried Forward:	£36,168	£34,380.62
Fixed Assets (at cost):		£21,026
of which:		
Land:		£ 8,412
Motor Mower and		
Tractor Equipment:		£ 3,190
Floodlight System and		
Covered Enclosure:		£ 9,424

Source: Moorhouse (1990: 10).

It seems likely that some retailers, particularly those occupying mobile outlets selling hot dogs, hamburgers, chips, etc., derive a substantial part of their income from football-related purchases. On match days some pubs – but by no means all – increase their revenue by a factor of five over non-match days. A 1989 survey of 766 retailers operating around 37 League grounds throughout England and Wales revealed that 27 per cent claimed that they increased their revenue on average match days with only 8 per cent experiencing a decrease (the majority – 65 per cent – claimed no change in revenue). The types of retail outlet benefiting from nearness to a football ground were fairly predictable – namely, food shops, tobacconists, pubs, and garages (Bale 1990).

As distance from the football club increases, the positive spillover effects on such retailers are likely to decline until a particular point is reached at which the club has no direct economic impact at all. Figure 4.9 illustrates such a simple relationship between distance from the club and its positive externalities which extend over the area whose radius is SP. I will amplify this diagram in the next chapter when a negative externality gradient is added to it in order to demonstrate the spatial impacts of both 'goods' and 'bads' generated by the club (see pp. 104–5).

Exactly how far away from the football ground retailers will continue to benefit from these spillover effects will vary according to the size, success and attraction of the football club. As I showed earlier,

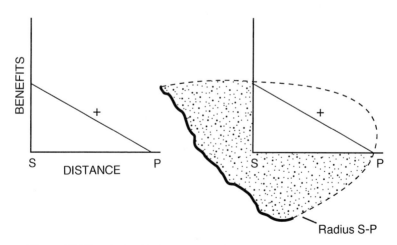

Figure 4.9 The relationship between benefits and distance from a football stadium

Manchester United has supporters' clubs all over the country and spending on petrol or coach hire generated by the club will benefit filling stations and coach hire companies considerable distances away from Manchester. But the spending generated by more modest clubs also has an impact beyond the urban area in which they are located. By mapping the area from which regular fans attend a home game we can get some idea of the geographical area over which the club provides various econ-

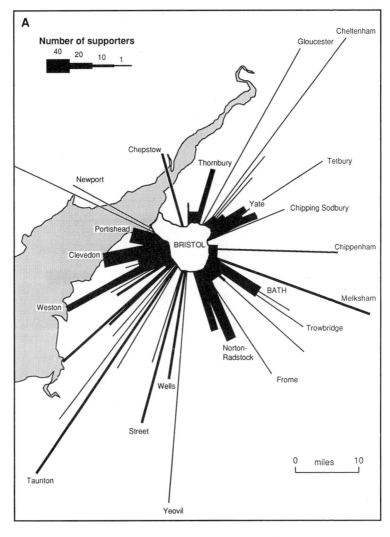

omic benefits to garages, shops and pubs in outlying areas on the way to the game, as well as in the town in which the club is found. As around 42 per cent of fans travel to matches by car (see next chapter), the football-induced spending on petrol alone will be substantial. Figure 4.10 (a and b) shows two examples of the spatial extent of this kind of spending, and, incidentally, reveals different ways of identifying the catchment area of a football club. One (4.10a) shows the origins of season

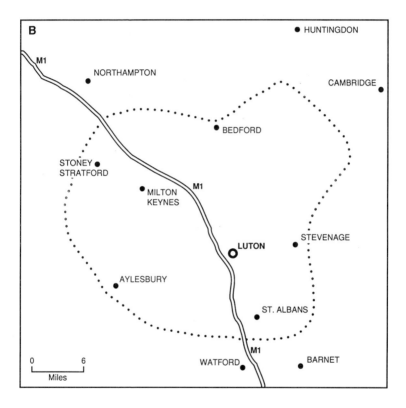

Figure 4.10 Trade areas of two League clubs. (a) Bristol City's trade area based on the residences of season ticket holders; (b) area over which fans are entitled to Luton FC membership. Such spheres of influence could be interpreted as 'positive externality fields'

Sources: (a) Peabody (1988), (b) Williams *et al.* (1989a).

ticket holders of Bristol City for the 1986/7 season, the other (4.10b) the area defined by Luton Town as that within which residents would be automatically eligible for club membership. In each case, the areas shown define the spatial extent of what might be called the 'positive externality field' of the football clubs concerned; within these fields, retailers obtain a free ride on the back of the football club for at least some of their sales.

It is extremely difficult to establish the net effect of football *per se* because some of the spending on, say, getting to the town centre from an outlying area could be spent whether football existed or not. Much more research is therefore needed to establish the exact economic impact of football on the areas within which clubs are found. This would involve identifying items of expenditure which would simply not be made were it not for the presence of a football club. A North American estimate suggests that for every game not played during the 1981 baseball players' strike the city of Boston lost $18,000 in taxes and $650,000 in spending 'near the stadium' (Johnson 1985). In the 1987 football strike, the city of Chicago lost over $1 million worth of spending in the stadium alone (see Table 4.3).

Other businesses in the urban area derive revenues from the football club itself. These will include legal, accountancy, catering, printing, and other companies which depend on the club for a proportion of their

Table 4.3 Economic impact in the Chicago area of the 1987 Football Strike (input data summary*)

In-facility expenditures:	
Tickets	$ 959,068.70
Concessions	167,903.44
Total	$1,126,972.14
Out-of-facility expenditures:	
Food/entertainment	$ 669,488.40
Lodging	265,670.00
Shopping	98,297.90
Parking	33,411.18
Public transit	25,813.20
Players' salaries	507,704.50
(after tax and consumption)	

Source: Miller and Jackson (1988).
Note: *Amounts are estimated impacts for the duration of the strike.

business. Players will spend money in the city on housing, food, clothing, etc. which they would spend elsewhere if the football club was not there. But I must repeat that no systematic economic studies have been undertaken on British football which would enable us to obtain a more detailed picture of the precise impact of football on the city.

I ought to stress at this stage that all the spending mentioned so far is simply the first round of expenditures which can be traced back to football. Part of the football-generated income of the hot-dog seller, for example, will be spent on something else, and so on and so on in a multiplier effect. If the multiplier is taken into account, then the economic impact of football is substantially greater than it first seems. The Atlanta Falcons study, alluded to earlier in this chapter, revealed that if the multiplier was applied to the nineteen-year period of the Falcons' presence in Atlanta 'the $291 million spent by the Falcons and out of town fans have stimulated $353 million in business activity, $269 million in household incomes, and $18.6 million in local government revenues' (Schaffer and Davidson 1985). The broad categories of spending were shown in Figure 4.8.

Other kinds of football-induced economic benefits can be attributed to other groups in the city. The fans of a particular club will benefit from savings in transport costs if they live within easy reach of the stadium, rather than some distance from it. Of the season ticket holders of Bristol City shown in Figure 4.10, 53 per cent lived within the city of Bristol itself. They can demonstrate their affection for their club at less cost than those living in, say, Bath or Taunton. For them, accessibility bestows an advantage for which they have to pay almost nothing in transport costs. Fans with accessibility to the club but who also happen to live outside the local political boundary within which the club is found, obtain benefits in a different way. They do not bear the costs of policing, road maintenance, etc. which are borne by the host community; 'home' fans living outside the city boundary create a 'free rider problem' – they obtain the benefits of being a fan without bearing some of the costs so imposed.

Another group of beneficiaries obtain much more indirect economic advantages. These are firms and businesses which derive unexpected gains when the local football club is doing well. An often cited example is quoted in Janet Lever's work on football in Brazil where it is noted that when São Paulo's most popular team won production in the city increased by over 12 per cent, but when it lost the number of accidents increased by over 15 per cent (Lever 1973). No such similar figures have been presented for British industry when such football victories occur but the success of Nottingham Forest during the 1978/9 European Cup tournament brought an estimated £880,000 worth of new business to the city's industries, resulting from a promotional campaign running alongside the club's fixtures (Hoare 1983). Researchers in Sunderland, following the 1973 FA Cup win over Leeds, observed that 'several people noted the effect of football success in shops, offices and factories: "It's done the town a world of good since they won the Cup. Industry, everything has picked up, everybody's talking about it"'. One company executive was certain that 'speaking for our company, [it has had] a tremendous effect. There's a different atmosphere in the place, they're all working a damn sight harder. They're much more enthusiastic'. A colliery near Sunderland noted a decrease in absenteeism and improved work rate and labour relations (Derrick and McRory 1973). For how long such diligence continued remains unrecorded.

FROM TOPOPHILIA TO ACTIVISM

Topophilia is generally regarded as the expression of love or affection for a place. Such affection can, however, be converted into activism if the source of affection is threatened. The love of place, in this case the stadium, can be graphically illustrated when the club considers relocation in either another part of the city or, worse, in another city altogether. I will deal with the pressures for relocation in Chapter 6. Of course, action against the stadium may come from those who dread the thought of a new football ground in their back yard. I will explore the implications of the NIMBY syndrome and football in the next chapter but will touch on it here in my illustration of a simple conceptual framework for exploring activism in the present context (see Figure 4.11).

So far I have discussed the various sources of topophilia which are generated by football. Fans are, by definition, favourably disposed towards the sport and the majoity of the local community are found in the left-hand sectors of Figure 4.11, obtaining minor gains (pride through association) or minor losses (nuisances of various kinds, dealt with in the next chapter). Such fans and residents are, for most of the time, politically passive in their relations with the local club; it is only when they 'move' into the right-hand sectors of Figure 4.11 that topophilia (or its opposite, topophobia) gives way to activism. It is the translation of an attitude of affection towards the stadium to active political engagement in defence of it that I now want to turn.

Football fans have frequently been presented as marginal figures in the affairs of the clubs, their influence being overwhelmed by the

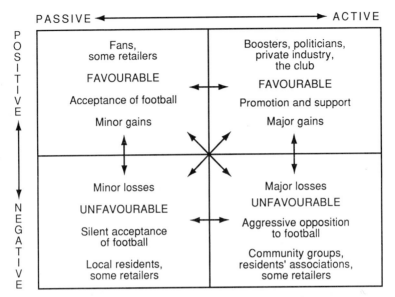

Figure 4.11 A framework for the analysis of the degree of community acceptance of a Football League stadium. Arrows show possibility of change
Source: Based on an idea in Hall (1989:231).

interest of capital, property developers, and other of society's dominant groups. This has certainly been the case in the USA. In Britain things have been done differently; Charles Korr reflects this view when he notes that British football clubs not only 'create traditions and a sense of permanency, they are also their captives' (Korr 1986: 19). In the 1990s, however, the traditional, fossilized picture of UK football is changing. For various reasons, which I will discuss in Chapter 6, the threat (or promise) of relocation is today blowing through the draughty wood-work of many of Britain's soccer stadiums. Localities which have long possessed a League football ground are facing the possibility of the kind of 'robbery' experienced by the Dodger fans of 1958 and those of the St Louis Cardinals thirty years later when 'their' team moved to Phoenix, Arizona. Though most of the drawing board scenarios have been for suburbanward moves, I will show later that some proposals have involved inter-city migrations.

The plans to relocate football stadiums reflect the rationalism, at a different level of geographical scale, which I described being applied to the inside of the stadium in the previous chapter. So does the suggestion that clubs should engage in ground sharing, as in the Charlton–Crystal

Palace arrangement which I consider in more detail below. Such suggestions make economic sense but they totally underestimate the strength of topophilic sentiment which the football stadium can create. When such much-loved elements of the urban landscape are threatened with closure, resulting from a decision to move the club or engage in ground-sharing, topophilia can be converted into resistance and activism, though such reactions are not inevitable.

To an extent, the emergence of the fanzines and the changes in fan behaviour – their dress and general 'style' – combine to make up a repertoire of oppositional strategies which serve to challenge the authority of society's dominant groups. Those strategies cited above are essentially symbolic in nature but the kinds of activism which I will describe below assume a more directly instrumental form of resistance and have resulted in some remarkably successful outcomes as the following case studies will show.

Perhaps the most well-documented UK example of successful action by fans in opposition to decisions made by their club is that of Charlton Athletic, a south-east London club formed in 1905. In 1920 the club occupied The Valley, a gigantic bowl of a stadium in Greenwich, the club having previously had four different sites. An unsuccessful move to Catford in 1923 led to a return to The Valley a year later where the club remained until 1985. The events leading up to the 1985 decision to leave The Valley and engage in ground-sharing with Crystal Palace at the latter's Selhurst Park ground, 12 kilometres away by the notoriously congested South Circular Road, await a diligent historian's insights. But the need for essential safety work on the stadium's ageing fabric, the non-payment of rent by the club on a ground that they did not own, the closure by the Greater London Council of the east terrace because of inadequate safety precautions, and the promise by the owners to develop the site for other uses, all contributed to the board's decision to leave The Valley.

The crucial point, however, is the way in which the fans responded. Often regarded solely as fund raisers and lottery organizers, supporters' love for The Valley was quickly converted into political activism. Their topophilic sentiments were encapsulated in comments in the fanzine, *The Voice of The Valley*, launched in January 1988 to orchestrate the fight to return the club to its 'home':

> It was just a football club leaving its ground, but to many, many people it was so much more. For the older fans it was the destruction of something that had run like a thread through their lives

and for those who knew the Valley's past only at second hand it was the crushing of a dream. Charlton's moonlight flit was a cruel human tragedy that fouind no expression in the accountant's figures.[18]

(Everitt 1989)

The Selhurst Park relocation was opposed with extreme vigour by Charlton supporters and illustrates the variety of possible forms of action in the case of locational conflict. Demonstrations, petitions, meetings with the club, and the formation of a fanzine and public meetings together combined to get the club to agree to forsake Selhurst Park and return to The Valley. Details of most of the Charlton campaign are shown in Figure 4.12.

In 1990 the club's plan to develop a modern all-seater stadium on the Valley site was rebuffed by the local council's planning committee on environmental grounds. It was suggested that a more modest scheme would be more sensitive to the needs of local people and the environment. Nevertheless, the fight to get Charlton back to Greenwich continued. In the May 1990 local council elections, activism assumed a more explicitly political character when, for the first time in British political history, a political party was formed by football fans. The party had 'no coherent ideology, little political experience and no manifesto save for one single pledge – to get Charlton home' (Everitt 1990). All sixty-two seats in the borough of Greenwich were contested in an attempt to encourage the council to reach a decision which would enable Charlton to return to The Valley. The party estimated that it would be fortunate to get 8,000 votes but, in the event, they obtained over 14,800, this amounting to 10.9 per cent of the votes cast. In one ward the party obtained 24 per cent and in another 14 per cent of the votes.[19] It was an astonishing display of fan power, supporters revelling in the fact that one of the deposed councillors was the chair of the planning committee which had denied the club a return to its home. The new chair supported a return to The Valley and in April 1991 the club was given planning permission to rebuild its traditional 'home'.

Although ground sharing and relocation appear to be rational plans for the future of football, several other examples show how well-orchestrated schemes to retain stadiums in existing locations have successfully contested the game's ideological realignment towards commercial consumerism. The case of Luton Town is different from that of Charlton in that in 1983 the Luton club, occupying an extremely cramped site with no potential at all for development and threatened by local road

HOW THE BATTLE WAS FOUGHT

December 1980: GLC threaten to slash Valley capacity from 67,000 to 13,000. Eventually a limit of 20,000 is agreed after Charlton promise to carry out essential safety work.

June 1982: Mark Julyer buys the club from Michael Gliksten, but not The Valley. An annual rent of £150,000 is agreed.

February 1984: Charlton are wound up in the High Court after penalty clause in Valley lease for non-payment of rent comes into operation.

March 1984: Sunley Holdings form a new company, Charlton '84, but fail to secure the freehold of The Valley. A rent of £70,000 is agreed with Gliksten.

July 1985: The GLC closes the East Terrace due to flaking concrete and serious defects in the crash barriers. Charlton fail to overturn the ruling in court.

September 3rd 1985: A leak to the *South London Press* reveals that Gliksten is reclaiming two acres of land behind the main stand for redevelopment.

September 7th 1985: Charlton distribute the notorious 'Message To Our Supporters' at the home match with Crystal Palace. A gleeful Ron Noades warns fans not to obstruct the move to Selhurst.

September 21st 1985: Charlton fans protest in vain at The Valley's final game. Wreaths are laid in the centre circle and the second-half is delayed as supporters protest in the middle of the pitch.

May 1986: Charlton are promoted back to the First Division after 29 years and John Fryer insists the club will 'never, never return' to The Valley.

October 2nd 1986: Abysmal attendances at Charlton's First Division matches prompt the *Mercury* to print a back page petition demanding a return home. The paper is besieged.

October 20th 1986: More than a thousand demonstrators take over the CASC AGM to demand a return to The Valley. Peter Cordwell hands over the 15,000 signature petition to Michael Norris, who claims the average attendances will rise to 11,000 before end of the season.

November 1986: Charlton fans, directors and Greenwich Council meet at Woolwich. The club say that it was always their intention to return to the borough and promise a further meeting in January to discuss progress.

January 1987: The club decline to meet supporters again as promised on the grounds that there is nothing to report. The long silence begins.

January 1988: Rick Everitt launches *Voice of The Valley* and calls the boycott. Fans flock to Sportspages bookshop in the West End to buy the first issue, which is reprinted after just ten days on sale.

February 1988: Steve Dixon joins *Voice of The Valley* and helps found the Valley Supporters' Club.

March 1988: News leaks that two directors, Michael Norris and Roger Alwen, have bought back The Valley. The boycott is called off. Celebrations end in confusion as the club announce that they do not necessarily intend to return there, but to a site at the Blackwall Peninsular.

June 1988: It is announced that Mike Norris and Roger Alwen now own the club. CASC, *Voice of The Valley* and the directors meet in London and agree that the VSC will be disbanded as a gesture of goodwill. Editors decline request to close *Voice of The Valley.* Directors agree to public meeting.

September 1988: Public meeting is a major success despite poor publicity and the absence of fresh news. Fans plead for The Valley, but Norris refuses to say whether it is possible to return there. He hopes to report back before Christmas.

November 1988: Richard Collins confirms speculation about the Thames Poly sports ground at Eltham being a possible site and tells the *Kentish Times* to expect an announcement before Christmas. Then he bans the paper for printing what he told them.

January 1989: Richard Collins is quoted in *The Mail On Sunday* as saying that the new ground will be a stone's throw from The Valley. An announcement is expected within a fortnight.

February 1989: An apology about the lack of news finally appears in the programme. It gives no details. Speculation grows about the involvement of ex-boxing promoter Frank Warren and a *Morning Star* story links Charlton with a crazy move across the Thames to Newham.

March 7th 1989: Roger Alwen unexpectedly succeeds Richard Collins as chairman, instead of Mike Norris as had been anticipated. Alwen is the fifth chairman in seven years. John Sunley is listed in the programme as a director for the first time.

March 16th 1989: *Mercury* reports that Charlton are set to announce plans to return to The Valley. Club could be back by middle of 1989–90 according to Peter Cordwell's story.

March 23rd 1989: Fans descend on Woolwich Town Hall to hear the news.

Figure 4.12 The 'battle for The Valley' was not won in March 1989 but continued into 1991 when the local authority finally agreed that Charlton Athletic should return 'home'. This followed The Valley Party's relative success in local elections in 1990 but the actual reoccupation of the ground did not take place until late 1992
Source: *Voice of The Valley*, no. 11, 1989, p. 24.

building programmes, considered a completely new location 35 kilometres north of the town in the new city of Milton Keynes. The proposal has been said to have 'caused a furore in Luton' (Williams *et al.* 1989a) – an overstatement perhaps, but it cannot be denied that supporters' opposition to the Luton move was substantial. To a degree the opposition was successful (though ultimately Milton Keynes decided it didn't want Luton – see Chapter 6) in forcing the club to look for another site within, or much nearer to, the town. 'A group of local fans, The Luton Town Supporters Club '83, orchestrated local opposition to the move. Protest marches were organized, leaflets distributed and fans boycotted matches' (Williams *et al.* 1989a).

Other examples of successful local activism in the face of plans to close down football grounds are not difficult to find. In 1983 the newspaper entrepreneur Robert Maxwell, the then owner of Oxford United, planned to merge the club with nearby Reading Town. The unlikely name for the new club was mooted as Thames Valley Royals and the even more unlikely location was suggested as Didcot. The plan was totally opposed by both sets of supporters and the idea dropped.

More dramatically, perhaps, was the messy scenario drawn up for the rationalization of the three clubs occupying the London Borough of Kensington and Chelsea, namely Queen's Park Rangers, Fulham, and Chelsea. In 1987 the three clubs were planned to be merged at Shepherd's Bush, with yuppie flats being erected by Marler Estates on the prestigious Thames-side site of Fulham's ground at Craven Cottage. This proposal precipitated the formation of another fanzine, *The Chelsea Independent*, and a 'public outcry embarrassed the property moguls into retreat' (Shaw 1989).

The future of Fulham was further brought into doubt when Cabra Estates bought the freehold of Craven Cottage from Marler. Cabra agreed to lease the ground to Fulham for a three year period which expired at the end of the 1989/90 season. It was then proposed that the site be developed as a luxury housing estate with no provision for Fulham FC. The subsequent involvement of the local authority revealed

91

the strength of local feeling when they proposed that a Compulsory Purchase Order (CPO) be placed on the site which would then be retained as a football ground with associated leisure and residential developments. The role of the club's fans followed a similar pattern to that of Charlton's by campaigning for the survival of Craven Cottage; their fanzine described the activism of fans in detail:

> Fulham supporters ... delivered leaflets in the Craven Cottage locality, to inform residents of the goings-on and to quash some of the false rumours that were circulating. A further 20,000 leaflets were distributed to other football supporters in London. ... Press packs were circulated to more than fifty concerns and as the enquiry neared so media interest intensified. Phone-ins took place on Capital Gold and LBC.
>
> (*There's Only One F in Fulham*, no. 10, 1990: 4)

The Compulsory Purchase Order was supported, it appeared, by the club's board of directors. Shortly after a public statement of support, however, it was disclosed they they had sold the site to Cabra Estates for £13 million; yuppie apartments on the site would result in real estate worth about four times that figure. The fans were naturally incensed, claiming that they had been 'sold down the river', the board effectively now siding with Cabra rather than the CPO. Meetings, demonstrations, media exposure, and local government support for the CPO followed. Letters of support for the club remaining at the ground were received from other League clubs all over the country while a letter to the enquiry from a former local vicar demonstrated the intense sense of local topophilia:

> The subtle influence of the football club on the neighbourhood has been much more important than the presence or absence of traffic. It has provided a focus of district loyalty, which peaked on Cup Final day in 1975 but which has affected a great many of us over the years.
>
> (*There's Only One F in Fulham*, no. 10, 1990: 4)

Fulham will ultimately have to leave Craven Cottage but the resistance provided by fans has ensured that they will stay within the borough and not be forced to relocate to the outer suburbs – a worst-case scenario which had been proposed by the club and a further example of the significance of distance and space in satisfying fan support. Clubs in Britain find it very dificult to move any distance beyond the town or borough in which they have traditionally been found.

These examples are sufficient to demonstrate that the passive affection for the stadium can be converted into activism when its survival, and hence the football-place bond, is threatened. I have shown that it is possible for fans to contest and counter certain prevailing tendencies in the world of football. Affection for football places and activism in support of them will need to be taken into account in scripting the scenarios for the brave new world of British sport in the twenty-first century.

CONCLUSION

The football club provides a potent force for community identification, though in the USA, where relocation has been common (see Chapter 6), there has probably been a weakening of the role of sport in the creation of any distinctive community consciousness (Karp and Yoels 1990: 93). In Britain, the football stadium continues to provide an undoubted source of topophilia for a sizeable minority of the population. Such sentiments result from its religious, home-like, scenic, and historic connotations. For some it also generates economic benefits. But the passive acceptance of topophilia can be changed into activism if the stadium is threatened, through either relocation or ground sharing. The strategies used to exert influence on clubs considering leaving their historic sites have mainly been sophisticated articulations (from petitions to fanzines) – or what is sometimes termed 'voice' – involving considerable time and cost. In the case of the Charlton group's opposition to relocation, one strategy did involve formal participation in the political process through the formation of a political party. Some of those who oppose a club's proposed relocation will inevitably resign themselves to the move but few appear to get involved in another possible strategy, namely that of engaging in illegal activity (Dear and Long 1978).

I have shown in this chapter that fan activism can be remarkably strong and in some cases apparently successful, at least in the short term. As Bill Osgerby has put it, 'the social groups from which football spectators have traditionally been drawn have not been easily moulded by the spirit of commercial consumerism' (Osgerby 1988: 71). The fan, therefore, should not be marginalized. I must stress, however, that topophilia has its opposite in topophobia – the dislike of place. For some people – and, indeed, some fans – the football ground connotes images of nuisance and fear. It is these negative aspects of the stadium that I want to explore in the chapter which follows.

5

WHEN SATURDAY COMES
Football as nuisance

In the previous chapter I showed how for some people football provides a kind of 'psychic income', a sense of place, and a source of topophilia which enhances their quality of life. In this chapter I will be looking at the rather more negative aspects which football brings to the localities in which it is found. In Britain it is probably these negative spillovers of the game which receive the most publicity, and in recent years the nuisance which has generated most media mileage has undoubtedly been the so-called 'football hooligan problem'. In this chapter I will be less concerned with hooligans and more with the people who possess negative attitudes (that is, the groups in the bottom half of Figure 4.11) – which can lead to political activism against football clubs and their grounds. For some people, their attitudes towards the stadium may well create feelings of fear; for many, however, it is more likely to be annoyance and nuisance. Nevertheless, just as topophilia can create 'psychic income', 'topophobia' can impose a 'psychic cost'.

In this chapter I will first explore the neighbourhood of the stadium as a latter-day landscape of fear. The remainder of the chapter will be concerned with building on some of the concepts introduced previously, adding a negative sphere of influence to the positive externality field described in the previous chapter, and looking at individual forms of 'football pollution' and the responses of individuals to them. This negative sphere shows that the stadium can be a 'good' and a 'bad' influence at the same time. In doing so, the widely discussed hooligan phenomenon will be set in a more realistic context than is often presented elsewhere.

FOOTBALL AND LANDSCAPES OF FEAR

For a large number of people the urban landscapes around Britain's football grounds are, for three or four hours every other Saturday, environments of nuisance. Although annoyance, nuisance, and disruption occur for only such short periods of time, it is, nevertheless, residents' leisure time and therefore likely to be highly valued.

It is not only local residents who experience the less-favoured face of football. A surprisingly large proportion of fans feel frightened when visiting certain football stadiums. I should stress, however, that the significance of fear at football matches should not be overemphasized. After all, it is still *the* most important spectator sport in Britain and for most of those involved the sport is relatively benign. Yet for some residents (a 'silent majority' in some cases) football can frequently constitute a nuisance and sometimes generate real fear.

Fans' fears

For many fans, some football stadiums present a strongly negative image. David Canter and his associates analysed the responses of 1,000 football supporters of ten clubs in the United Kingdom (Canter *et al.* 1989).[1] Sizeable percentages of those interviewed stated that they were worried about safety at both home and away games but in only three of the ten clubs did a large number cite worries about safety at home matches. For 8 of the 10 groups of supporters, over 35 per cent considered that away games created safety worries, while in the case of three grounds the respective figure exceeded 50 per cent. The kinds of concerns mainly involved events *inside* the stadium. Over 33 per cent had at some time been worried about safety. Crushing caused by crowds, police, and horses were mentioned as possible sources of fear.

Data collected by the Leicester University sports sociologists showed that 70.8 per cent of members of the Football Supporters' Association (FSA) expected to be crushed or feel uncomfortable at matches on a number of occasions throughout the season, while 70.1 per cent felt that some grounds were dangerous to visit (Sir Norman Chester Centre for Football Research, 1989b). Of fans interviewed, 57 per cent had at some time felt threatened at away games, a figure rising to 68 per cent for members of the FSA in a survey undertaken by Liverpool City council.[2] The latter survey also showed that 43 per cent would not go to some grounds because they perceived a serious hooligan problem to exist. The football grounds with the most severe stigma were identified by the Leicester group. These are shown in Table 5.1 and include several grounds in London and the north-west. Fans also possess well-defined cognitive maps of the areas of cities which they perceive to be unsafe to visit when supporting their team at away games. Some pubs will be safe enough to allow fans to mingle and exchange greetings with their peers from the home team. Other parts of the city are seen as threatening and hence branded as places to avoid. Such acknowledged places of fear will be avoided on match days by all but the uninitiated.

An example of a cognitive map of fear is shown in Figure 5.1 and indicates the areas to be avoided in Cardiff by visiting fans on their way to watch games at Ninian Park. Although Cardiff City FC have been languishing in the lower divisions in recent years, Cardiff hooligans have, over the years, developed a reputation for 'hardness'. The map, constructed by a number of hard-core Midlands supporters, shows that the most direct route from station to ground should be avoided by visiting fans, as should the Canton area and the western side of the stadium. Fanzines often include maps which show the location of the best pubs to visit at away games but maps such as that in Figure 5.1 might be of equal, or greater, value to fans of all clubs in their visits to away grounds.

Table 5.1 Stadiums of stigma*

Club	No. of fans citing club (%)
Liverpool	21.3
Chelsea	12.4
West Ham United	12.1
Everton	9.8
Leeds United	6.8
Manchester United	6.1
Tottenham Hotspur	4.3
Newcastle United	4.1
Millwall	3.4
Manchester City	2.2

Source: Williams *et al.* 1989a, Appendix, p. 5.
Note: *Football clubs at whose stadiums more than 2 per cent of fans (n = 324) feel threatened.

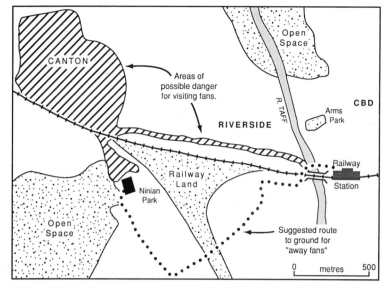

Figure 5.1 Landscapes of fear around Ninian Park, Cardiff, as perceived by a group of fans from the East Midlands. The map shows places to be avoided by visiting fans

The stadium as a place of confinement

The English football stadium, which I discussed in Chapter 2, has changed from being a place of assembly and interaction to one of confinement, security, and surveillance. The wish to place fans in particular spaces, separated from others on the basis of not only social class but also club affiliation, plus the ubiquitous police surveillance at such grounds, has, as was noted in Chapter 2, produced in the football stadium the panoptic features that have long characterized schools, prisons, and hospitals (Foucault 1973, 1979). Inside the stadium the rigid demarcation of space defines very explicitly those areas which are to be feared and avoided by fans of different affiliations. As noted earlier, the most frightening practical effect of the containment of spectators was felt during the Hillsborough (Sheffield) tragedy of 1989 when the very fences designed to control crowds actually contributed to the deaths of ninety-five people. Around many stadiums the fences (especially those topped with spikes or barbed wire), narrow entrances, and threatening graffiti may subliminally induce, in fans and passers-by, feelings of fear

97

and trepidation (see Figure 5.2). As the Taylor Report (1990) noted, 'the spectacle of these cage-like fences is inconsistent with a sports ground being for pleasure and recreation. ... Having to stand in a cage for your Saturday afternoon recreation inevitably causes resentment'. The introduction of the ominous and surveillant 'hoolivan', akin to an armoured military vehicle, patrolling the streets around stadiums, was argued to be undesirable, even by a former Conservative Minister for Sport (Macfarlane 1986). The image created is hardly welcoming!

The perceptions of the public

In Britain many people perceive the football stadium to be a noxious facility which generates unwanted nuisances in the urban area. Most people feel that if they lived near a football ground they would experience nuisances of various kinds on average match days. Perhaps the traditionally negative images of fear connoted by crowds become enhanced at football matches, where crowds have received massive negative publicity in the popular press. The drab files of regimented fans being herded from railway stations to stadiums do tend to give the impression of being more like Van Gogh's *La ronde des prisonniers* than

Figure 5.2 On seeing this view of Ninian Park a French sociologist likened it to the entrance to a concentration camp

L. S. Lowry's purposefully striding, but diffuse, crowd in *Going to the match*. A survey conducted in 1989 showed that 96 per cent of a random sample of adults felt that *if they lived* within 500 metres of a football stadium they would experience nuisances of various kinds; if they lived 2 km away from a stadium, 32 per cent still felt that nuisance impacts of the sport would be experienced (Bale 1990).

The trepidation with which the general public react to the prospect of living near a football stadium can be contrasted with the attitudes of those who *actually do live* in such locations. As part of the same project referred to above, over 4,500 residents who lived within 2 km of one of thirty-seven Football League grounds were asked if, living where they did, they experienced nuisances on match days. Compared with the 96 per cent of the general public who felt that nuisances would be perceived if living within 500 metres of the ground, the respective response of residents who actually did live that close to grounds was 52 per cent. Similarly exaggerated images were felt by the general public with respect to three 500-metre distance zones away from the ground (see Figure 5.3). About twice as many members of the general public think that nuisance will occur near football grounds than the number of people who live near the grounds who perceive such nuisances to actually exist.

Exemplified here is what I referred to earlier (see p. 29) as 'deviancy amplification' and 'moral panic'. Those who do not visit football matches and receive information about the sport from secondary sources, overemphasize the nuisance impact of the average game. This is

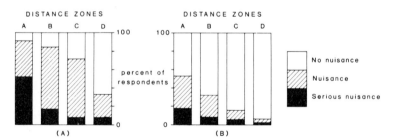

Figure 5.3 (a) percentages of a sample of the general public who felt that living near a football ground would involve the experience of nuisances on match days, and (b) percentages of a sample of residents living near football grounds who perceived football-related nuisances
Source: Bale (1990: 326).
Note: A, B, C, and D represent 500-metre-wide concentric rings centred on the football ground.

not to say that no nuisances exist – far from it – for much of the remainder of this chapter is concerned with examining their nature and extent, and what residents can do to repel them.

In the above discussion I have dealt with an aggregated public perception, without distinguishing what various sub-groups feel about the game. Little evidence exists to suggest that gender differences influence whether football is perceived a nuisance or not. What is much more important is whether one is a fan or not. Indeed, it has been suggested that there is twice as much chance of perceiving something connected with football as a nuisance if you are a non-fan than if you are a fan. Of 470 residents living on the western side of London, 50 per cent of those who were not fans of either Queeen's Park Rangers, Fulham, or Chelsea (the clubs around which the survey was held) perceived football to generate nuisances; the equivalent figure for those who were fans was 25 per cent (Bale 1990).

Some of the most graphic images of how people perceive the 'people's game' has come from children. A notable series of essays have been written on what they thought about the game by schoolchildren in a major comprehensive school in Liverpool (Sir Norman Chester Centre for Football Research 1987a). Two generalizations emerged from this work. First, boys rather than girls tended to concentrate more fully on issues of spectator violence and misbehaviour. This may not be very surprising given the more aggressive cultural conditioning in boys. Second, and perhaps more interestingly, those who did *not* attend games had violence as a central theme in their accounts of the football ambience to a greater extent than those who were regular attenders. This finding lends further support to the 'moral panic' argument described earlier, since those who were not regular attenders would have obtained their (amplified) images of the sport through secondary sources, obtaining a more violent image of the game than those who regularly attended. The graphic nature of such images is well illustrated in a similar survey undertaken with primary school children in Stoke-on-Trent. One 10-year-old girl who had never attended a football match wrote that she had 'seen police on the telly *killing people* at football matches with sticks'. Another who never attended said that she 'would love to go to Stoke City but I can't because of *all the violence*. Football is boring on TV but it would be great if there was no fighting or people getting killed' (Cooper 1990).

PANIC IN THE STREETS?

The most detailed single study of the actual, as opposed to the imagined, impact of football on an individual locality was undertaken around the ground (The Dell) of Southampton FC in the early 1980s. It was noted that 'although media coverage has increased the level of public awareness of the problem of "hooliganism" among football spectators, it nevertheless presents a distorted picture of its significance' (Humphrys *et al.* 1983). This can be illustrated by the fact that local residents around The Dell most frequently cited traffic and parked cars as football-induced nuisances in each of three 500-metre zones away from the the ground. Indeed, in each zone the hooligan nuisance possessed a 'nuisance score' of less than the zonal mean (see Figure 5.4).

A more recent study of a larger number of localities elicited a similar conclusion. Of over 4,500 residents living within 2 km of thirty-seven football stadiums, 10 per cent cited hooliganism as a nuisance, while the respective figures for car parking and traffic were 18 per cent and 22 per cent; twice as many people cited football-induced traffic than hooliganism as a nuisance (Bale 1990). Although these percentage figures were higher within 500 metres of the stadium, the rank order of frequency of response was the same.

In only a small number of cases did the percentage of residents perceiving football hooliganism/vandalism as a nuisance exceed that perceiving traffic and parked cases as nuisances. In Figure 5.5. each point or cross on the graph refers to the percentage of respondents in each locality citing traffic or parked cars respectively, graphed against the percentage citing hooliganism. If each spillover was perceived as a nuisance by the same percentage of respondents in each locality, all the points (and crosses) would lie on the 45 degree line. Clearly this is not the case. As well as the number mentioning hooliganism being consistently less than that citing traffic and parking, the percentage mentioning noise and pedestrians exceeded that mentioning hooligans in a number of cases (Bale 1990).

Nuisances as negative externalities

Just as the benefits, topophilic and economic, which were described as being generated by a football stadium in Chapter 4, were not spread equally over the urban area, so too the nuisances associated with football tend to be concentrated rather then distributed at random. Like the positive spillovers from football, the value of those of a negative nature

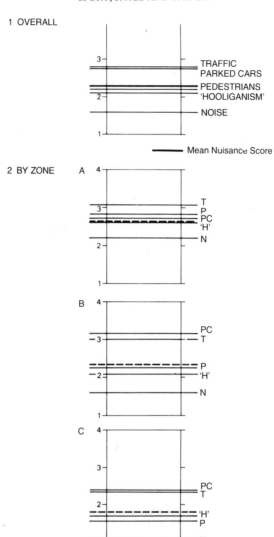

Figure 5.4 Ranking of football nuisances by zones around The Dell, Southampton, in the early 1980s
Source: Humphrys *et al.* (1983).

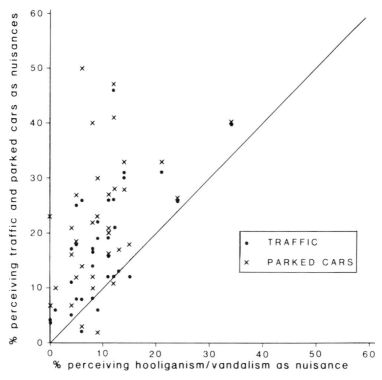

Figure 5.5 The percentage number of residents living near Football League grounds who perceive hooliganism/vandalism as nuisances plotted against the percentages who perceive traffic and parked cars as nuisances
Source: Bale (1990: 328).

tend – and there are exceptions – to decline fairly regularly away from the stadium. It is possible, therefore, to modify the diagram of the positive externality gradient (see Figure 4.9) by adding to it a hypothetical negative gradient as in Figure 5.6. Whereas the positive externality gradient extends as far away from the stadium as SP, the negative one only reaches SN. What is more, between the stadium and point L, the negative externalities actually exceed the positive whereas beyond that point the positive exceed the negative. This conventional presentation of the relationship between positive and negative externality gradients (Kirby 1982, Pinch 1985; see also Harrop 1973) emphasizes that people may gain from *accessibility* but suffer from *proximity* to football stadiums.

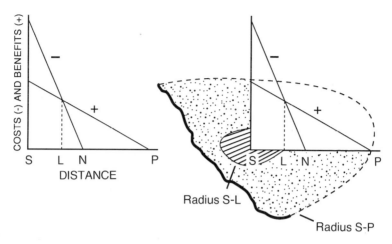

Figure 5.6 Positive and negative externality gradients in relation to a football stadium

It should be stressed that this is a very general model which could be applied to a wide variety of facilities, from a nuclear power station to a motorway. It is also a generalization in the sense that different people will possess different attitudes to a given facility and that different examples of the same facility (that is, a stadium) may have different gradients. For example, a minor club, with few supporters and limited traffic generation, may generate some nuisances which decline with distance from the stadium but the gradient drawn to represent them might lie *below* the entire length of the positive gradient, showing that at no point do negative externalities exceed the positive.

Operationalizing these concepts is far from easy but just as I was able to show in the last chapter the spatial extent of fans' travel to clubs using this sphere of influence as a sort of 'surrogate' positive externality field, I will spend the next part of this chapter exploring the spatial extent of football nuisance fields.

Nuisance fields

The spatial extent of football-induced nuisances may extend a considerable distance from the stadium. Figure 5.7 shows the areas around the grounds of First Division Queen's Park Rangers and Fourth Division (at the time of the survey) Crewe Alexandra, over which residents perceived that on average match days football generated a 'nuisance' or 'serious

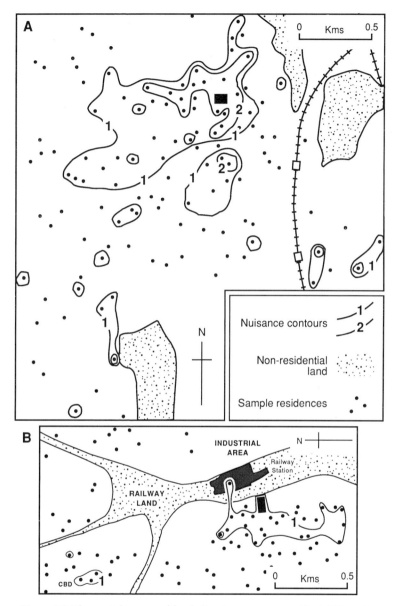

Figure 5.7 The spatial impact of football nuisances generated by (a) Queen's Park Rangers (First Division), and (b) Crewe Alexandra (Fourth Division) as perceived by local residents in early 1989. Points on the map refer to sample residencies. The '1' contours indicate the spatial limits of respondents who perceived football 'nuisances', while the '2' contours enclose those perceiving 'serious nuisances'

105

nuisance'. The surveys were conducted by asking samples of local residents whether living where they did, football constituted 'no nuisance', a 'nuisance', or a 'serious nuisance'. Respective scores of 0, 1 and 2 were then given to each sample point and 'nuisance contours' interpolated. I need to stress that the spatial limit of the nuisance field is based on local residents' *perceptions* of nuisance. What might be a nuisance to one person may be salutory to another and what produces activism and conflict is what people *perceive* to exist, not the origins of the perceived nuisances in themselves.

Figure 5.7 shows that in the case of Queen's Park Rangers, residents' perceptions of nuisances extended up to 1,500 metres from the ground. In the case of Crewe, however, nuisances were much less in evidence and the 'field' is consequently much less extensive with the 'nuisance surface' being much lower. In this case the spatial extent of nuisances is reduced by the nearness of the railway station to the ground and the relatively compatible land uses nearby. In some cases nuisances have been 'relocated' so that the immediate area around the stadium is relatively trouble-free, the result of rigid car-parking restrictions and intensive policing. Around the most lowly grounds of the lower divisions, virtually no nuisance impact is felt.

The two clubs and the extent and intensity of their respective nuisance fields shown in Figure 5.7 are part of a spectrum, a clear – but not perfect – relationship existing between the divisional status of a club and the proportion of the local population which perceives it to generate nuisances on match days (see Table 5.2). The implication of these divisional differences is that as clubs move between divisions their nuisance

Table 5.2 The relationship between divisional status of clubs (n = 37) and the average percentage number of residents perceiving football-generated nuisances

Division	Average percentage of residents perceiving football as a:	
	Nuisance	Serious nuisance
1	45	13
2	39	10
3	29	9
4	22	4

Source: Bale (1990: 330).

impact increases and decreases, nuisance being a function of divisional status. For some residents the thought of their local club experiencing upward football mobility is looked upon with horror.

But there is not a simple one-to-one relationship between extent of perceived nuisance and divisional status. More residents around southern grounds, for example, tend to view football spillovers as nuisances than do residents in the north of England (Bale 1990). As the balance of football power has shifted south (see p. 136), what amounted to little more than recreation grounds in leafy suburbs have, in a few cases, gained the status of Football League grounds – with annoying results for local residents. In addition, it is likely that increased negative images of the areas around stadiums would be generated if clubs engaged in ground sharing on a substantial scale. Of the thirty-seven clubs examined in the 1989 survey alluded to earlier, the ground around which the largest percentage (73 per cent) of local residents perceived nuisances to exist was Selhurst Park, a ground at which football was played every weekend as a result of ground sharing between Crystal Palace and Charlton Athletic.

The externality fields shown in Figure 5.7 are, of course, aggregates of various individual nuisances, each of which has its own 'field' which defines the spatial extent to which it is perceived to be a nuisance. The Southampton study (see pp. 101–2) delimited areas of individual nuisance, and just as the hooligan nuisance was cited by fewer people so too was it cited over a smaller area than the traffic and pedestrian nuisances. The smallest nuisance field of all, however, was that generated by noise (Humphrys et al. 1983).

The spatial extent of football nuisances can be conceptualized as a negative externality field which can be delimited in the way outlined above. Such fields are obviously of more limited spatial extent than the positive fields; in many cases the nuisance fields are quite small and scattered around the urban area with well-defined 'outliers' rather than being concentrated solely around the stadium. Traffic and parking are viewed by more residents as nuisances than is hooliganism. Having looked at the way in which people perceive football nuisances, I now want to explore the impact of individual spillovers in rather more detail.

THE NATURE OF FOOTBALL NUISANCES

The overall nuisance imposed by local football matches is made up of a variety of individual nuisances, some of which will assume greater importance than others in particular circumstances. I now move away from people's perceptions of such nuisances and explore the main sources of 'football pollution' in somewhat more objective terms.

Traffic

Traffic is perceived as a nuisance by many residents living around British football grounds. For thirty-seven localities around League grounds explored in 1989, more than 20 per cent of residents living within 2 km experienced traffic nuisances around fourteen of them. Within 0.5 km of some grounds as many as 80 per cent of local residents perceive traffic nuisances to exist (Bale 1989b). Such a perception is hardly surprising when it is recognized that a football crowd of 58,000 people may generate over 2 million person-miles of travel (Grayson 1971).[3]

Several studies have shown that about 42 per cent of fans in Britain travel to matches in cars (although less than half of these are actually driving, car occupancy being about 2.5 per car), creating considerable traffic pressure on the residential environments around stadiums. Large proportions of the remaining fans travel by coach or bus. It should be noted, however, that the above figure is typical of stadiums which are not served by alternative forms of urban transport systems such as underground railways. Where the underground exists, it tends to replace coach or bus travel as the second major mode of transport. A 1970s study of the mode of travel to Chelsea FC noted that as many as 39 per cent of fans travelled to Stamford Bridge by underground, while nearly 30 per cent of fans going to Ibrox benefit from good access to underground and railway stations. Road vehicles are nevertheless the typical mode of travel at most clubs (see Table 5.3), and the effect of congestion is to reduce traffic speeds (see Figure 5.8) and hence increase the real cost of going to the game. The congestion also increases the transport costs of non-fans who happen to be in the urban area at the time.

It should be stressed, however, that the figures for at least three of the clubs shown in Table 5.3 refer to travel to games which produced very large crowds. Such matches would have attracted a large number of occasional spectators and Michael Grayson's research in the early 1970s showed that those who went to matches least frequently were more likely to use an available car than those who went to matches regularly. For matches attracting smaller crowds, therefore, the proportion using cars might be significantly less (Grayson 1971). What is more, car use is associated with distance travelled. Non-use of an available car is high for trips of less than 3 km but 'suppression' of car use is less for long

108

Table 5.3 Travel modes to selected English and Scottish League grounds

	1 Old Trafford	2 Maine Road	3 Stamford Bridge	4 Ibrox	5 Pittodrie	6 Easter Road	7 The Shay
	(early 1970s)				*(early 1980s)*		*(1990)*
Car	42	42	44	44	63	41	62
Coach/bus	41	44	8	23	17	34	15
Train*	12	14	39	27	4	6	2
Other	5	–	8	7	16	16	16

Sources: 1 and 2 (Ferrier 1975); 3 (Grayson 1971); 4–6 (Centre for Leisure Research 1984); 7 (Sir Norman Chester Centre for Football Research 1990).
Note: Figures refer to percentages of spectators using each mode of transport (*includes underground).

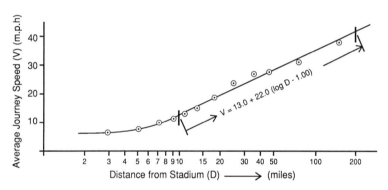

Figure 5.8 The relationship between distance from Stamford Bridge (home of Chelsea FC) and average car journey speeds in the early 1970s
Source: Grayson (1971).

distance trips of more than say, 80 km. For medium distance journeys to spectate, car use is deterred by the prospect of finding suitable parking space.

Arrivals at major games are spread over a considerable time period, the first fans beginning to enter the ground about two hours before the start of the game. In the case of the major clubs, were it not for the staggered nature of such arrivals, the public transport system, which is often responsible for bringing sizeable proportions of fans to the ground, simply could not cope.

Traffic problems tend to be greater after matches than before because crowds take much less time to vacate the stadium than to enter it. Such post-match crowding can again create severe problems for facilities such as rail and bus transport. In a period of 30–45 minutes after a Chelsea match which attracted 58,000 spectators in the early 1970s, it was estimated that 4,500 and 23,000 wanted to board a bus or underground train respectively (Grayson 1971). Because this figure far exceeded capacities, many people experienced the additional costs of long delays and severe discomfort. One of the results of reduced stadium capacities is that the figures cited above are no longer typical, but they illustrate graphically the problems faced by fans and other urban travellers near major stadiums located in areas of inadequate transport infrastructure.

It has been suggested that some sort of post-match entertainment ought to be provided in the stadium so that fans do not all leave at the same time. While seeming sensible in theory, nothing of any consequence has been tried in Britain to prevent the mass exodus usually associated with football crowds.

The cost of football-induced traffic delays to the community is notoriously difficult to infer. Grayson's early 1970s research into the impact of Chelsea FC on the local environment analysed the composition of traffic flow speeds on match and non-match days. By taking one-third of the national average wage rate of £1 per hour as the value of leisure time, he estimated that the cost of one hour's delay to the non-match travellers in the local community was over £1,170 (Grayson 1971). This was probably an underestimate of costs since it excluded costs of discomfort apart from delay.

Costs of discomfort also accrue to fans travelling to the game, though their spatial behaviour (that is, time spent travelling, waiting for the game to start and then getting home, may take 3.25 hours compared with only 1.75 hours actually watching the match) suggests a low valuation on time savings. Costs of discomfort may be high, however, since travel is often by car and late arrival may mean parking as far as 2 km from the stadium.

Parking

Many, but (as I will show in the next chapter) by no means all, of the English Football League grounds are sited in densely built-up residential areas of the urban region. Late-nineteenth- and early-twentieth-century housing often surrounds these stadiums, the areas possessing very little parking space. The tendency for the suburbanization of the football industry, with its associated vast parking space, is well advanced in other service industries and in the USA but has barely started in British football where a twentieth-century industry is still frequently found in late-nineteenth-century locations.

Parked cars were seen as a nuisance by more than 20 per cent of residents living within 2 km of half the thirty-seven League grounds explored in 1989 (Bale 1989b). Such widespread objections are not surprising when it is realized that a well-attended football match can attract about 10,000 parked cars to areas which on non-match days would have less than 600 (Ferrier 1976). As the size of the crowd increases, the spatial extent of parking increases too. It has been estimated for London's Chelsea FC that for a crowd of 20,000 fans, the radius of the zone of parked cars would extend 850 metres from the stadium; a crowd of 60,000 would result in a respective figure of 2,000 metres (Grayson 1971). An intensive study of the locality around Manchester City's ground, on the occasion of a match against Birmingham City in the mid-1970s, showed that 90 per cent of the 4,500 vehicles generated by football were parked in primarily residential areas. Another Manchester game, between United and Newcastle in the same year, attracted a crowd of 52,000 and resulted in 45 per cent of the vehicles generated by the game being parked in residential streets, despite the fact that Manchester United has substantial parking space in a nearby industrial area. In this area over 2,100 vehicles were parked; the following Saturday there were 15. In streets around the stadium the respective figures were 3,840 and 503 (Ferrier 1976). In such situations much illegal parking takes place. More recently, the police have cordoned-off side streets to protect residents, and when Liverpool played Arsenal at Highbury in the late 1980s it was thought necessary to place a police cordon at an 800 metre radius around the stadium with local residents having to establish their identity (Taylor 1990).

Fans visiting away games seem more disadvantaged than home fans with respect to the quality of travel and parking near grounds. It has been shown, for example, that whereas at *home* matches 41.4 per cent of fans found parking and travel near the ground to be excellent (8.6 per cent) or good (32.8 per cent), the respective figure for away fans was 13.9 per cent (0.6 and 13.3 per cent excellent and good, respectively). Ease of access to, and of leaving, the ground is similarly found to be better for home fans (Sir Norman Chester Centre for Football Research 1989b).

For the people living around such stadiums the impact of high residential parking densities can become intolerable. An invasion of cars into a residential area poses several actual and potential problems. These include:

1 Vehicular access and often egress is almost totally denied to residents in the area. Their traditional parking spaces may be taken by fans, their driveways blocked hence preventing them getting their cars out or resulting in them having to park their cars in spaces distant from their homes.

2 The movement in and out, at very slow speeds and combined with the parking problem, creates environmentally intolerable conditions for about 66 hours per season (assuming the nuisance lasts for 3 hours and there are 22 home games per season – a low estimate for some clubs).

3 There is the danger of impeding emergency vehicles such as ambulances and fire engines in highly congested streets, with the distinct possibility of injury or even fatality.

4 Streets which, even in these days, might otherwise be used for children's play space, are denied by the presence of parked cars and traffic which also creates danger.

These problems invite solutions based on park-and-ride principles but, with a small number of exceptions, this has not proved popular in English cities.

Hooliganism/vandalism

The significance of hooliganism as a nuisance can be placed in perspective by noting that of localities around thirty-seven Football League grounds in England in only four was hooliganism perceived as a nuisance by more than 20 per cent of residents living with 2 km of the grounds, and around only six grounds did 30 per cent or more of residents living within 500 metres view it as a nuisance (Bale 1989b). To be fair, around some grounds between 30–45 per cent of residents perceive hooliganism to be a nuisance which, on occasions, can be extremely frightening, annoying, and damaging to property as well as contributing to considerable psychological stress.

Football hooliganism and the anti-social behaviour of fans must not be under-rated as a problem; but neither should it be over-rated. Only eleven arrests were recorded outside the Third Division ground of Bristol Rovers during the 1989/90 season (out of 93,000 fan visits) (GMA 1989), and arrest figures for football fans in the streets around stadiums are generally very low – just as they are for arrests inside grounds (see pp. 29–30). In the Strathclyde region of Scotland which contains fifteen Scottish League clubs, arrests at 346 games in 1987 totalled 756 inside and 845 outside the grounds. This represented an arrest rate of 0.07 per cent – twice as high as that for England but still astonishingly small given the media hype concerning hooligan behaviour (Scottish Education Department 1977). Indeed, Eugene Trivizas (1980) has suggested that people committing offences in football crowds are dealt with more severely than those committing similar offences in other circumstances, suggesting that the tiny percentage noted above is somewhat higher than might otherwise be expected. A study in Bristol reported that of 478 assaults resulting in accidents to people of 16 and over recorded in the city's Royal Infirmary in 1986, only 2 per cent reported football hooliganism as a cause of the violence. This represented a smaller number than those reporting violence resulting from road traffic disputes! (Shepherd 1990).

Annoyance and nuisance is much more widespread, of course, than the arrest or accident figures suggest. Noise, crowding, harassment, litter, various incidents, disturbances, and generally anti-social behaviour are not reflected in the arrest figures. A widespread and upsetting occurrence before or after many games is the propensity of some supporters to urinate against doors or walls of houses and in front gardens and to throw litter on to other people's property. These practices are surprisingly widespread and produce angry responses from residents from Brighton to Birmingham.

Hooligan incidents, though currently being distanced to some extent from the immediate vicinity of the stadium by intensive local policing, do seem to remain dominantly within the neighbourhood of the ground where crowd density is at its greatest and where confrontations are most likely to exist. Local residents therefore bear the brunt of such disturbances. Figure 5.9 shows how 'hooligan incidents' reported in the *Portsmouth Evening News* on two Saturdays in August 1987, associated with Portsmouth games against Chelsea and local rivals Southampton, were concentrated around Portsmouth's Fratton Park ground (though it must not be assumed that newspapers include reports of *all* such incidents). The precise location of hooligan incidents and other football nuisances, however, may be strongly related to the particular properties of the urban environment such as adjacent land uses, surveillance and street layout, as well as to the level of police activity and efficiency. This is not to say, of course, that *all* such incidents are spatially confined. The infamous visit of Leeds fans to Bournemouth at the end of the 1989/90 season on a May Bank Holiday weekend resulted in several days of

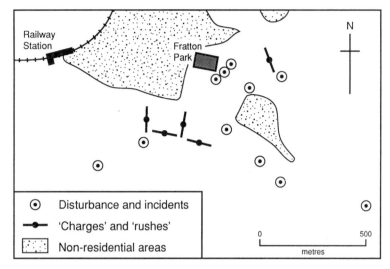

Figure 5.9 Two Saturdays in August 1987: the geography of hooligan incidents
reported in two issues of the *Portsmouth Evening News*
Source: Peabody (1988).

hooliganism and vandalism over a much larger area, including places as
far afield as Poole and Christchurch.

Football-related vandalism, which may include damage to vehicles,
residences and retail property, is rarely fully recorded and its extent is
unknown. In the 1960s considerable attention was devoted to football
vandalism on trains and coaches. The 'Harrington Report' of 1968 felt
that vandalism on 'football specials' had peaked in 1962 with 4,641
cases reported and 811 arrests in that year. These compared with
respective figures of 3,689 and 533 by 1966 (Harrington 1968). The
cost of such vandalism was about £6,500 per annum (£5,000 resulting
from events in Scotland) – a surprisingly low figure, Harrington pointed
out, in view of the fact that the cost of vandalism in the city of
Birmingham was £1,000 *per week*.

The effects of a single match can, in extreme cases however, cause
much more damage than this. At the infamous Luton–Millwall game in
March 1987, £15,000 worth of damage was inflicted inside the ground
as seats were ripped out of stands and a pitch invasion was televised
nation-wide. 'An estimated £10,000 worth of damage was also caused
outside the ground where local residents were attacked and their cars,
homes and shops were wrecked. British Rail estimated the cost of
damage to trains taking Millwall fans back to London at £45,000'

(Wesson 1987). Associated with the Bournemouth–Leeds game noted earlier, damage variously estimated at between £40,000 and £100,000 was inflicted on the rather genteel southern resort by the northern fans.

Because fans are today herded by police from station to stadium – a further example of the containment and surveillance described in Chapter 2 – events such as those described above are, thankfully, exceptional. Around grounds the damage to property is a relatively infrequent occurrence, though this is not to ignore the distress such damage can create. One aspect of so-called vandalism which is more enduring, however, is football-related graffiti. While some regard this as a visual legacy of vandalism others see it as art, a statement of territoriality, a means of insulting opposing teams, the visual defence of 'turf' or a form of resistance by one of society's marginalized groups. Virtually no territorial analyses of British football graffiti has been undertaken in the spirit of the seminal study of Philadelphia 'gang turf' graffiti by geographers David Ley and Roman Cybriwsky (1974). While graffiti such as that in the Ley–Cybriwsky study displayed a pattern of concentration at the centres of gang turf (similar to the way 'political' graffiti is concentrated around universities) promoting the gang and at the peripheries of turfs where space is actively contested, football-related graffiti seems to assume less predictable patterns.

Rather paradoxically, what is perhaps the most interesting study of football graffiti has been undertaken by an American historian working in Russia. John Bushnell's (1990) study of football graffiti in Moscow is part of a broader study of the growth of graffiti in that city since the mid-1970s, before which it was largely absent. Although Bushnell identified concentrations of football graffiti around the stadiums of the major Moscow clubs, it was not aggressively territorial in the sense found in gang graffiti in US cities. Other studies suggest that football-related graffiti is located where space exists and opportunity arises and that it is not particularly concentrated around the stadium (see Figure 5.10). If the city of Osnabrück in Germany was typical, football-related graffiti would account for only about 4 per cent of all urban graffiti – tiny in comparison with that devoted to politics (35.5 per cent), for example (Hard et al. 1984). It should be noted, however, that political graffiti is probably more prominent in Germany than in Britain, though this speculation is based on nothing more than intuition. It might also be noted that football graffiti was, 'for a long time the most numerous accounting for at least half of all public graffiti in Moscow until the middle of the 1980s' (Bushnell 1990: 30).

One effect of football hooliganism and vandalism on the urban scene

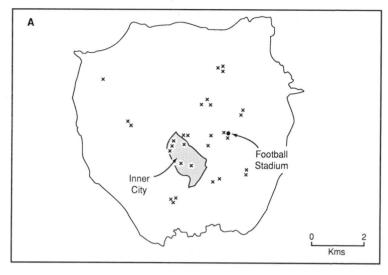

Figure 5.10a The incidence of football-related graffiti in Osnabrück, Germany,
September 1983
Source: Hard *et al.* (1984).

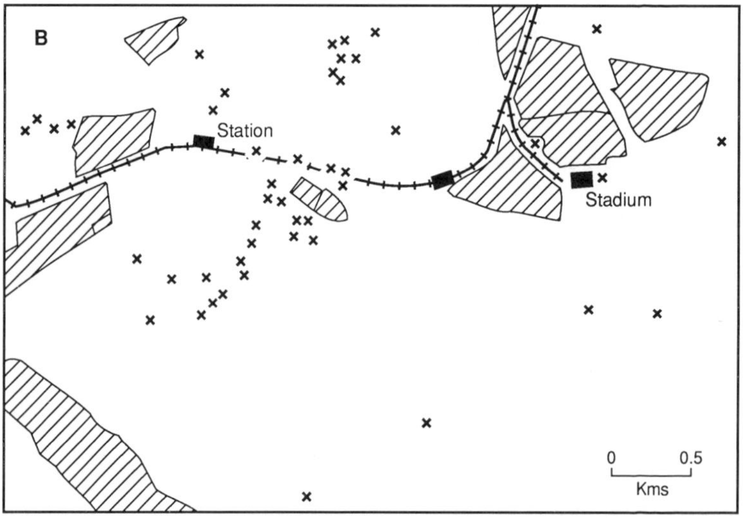

Figure 5.10b '625 Crew' graffiti in Portsmouth
Source: Peabody (1988).

116

Figure 5.10c Graffiti in Wenceslas Square, Prague, in early 1990 indicating support for both political changes and the perennial Czech champions, Sparta

Figure 5.10d Graffiti near the Stadio Communale in Florence denigrates teams from Turin, Bologna, Milan, Rome, and Naples

117

is to change the normal pattern of disorderly events in the city. Most disorder occurs late at night (Parkes and Thrift 1980: 344–5); in Britain football hooliganism occurs between 1400 and 1800 hours, hence bringing disorder at an otherwise orderly time of day. But nevertheless, the hooligan events of late Saturday afternoon are not significantly greater than the disorder that occurs on an average Saturday night, if the results of a study by police in the Glasgow area of Scotland are typical. Strathclyde Police, in Scotland, noted that 'the fact that there are 1.6 per cent more crimes committed when football matches are played than when they are not hardly seems a cause for concern' (Scottish Education Department 1977).

Noise

The noises from a football match which effect local residents include those emanating from traffic before and after a game, amplified music in the pre-match period, and the shouting and cheering of the crowds. If the stadium houses non-footballing events, such as rock concerts which take place at night, the noise impact can be intolerable (see pp. 125–6). Normally, however, the noise impact is less than this but can, nevertheless, cause annoyance.

Objective records of the impact of noise can be made by a sound level meter, noise levels being measured in decibels. A very noisy residential area would have an average decibel value of 58 while decibel values regarded as 'very loud' would be between 90 and 100. Higher values are regarded as 'uncomfortably loud' (Berry *et al.* 1974: 214). Observations of football-induced noise from a 1989 Third Division game between Bristol Rovers and Swansea City, attracting 5,600 spectators at Twerton Park, Bath, revealed a decibel level of around 70 during exciting parts of the game. This contrasted with a level of 45 ('quiet') at 11.40 on the morning of the game. These values were recorded in a residential area about 100 metres from the centre of a ground which possesses rather poor noise insulation with an absence of high surrounding walls (GMA 1989).

On the face of it such noise levels, for relatively short periods of time, are not particularly objectionable. On the other hand, were a similarly located stadium occupied by a club attracting larger crowds, the noise level could reach levels which could give cause for residents' concern and it is salutory to note that American guidelines suggest that for proposed outdoor spectator sports facilities generating noise levels such as that at the Bristol–Swansea game cited above, no such development should take place in an urban area (Berry *et al.* 1974). It is also interesting to note that in cases such as that at Luton, where unruly behaviour has been considerably reduced by the 'home only' supporters scheme, a larger number of residents living around the ground have been found to perceive noise to be a nuisance than hooliganism (Mason and Robins 1991).

Retail impacts

Another negative effect of proximity in relation to a football ground may be reduced retail sales of nearby shops. Retailers in Luton emphasized that an increase in revenues followed the decision by Luton Town FC to ban away fans from Kenilworth Road. In 1984 major stores 'found their takings down, sometimes by thousands of pounds, when the most notorious teams came to Luton' (Williams *et al.* 1989a). A secretarial college near the ground was forced to cancel courses and lock students in for fear of harassment (Williams *et al.* 1989a). But following the ban on visiting fans, the president of the town centre Arndale Traders' Association reported no troublesome incidents and 'significant increase in Saturday afternoon takings at the centre' (Williams *et al.* 1989a).[4] Two stores noted an increase of 14 per cent and 30 per cent respectively, compared with the previous, pre-ban season, while other retailers quoted figures as high as 150 per cent.[5] Traders and public were felt to be less nervous following the ban on visiting fans.

If the above evidence was typical it might be reasonably concluded that 'normal' (that is, non-Luton) football crowds only generate negative spillovers for the retail trade. Even in the Luton case, however, some traders reported reduced takings following the ban, and a 1989 survey showed that of 766 shopkeepers located around thirty-seven League grounds, only 8 per cent claimed that they suffered a reduction in revenue on average match days with only 15 per cent stating that an increase in shoplifting occurred at such times (Bale 1990). Again, it seems possible that the negative impact of football on local retailing may have been exaggerated. The Taylor Report (1990) noted that 'shops may be pillaged' on match days, but strong emphasis ought to be placed on *may be*. The losses in retail takings in some shops on match days are greatly exceeded by the overall increases in revenue described in the previous chapter.

House price effects

The effect on the price of houses which are in proximity to noxious facilities is relatively well known. Just as proximity to a golf course tends to raise the average price of property, proximity to a stadium tends to reduce it. Of course, this is a claim based on an 'all other things being equal' assumption, and as the price of a house is based on variables other than simply its site, it is often very difficult indeed to isolate the sole effects of, say, a nearby football ground.

The best evidence of a negative impact on house prices is provided by work done in the early 1970s in suburban London. Statements from a sample of estate agents led Bowen (1974) to conclude that the percentage decrease in house prices tends to decrease from the higher to the lower end of the price range, proximity to a stadium producing a 13 per cent reduction for the most expensive type of house if so located, figures of 5 and 3 per cent reductions being applied to the middle and low end of the range residences. One estate agent has estimated the reduction in value on one property near Oxford United's ground of 8 per cent resulting from the location of a floodlighting pylon, with another losing nearer 10 per cent in value because of nearby access gates to the stadium (Goodey et al. 1986).[6] Unlike the situation in relation to clubs in working-class areas of the city, it may be more difficult to sell a middle-class residence next to a football ground.

Community costs of policing

Although the club (helped by funding from The Football Trust) bears the costs of policing inside the football ground, the police activity in the streets around the stadium is borne by the public, via local taxes. Traditionally it was felt that policing outside grounds was relatively insignificant compared with that inside grounds, but in recent years the balance has changed dramatically.

For a club like Luton Town, for which police costs inside the ground are currently negligible due to the club's insistence on a ban on away fans and a club membership scheme, the police cost to the community was on average about £1,620 per match in 1987/8. Because of the ban on away supporters only 50–70 police officers are required on duty at the ground and in the town on match days, whereas in the previous season, before the introduction of the home-only scheme, an average of 184 police officers were involved each match. Of course, Luton Town is exceptional and its average 1987/8 charge per match of £1,620 for policing should be compared with the First Division average of £3,990

(Williams *et al.* 1989a). In 1988/9 the total costs of policing football in London was some £10 million of which only £1.6 million could be recovered by the clubs. For Scottish League and GM Vauxhall Conference, the cost to clubs in the same season was £4.9 million. Such figures refer to policing inside the ground and the costs of deploying police outside the ground is much more. Typically, 5,000 police officers may be engaged on football duties on a Saturday during the football season and it has been estimated that the cost of deploying these officers is between £200,000 and £300,000 each Saturday (Williams *et al.* 1989a). Evidence from the USA indicates that 1983 expenditure on police attributable to professional baseball and football in Baltimore amounted to over $714,000 – an average expenditure of about $8,000 per game (Johnson 1986).

Other football nuisances

A number of other nuisances exist, the costs of which are difficult to ascertain. Smells from food vendors can create a negative impact on some local people. A more recently studied phenomenon, that of 'light pollution', can also be generated by football when played outside daylight hours, the floodlights increasing the natural brightness of the sky. At the present time, however, little is known to provide guidelines about acceptable levels. The development of new stadiums in greenfield sites would also possess ecological impacts, the 'cost' of which virtually defies quantification but, according to 'deep ecologists' would typify the 'anti-nature' character of much modern sport (Galtung 1984, Mützelberg and Eichberg 1984).

These, and all the other impacts discussed in this chapter, can be interpreted as costs imposed on the community by football; the spillovers are parts of the 'production' of a football match but their costs are paid by the community. But I should also note that the congestion, parking, and associated problems described above affect fans as well as residents. Indeed, the real cost of a football match to the fan makes the cost of entry to the game look relatively modest. The cost of time is difficult to ascertain for a fan but if it is assumed that an hour is taken up in travelling, 50 minutes is spent waiting for the game to start, 15 minutes taken in getting out of the stadium, 30 minutes taken up in traffic delays, and another 60 minutes taken to get home, it becomes clear that the fan has 'wasted' 3.5 hours for 1.5 hours football. In other words, 5 hours are required for many (home) spectators to attend and watch upper division matches.

At this point I need to stress that football nuisances would be likely to be substantially reduced if non-residential spaces existed around football grounds to isolate or internalize potential externalities. As the figures depicted in Figures 5.3–5.5 show, and as much of this chapter has implied, however, the fact that many (but by no means all) football grounds *are* sited in residential areas means that residents often consume more football, and its spillovers, than they would freely choose. But this is only a partial picture and a number of other factors need to be considered in assessing the particular impacts of particular clubs. These include the club's history and its changing relationship with the locality in which it is sited. Let me illustrate what I mean by considering two clubs, Oxford United and Nottingham Forest.[7]

Nottingham Forest is one of the oldest football clubs in the world, having been formed in 1865 when its games were played on the Forest Racecourse. Five other grounds, including Trent Bridge Cricket Ground, were occupied until 1898, the year in which it moved to the City Ground which has been its home ever since. The City Ground is a classic centrally located stadium, very close to the city centre and easily accessible to the main railway station. Transport routes have developed gradually, with the centrally located ground as a major focus, so that it is only the stadium's immediate area that is affected by crowds. Even car parking space has been developed on land which has been purchased from the local authority after slum clearance.

The City Ground has low-priced terraced housing on three of its sides and the River Trent on its fourth. It could be argued that because the ground has been there longer than any local residents, the latter have had an element of choice about living so close to a football stadium. Indeed, the fact that some of the houses are painted in red and white suggests that some residents enjoy this association by sporting the club's colours. The ground is well-established in the popular psyche.

Oxford United, on the other hand, is a comparative newcomer to the League. The club was founded as Headington in 1896 but did not turn professional until 1949, not being admitted to the Football League until 1962 following the resignation of Accrington Stanley (a classic reflection of the changing economic fortunes of the nation). A combination of its location in an affluent part of England and the aggressive policy of upward footballing mobility by its chairman and media magnate, Robert Maxwell, led to speedy movement between the divisions of the League and by the early 1980s it was in the First Division. It was now a major league club occupying a non-league site.

Such a rapid rise, from non-league status to one which attracted visiting clubs from London, Manchester and Liverpool, created problems which Nottingham has never really had to face. For a start, the Oxford club was sited in an established middle-class residential area which has seen no planning provision for a First Division football club and its stadium. While Oxford and Forest may each occupy a ground with an entrance at the end of a residential street (see Figure 5.11), the perceived impact if 14,000 fans on a Saturday afternoon on what was a quiet middle-class housing area may be different. Oxford railway station is on the other side of the historic city and opposition fans, even if escorted by police, are capable of bringing the whole of Oxford's central business district to a standstill; the entire infrastructure strains when there is a major game at the Manor Ground.

Newly found status may have other negative implications for local residents. Should clubs wish to increase the size of their grandstands, for example, the potential impact of architectural change needs to be anticipated. In Copenhagen, for instance, it has been shown how an increase in size of the stadium next to the Brumleby area of the city will produce a substantial increase of the area of residences in shadow, a small but important impact on the quality of residents' lives (Nagbøl 1991).

NON-FOOTBALL NUISANCES OF FOOTBALL GROUNDS

Football stadiums are highly underutilized. In a season extending from mid-August to early May income-generating matches are played on an average of only twenty-six occasions. A survey undertaken in 1987 indicated that of 42 League clubs examined, 15 (or 35 per cent) used their grounds for non-footballing activities ranging from pop concerts, religious festivals (for example, Billy Graham's 'Mission England', Jehovah's Witness conventions, the visit of Archbishop Desmond Tutu), to sporting events other than football (Oliver 1986). Rugby League clubs have played on the grounds of Leeds United, Carlisle, Cardiff and Fulham, among others. Stockport County's ground was used for the lacrosse world cup, floodlit cricket has been hosted at Chelsea's ground, and world championship boxing has been held at Queen's Park Rangers. But non-footballing activity is inevitably limited because of the potential damage to the grass playing surface, and as a result such activities tend to be few in number and usually restricted to the summer close season.

This constraint can be overcome, of course, by the installation of an

A

B

Figure 5.11 Football and residential land use; (a) Nottingham Forest's ground from Colwick Road, and (b) Beech Road, Oxford. (Photographs by courtesy of Brian Goodey)

artificial pitch. In the case of Luton Town, the club spent £350,000 on a synthetic pitch but generated £100,000 of additional income in only eight months by renting the stadium for such events as hockey, bowling, women's football, gridiron football, and various exhibitions. At Port Vale's ground a weekly market, held in the concourse area outside the stadium, contributes £140,000 to the club's finances each year (*Evening Sentinel* (Stoke), 8 January 1991). In other cases some clubs have sold or leased land for development. Brentford built forty-eight houses on the site of a stand and car park which back on to a new, smaller stand, while Crystal Palace leased a bank of terracing to Sainsbury's retail chain. Similar developments have taken place at Hull City and Bolton Wanderers and are likely to become widespread given the need for revenue to implement the Taylor Report's recommendations.

The question posed by such non-footballing events and developments is whether they create greater or lesser nuisances to local residents than the football which normally takes place. It is also salutory to consider whether, if football grounds should be sold and converted into, say, supermarkets, local residents would be consuming greater, and more frequent nuisances than hitherto. The only available evidence, from a study of football in the Scottish city of Perth, suggests that non-footballing (in this case, retailing) use of former football stadium sites is perceived to generate fewer nuisances than football formerly did (Moncrieff 1991).

It is clear, however, that certain non-football uses of existing stadiums can create intolerable annoyance to local residents, far in excess of the normal football nuisances. Two examples clarify these situations. Aston Villa is one of Britain's most legendary football clubs. Proximate to its imposing Villa Park stadium is a mixed area of residential and retail development, the local properties being occupied by a mix of traditional residents and a newer Moslem community. Many of the long-standing residents no longer visit Villa Park, and the Moslems are simply not interested in football. Regular Saturday First Division games in one of Britain's premier stadiums create almost intolerable negative effects but most residents concede that the club was there first.

The club already has an indoor cricket centre next to the ground, plus a nearby sports and social club, and in 1988, as a means of diversifying further its sources of revenue, it hosted a rock concert featuring Bruce Springsteen. From the club's point of view the concert was a considerable success but according to local residents the two-day event led to a local 'state of siege'. The environmental impact of this event was graphically described in the following terms:

For the duration of the performances and extending in various ways through the preceding and following 24 hours, floodlights, noise, traffic and the mass of people coming into the area brought ordinary activity to an end. Some businesses had to close through lack of parking space. Residents over a substantial area had great difficulty reaching home. Once there they could not sleep or hear ordinary speech. The presence of a mass of people, *far exceeding football crowds* at the ground, sometimes behaving badly under the influence of alcohol, was intimidating. There was widespread urinating in doorways and a deluge of litter. Elderly people were frightened.[8]

Clearly, the widespread use of stadiums set in residential areas for concerts involving the playing of highly amplified music and attracting a larger number of people than occupy the stadium for football, is not to be welcomed.

In other cases, however, it is clear that non-football uses of stadiums create far fewer nuisances than football. A study of the external effects of football and non-football uses at Kenilworth Road, Luton showed that 'the general nuisance field created by ... non-football uses is both significantly less intense and smaller in extent that the football-generated nuisance field' (Mason and Robins 1991). At the same time, the overall ranking of nuisances is the same for football and non-football uses, traffic congestion and pedestrians being the major problems as perceived by residents. But for every type of nuisance the spatial extent of the externality field is at least three times smaller than that for the comparable football-generated nuisance. It should finally be noted that the Luton research showed that non-sporting uses generated nuisances for a smaller number of residents than either football or other sporting uses – though it should be stressed that this finding is specific to Luton's particular ground uses (see Figure 5.12). Also, I must emphasize that given the great variety of site characteristics of football grounds and the great variety of possible uses to which stadiums theoretically can be put, broad categories of usage will include an equally broad range of resident responses. The Aston Villa example shows that some non-sporting uses can create very serious nuisances indeed.

FROM TOPOPHOBIA TO ACTIVISM

It should be stressed that for many football grounds in Britain, the level of nuisance is very low indeed. For clubs such as Crewe, Hartlepool or

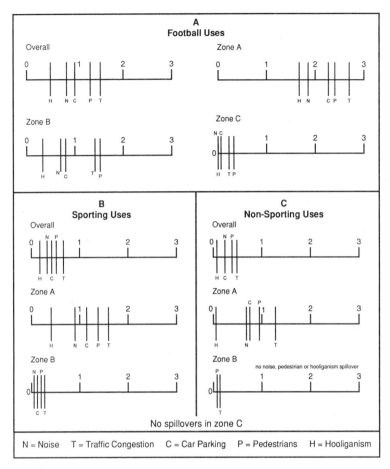

Figure 5.12 The impact of football and non-football nuisances generated by events at Kenilworth Road, Luton. Diagrams show the ranking of negative externalities as perceived by local residents
Source: Mason and Robins (1991).

Rotherham, for example, very low, or non-existent levels of 'serious nuisance' are perceived by local residents while 'nuisances' fail to be perceived by more than 25 per cent of residents, even within 500 metres of the ground (Bale 1990). This is not to deny that nuisances which create annoyance do exist, and I have spent most of this chapter discussing them.

It is difficult to envisage people trying to distance themselves from positive externalities (indeed, proximity to them is usually regarded as highly desirable). It tends to be the existence, or threat of, negative externalities that generate conflict and it has been noted by Brian Robson that 'what prompts residential conflict is almost invariably a concern with minimizing the negative externalities which are represented by the real or perceived threats of land use or social changes in an area and with maximizing the converse positive externalities' (Robson 1982: 45). While in some cases it is possible for the community to present a 'common front' against the source of the negative externality, this may not be so easy in the case of the football club because the community may include fans whose support for football verges on the religious (see Chapter 4). What may generate negative externalities to some may create positive externalities to others. As noted earlier, a fan is less likely to perceive football as a nuisance than a non-fan; at the local scale a stadium might be a nuisance to residents but at the city scale it may provide pride in place for civic elders.

Because of the limited environmental impact of many clubs, neighbourhood activism and resulting conflict between club and community is also limited. Nevertheless, there is a range of possible responses to the football nuisances discussed above, ranging from mild annoyance to vigorous legal action, the former being associated with slight nuisances and the latter with extreme nuisances. The former are common; the latter, which bring residents into conflict with the football club, are rare. The recourse to legal action involves a cost, through the use of spare time and the establishment of a well orchestrated campaign, to the community group involved. Examples of neighbourhood activism towards the activities of football clubs can now be briefly outlined.

EXAMPLES OF ACTIVISM

Football grounds may give rise to local activism and involve conflict for limited periods of time, the presence of grounds being less a cause for concern than the changing spatial extent and intensity of their negative spillovers. Such changing impact is common among football clubs because of the dynamic nature of their divisional rankings. A club languishing in the Fourth Division is less likely to generate nuisances than clubs in the First or Second. Neighbourhood conflict with the club, therefore, varies with its divisional status.

A typical example is provided by the case of Cambridge United. In the late 1970s and early 1980s the club found itself in the Second Division of the Football League, a somewhat untypical situation for a club which had entered the League as recently as 1970. While a member of the Second Division, crowds exceeded 8,000 whereas before their entry to this higher division, and in subsequent years, they averaged about a quarter of that figure.

In 1981 the *Cambridge Evening News* graphically summarized the situation for residents of parts of the city *en route* to the football grounds in these words:

> Not very long ago the people of Newmarket Road, Cromwell Road and Mill Road could look forward to Saturday as a day of relaxation. That was before Cambridge United became a Second Division football club, attracting large numbers of visiting followers who, having arrived at the railway station, somehow feel compelled to shout obscenities at residents, pelt them with stones, bash up their cars parked in the streets and throw bricks through their windows. Many pubs en route to Abbey Stadium have had to make special arrangements for match days, locking front doors against gangs of visitors. On Saturday some Newmarket Road shops closed early rather than risk a looting or a beating. On Saturday the homes of 30 Cambridge people were damaged by visitors on their way to see Chelsea play United. Police estimate the damage at around £3,000.[9]

The above quotation may contain an element of hyperbole but it nevertheless illustrates the public response to football nuisances being injected into what had traditionally been a nuisance-free area. The Cambridge public's response to such a situation was to engage in various forms of local political activism, not so much against the club *per se* but against the impact which visiting fans had on their neighbourhood.

Such activism illustrates the forms assumed by political involvement in local conflicts. A petition was sent to the Environment Committee of the City Council, calling for a railway halt to be built to prevent fans spilling over into city streets. Complaints by residents to local councillors were widespread with suggestions for a free bus service from central station to stadium. A year or so after these complaints Cambridge United began to lose form and lapsed into the lower divisions again. With their decline the spatial extent of the nuisance field was reduced and activism was replaced by occasional annoyance, notably in the event of local derbies against rivals Peterborough United. With another upward surge to the Second Division in the early 1990s residents again faced the problems which they thought had disappeared.

The voicing of grievances by writing to the Press or by submitting petitions and complaints to local councillors represents a low level of activism. The collective formation of local residents groups infers greater commitment and results perhaps from greater nuisance, with activist groups tending to form only after *at least* 20 per cent of a locality's population are annoyed by the nuisance (Berry *et al.* 1974). Two recent examples serve to illustrate such collective action against football clubs which have been perceived as having pushed the level of annoyance beyond tolerable limits.

Let me return briefly to the experiences of residents around Villa Park alluded to earlier. Following the success (from the viewpoint of the club) of the Bruce Springsteen concert held in 1988, the club announced in 1989 that it planned to hold two further such concerts. This had the effect of pushing local residents from a passive-unfavourable to an active-unfavourable attitude towards the club (as in the lower half of Figure 4.11). In order to understand why, it is important to recall the nature of the impact of the first Springsteen concert, held in 1988 and alluded to on p. 126. The prospect of two further such events served to galvanize local political involvement to the extent that twenty-one local community groups (including the Federation of Aston Residents Associations, the Aston Churches Working Together Group, Mosques, and other religious leaders) got together and successfully opposed the club's application to the city council to hold the events. The residents' case was based on a detailed list of concert-induced nuisances which included community stress, noise, illegal street trading, and inadequate sanitary arrangements, all expertly presented at a meeting of the council's General Purposes Sub-committee by a solicitor employed for the occasion. The club's case, on the other hand, was presented in an ill-prepared and aggressive way. It was an example of community activism triumphing over the forces of capital.

The nearest example in recent years to successful community opposition to the continuation of football (rather than to the kind of diversified activities of clubs as described above) is probably that of the North Charlton Community Project which vigorously opposed the return of Charlton Athletic to its traditional home at The Valley in the London borough of Greenwich after three unhappy years of ground-sharing with Crystal Palace. The campaign of those supporting a return to The Valley has already been described (see pp. 88–90) but I here want to stress that having set in motion a campaign to return the club to its former home, opposition from local residents ('silent acceptors' of the club while it was there) became much stronger. It has been suggested that much of this new anti-Charlton activism was generated by a newer, yuppified population which had moved into the area around the ground, following Charlton's move to Selhurst Park. Four basic arguments were used to oppose Charlton's return. These were:

1   The diversification of the club's activities to include in the stadium complex office accommodation and banqueting facilities would intensify the use of the stadium and hence increase the negative traffic and noise spillovers.
2   Lack of adequate off-street parking would conflict with the council's planning policies regarding movement and environment.
3   Office development and banqueting facilities would result in the loss of land defined as Community Open Space and would set up an undesirable precedent for the further reduction of such open space.
4   The excessive height of the north and south stands of the proposed stadium would be obtrusive and out of scale with the surrounding residential properties, hence creating a feeling of 'enclosure' for local residents.[10]

At Woolwich Town Hall in February 1990 the Development Control Sub-committee of the borough council agreed unanimously to ratify the decision of the Planning and Transport Committee to redevelop Charlton's traditional home, an apparent success for local residents against the activities of the football club. As shown earlier, however, the success was short-lived, and following The Valley Party's local election 'success', plans to refurbish The Valley for football got underway (see pp. 88–90).

In late 1991 community opposition to the spillovers of local football clubs reached a new level of activism with the formation of a National Federation of Stadium Communities to which local community groups could affiliate and pool experience for mutual benefit. Among other things, the Federation sought to ensure that neighbourhoods and communities in the shadows of major football stadiums would be recognized by the various levels of government, to lobby for sufficient funds to be invested in such communities so that they could continue to function despite the number of fans they attract, and to look after the interests of community and neighbourhood when plans are drawn up for stadium development or change.[11] Among the first contestations with clubs following the Federation's formation were those between residents around Highbury stadium (home of Arsenal) who opposed the brutal architectural style of a proposed new stand. The community around the Hillsborough Stadium in Sheffield, on the other hand, concentrated on improving the still-tarnished image of the neighbourhood resulting from the 1989 disaster. The progress of both these grass roots activist groups, and others, was monitored and given an additional 'voice' by the newly formed Federation newsletter, *The Shadow*.

I have provided some evidence which shows that residents *can* successfully oppose the activities of existing football clubs but I should emphasize that most opposition appears to have come from the *threat* of potential football grounds coming to the back yards of residents, rather than from residents who already have the grounds there. Such threats, if converted into activism, can influence the extent to which the suburbanization of the football industry will take place, a subject I turn to in Chapter 6.

CONCLUSION

This chapter has highlighted some negative impacts of the English football stadium. There can be no doubt that for some people football contributes positively to their quality of life. But for many people, the 'silent majority' perhaps, the combined effects of traffic, parking, noise, and hooliganism make football a nuisance – an annoying, and sometimes frightening, experience. In conceptualizing the football ground as a 'noxious facility' it is worth stressing that, unlike other such facilities as prisons, mental hospitals, or drug rehabilitation centres (to which popular response is also 'not on our street'), the football stadium is not viewed as noxious by those both inside and outside. Fans are not consciously coerced to go to stadiums in the way prisoners are to prisons. And because of the nature (and local presence of at least part) of football's fandom, a larger proportion of local residents support the stadium than would welcome the local presence of, say, an asylum.

This chapter has shown that hooliganism is almost certainly overestimated as a problem, though this is not to deny its seriousness when it does occur. Football has an exaggerated negative image and I have demonstrated the existence of a moral panic by contrasting what is generally perceived to be the impact of football with that which local residents around grounds see it to be. It cannot be denied, however, that for some people (a minority around most grounds) what should be a landscape of fun has been turned into a landscape of fear. In rare examples the voice of the community is able to influence the outcome of club-community conflicts over negative externalities. In selecting new stadium locations for the future urban geography of English football the negative impacts, as well as the positive, will need to be taken into account. The problems of internalizing nuisances will need to be considered before locations for new stadiums are chosen, and in finding the answers to such problems questions relating to landscape, distance, and location will be crucial. As I shall show in Chapter 6, many suburban residents are only too well aware of the negative impacts which such stadiums could bring.

6

QUESTIONS OF LOCATION AND RELOCATION

L. S. Lowry's painting *Going to the Match* reveals the stereotypical English football ground located amid rows of Victorian terraced houses in a somewhat bleak industrial landscape. It is a landscape in which men appear to outnumber women by about five to one, confirming Bruce Kidd's assertion that stadiums might be better called 'men's culture centres'.[1] This landscape of blue-collar masculinity, cloth caps, and fish and chips is a landscape of the northern inner city, or at least the English equivalent of what E. W. Burgess (1925) would have termed the 'zone in transition', an area of changing land use and changing residential status. Other, sub-Lowry, representations of the football ground, such as those by Harold Riley, present its environment in similar terms. Just as artists and writers have mythically projected the cricket landscape as a rustic idyll (Bale 1988), the far fewer who have addressed the football landscape have consistently projected an inner-city and industrial stereotype. It is often upon such myths that our images of the national sport are based.

But following the Hillsborough disaster in 1989 the brave new world of British football was projected as one to be located in, or preferably beyond, the suburbs, with massive amounts of car parking space, surrounded by a girdle of sterile land where negative spillovers could be neutralized. Of course, the Hillsborough tragedy did not, of itself, initiate discussion on the suburbanization of the sport. The post-war period has seen a substantial move towards peri-urban developments in the service sector and even in Britain with its relatively stringent planning mechanisms, retail parks and leisure complexes are far from absent from the suburban scene.

The suburbanization of football can be interpreted as part and parcel of what Chris Philo has called 'the planned obliteration of variety in the urban scene' and in a football context is uncannily reminiscent of

Foucault's 'great confinement' in which various transitional, deviant, or marginal groups in society were, from the seventeenth century onwards, physically isolated (Philo 1986). The dislike of a mixed use of space breeds the notion of a place for everything and everything in its place, something that I have already described as being well under way inside the modern football stadium.

The Economist argued that 'the need for larger all seated stadiums and adequate parking for today's car-owning spectators would force many clubs to acknowledge that, stranded in the middle of 1920s council estates, they are simply in the wrong place'. 'Ancient club loyalties' were seen as 'sentimental' and shared grounds in suburban sites were suggested.[2] Apart from the geography of football grounds being all wrong (how many are in inter-war council estates?) this kind of comment not only disparages community loyalty but also underestimates its strength when mobilized into activism. The stadium as a sacred place, as described in Chapter 4, is part of a family of homes or family hearths belonging to a tradition which, according to Tuan 'once secured in a certain spot ... could not lightly be moved' (Tuan 1975: 24). This may not always have applied to professional sports franchises in the USA and it is not to deny the need for a new locational strategy for football in Britain, but what might work in the United States might not necessarily work on the other side of the Atlantic.

In this chapter I want to explore the pressures for, and the resistance to, the suburbanization of British football. The European and US model of big stadium complexes is a world inhabited by rational, profit-maximizing entrepreneurs and equally rational, discriminating consumers of football who would be prepared to travel over considerable distances to see a good game rather than support just one club. This is not to say that relocations have never occurred in British football and it could be argued that those who run football clubs have, at certain points in time, demonstrated through their locational decision-making a degree of economic rationality or profit-maximizing behaviour. Indeed, part of my purpose in this chapter is to describe past locational changes and the prospect of more in the future. But I do not simply want to chart the changes; I want to describe the pressures for geographic change and the prospects and problems involved in the re-drawing of the map of British football. In such spatial re-drafting of football the voices of local political interests may prove critical. What is certain is that such scenarios for geographical change will be contested.

LOCATIONAL CHANGE

Two basic kinds of locational change have taken place in the British football industry. The first is the national distribution of clubs and the second is the intra-urban pattern of location. At the national scale, professional football started in the north of England and gradually diffused to embrace the entire country (Bale 1978). The concept of a league was also a northern innovation, an indication of the seriousness with which the northerners took the game in contrast to the more gentlemanly mode of organization in the south: the fixture list. Despite the northern origins of many innovations in modern football, the centre of gravity of League club location has shifted south since the 1920s. In 1930, 64 per cent of First Division clubs were in the north whereas by 1990 the figure had dropped to 25 per cent (Bale 1989a: 97).[3] As clubs enter and leave the League its balance has shifted from the focal points of nineteenth-century industry to towns of the more service-oriented economy of the post-war years.

The second type of spatial change which has occurred in the football industry has been at the intra-urban scale. Broadly speaking, two periods of locational activity can be identified. These are readily seen in Figure 6.1 which graphs the dates at which the present members of the Football League (1988/9) have changed locations. It is clear that the overwhelming number of ground changes took place between the early 1870s and 1920. Indeed, of the 179 moves which I have been able to identify, 88 per cent had been made by the start of the second decade of this century. Since then, the football industry has been locationally static, clubs having appeared relatively settled in grounds that have become 'home'. Whether the twenty-first century will witness a second period of locational flux remains to be seen, though it seems possible following the 1990 Taylor Report and from the fact that clubs have a choice of spending money on modifying their existing stadiums or realizing the assets on them and spending only slightly more on new, relocated all-seater stadiums.

In this chapter I will first review some of the events of the late nineteenth century, drawing attention to the kinds of pressures for relocation, pressures which possess remarkable similarities with those of today.

The early days

The large number of moves in the British football industry which occurred at the end of the nineteenth century, and continued into the

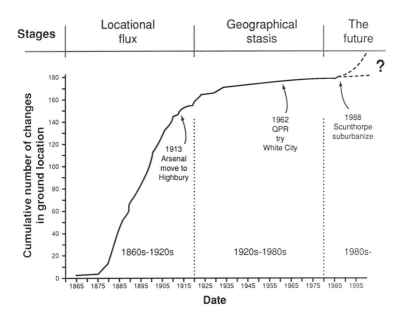

Figure 6.1 Cumulative frequency graph of locational changes in the clubs of the Football League, 1865–1991

early twentieth, are not untypical of the spatial behaviour of a growing, but fledgeling, industry. It was also typical, to an extent, of clubs which were prompted by the desire for profit and more profitable markets – though not quite to the extent of the American experience. Clubs were often sited initially on space which they could not call their own, and their migratory behaviour simply reflected the search for a more permanent home. But they were not totally free to move where they liked and, furthermore, there was often pressure for them to move from those with a dislike of football. At the end of the nineteenth century some clubs faced the kinds of topophobic sentiments which they face today.

Charles Korr, in his meticulous 1986 historical study of the history of West Ham United, has highlighted the nature of locational change at the end of the nineteenth century. Originally, the team of the Thames Ironworks used 'a nearby football ground' and its first ground which could be called 'home' grew out of the desire of the owner of the ironworks to improve the club's status from one with a local, to one with a regional, impact. The new Memorial Ground was occupied in 1896, a splendid provision, incorporating cycling and tennis facilities for the workers. But as the football club became more commercially oriented and distanced from the works which gave it birth, the need for access to a larger population became apparent. In 1904 West Ham took occupancy of the Boleyn Ground, their home ever since. As Korr says:

> West Ham's new home was everything the Memorial Ground had not been. It was easily accessible for large numbers of spectators, as it was within walking distance of the industrial suburb of West Ham and the residential areas of East Ham and Barking, and in easy reach of Canning Town ... and the suburbs of Ilford and Stratford, because the ground was close to a railway station and the tram stopped less than a five-minute walk away.
>
> (Korr 1986: 11–12)

This paragraph encapsulates two of the prime location factors influencing early football grounds, factors which are not very different from those operating today – namely, access to a public willing to buy the service they were offering and access to transport nodes, in this case the railway station. Such factors were seen to be essential for increased profits and in their first season at the Boleyn Ground, West Ham turned a previous season's loss of £800 into a profit of £400 (Korr 1986: 13).

Most moves during the late nineteenth and early twentieth century were over relatively short distances, though what might appear short today may have been long in time-distance terms if direct public transport networks were non-existent, and it is not clear how faithful fans were to a club which moved several miles to a new site. But there were exceptions to the prevailing tendency for short-distance moves. Easily the most dramatic was the move of Arsenal in 1912 from Woolwich, in south-east London, to Islington in the north-central part of the metropolis. Residents of the area in which the club was initially sited did not have much enthusiasm for football and the desire to increase profits through a greater share of the market led to the risky decision to move closer to the central city. Wray Vamplew (1989) regards the Arsenal move as illustrative of the profit motive possessed by the football businessmen of the early twentieth century. The 1899 move of Sheffield Wednesday from Olive Grove to Hillsborough was indeed an exercise in risk taking, as was that in 1923 of Manchester City moving from Fallowfield to Maine Road. In the former case, however, 9,000 supporters took part in a poll to indicate their locational preference. Hillsborough was, at the time, well beyond the city boundary and poorly served by public transport. Few residences existed nearby and it was a long walk from the city centre. Yet Sheffield Wednesday's fans seemed

138

dedicated and average attendance rose following the move (Farnsworth 1982).

Opposition to clubs moving to new locations shows that local community activism is a far from new phenomenon. In Arsenal's case Islington Borough Council did not want them, arguing that a major football ground would reduce local property values and local residents were well aware of potentially 'undesirable elements of professional football' (Vamplew 1989). Despite a campaign to oppose the new football ground, Arsenal's gamble paid off with a new stadium virtually next door to a major location factor, a London underground station.

In some cases community activism could be successful enough to lead to a change of ground. In the case of Queen's Park Rangers, one of Britain's most mobile clubs, it was thought by local residents living around their 1902 ground in North Kensington that the club lowered the tone of the neighbourhood and they complained about the negative spillovers generated by the game. Indeed, they took the club to court, which ruled against it, forcing a move back to a formerly occupied site at Kensal Rise Athletic Ground (Inglis 1987).

The inter-war years and after

The years immediately after the First World War witnessed a few more club relocations but the inter-war period was essentially one of geographical stasis in the football industry. What changes did occur were in the geography of the composition of the Football League, not in the location of the clubs. Places caught up in a negative economic multiplier, in areas of the severest industrial depression, found that their football clubs, like their corner shops, went out of business. The demotions from the Football League since 1920 include places like Aberdare, Merthyr Tydfil, Barrow, and New Brighton. The newcomers, on the other hand, included Oxford, Cambridge, Wimbledon, and Bournemouth. These two groups of place names are redolent of industrial and post-industrial Britain respectively.

During the inter-war period many clubs achieved their record ground attendances. Plymouth Argyle, today restricted to 28,000 (16,800 if it becomes all-seater), attracted 43,600 to its Second Division game against Aston Villa in 1936; Burnley recorded an attendance figure of 54,776 in 1924, and Bolton Wanderers 69,900 in 1933. With attendances such as these there could have been little incentive to move. Nevertheless, one or two interesting developments did occur in the immediate post-war period. For example, Port Vale's ground was sited

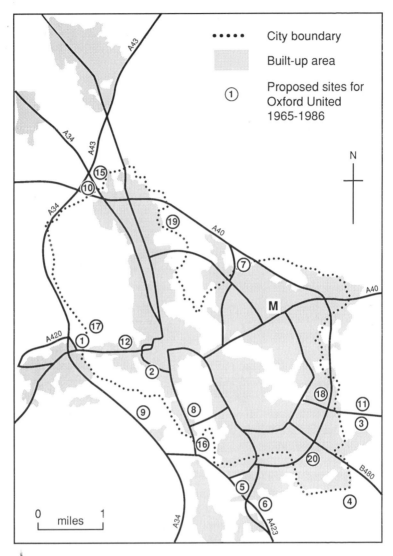

Figure 6.2 Sites considered for Oxford United, 1965–86. 'M' indicates the existing Manor Ground

extremely close to the city centre of Stoke-on-Trent until 1950 when a decison was made to move when the lease on the corporation-owned land ran out. The new location was on derelict land, of which there was no shortage in the Potteries of the early 1950s. The other post-war relocations included that at Southend. More recent moves by Scunthorpe, Walsall, and St Johnstone are discussed below (see pp. 147–9).

PRESENT-DAY PRESSURES FOR CHANGE

At the present time, and especially following the Taylor Report, British football faces three kinds of geographical pressures. I have already described the pressures upon clubs for micro-spatial changes to the internal geography of their stadiums. There are, in addition, pressures to find new locations (that is, new spaces) and also new sites (that is, particular places within those spaces). As noted at the start of this chapter, it has been argued that the 'location factors' for stadiums have changed, those suiting stadium development in the late nineteenth century being no longer the same as those favouring location today. In addition to traditional locational 'pushes' and 'pulls', however, the forces of local political activism also need to be taken into account in any exploration of the current geography of British football.

Before doing so it is worth noting that the Lowry stereotype of the inner-city stadium is not invariably accurate in the case of the British football landscape. Clubs like Leeds, Cardiff, and West Bromwich can hardly be described as 'inner urban'. Plymouth Argyle's ground is located in the centre of a recreation ground, and AFC Bournemouth is adjacent to suburban, detached residences more redolent of the poetry of John Betjeman than the novels of Arnold Bennett. British football stadiums were not (as the normally meticulous Allen Guttmann would have us believe) 'nearly all built ... in what might be anachronistically called the "inner city"' (Guttmann 1986: 106). Indeed, of forty-six football club representatives questioned in the mid-1980s about the spatial characteristics of their stadiums, twenty-three declared them to be 'excellently located' (Oliver 1986), hardly consistent with the view of Lord Justice Taylor or many of the 'outsider' pundits. It is not surprising that over 60 per cent of fans questioned in one survey felt that their clubs' grounds were all right where they were and had nothing to gain by moving to a new location (Sir Norman Chester Centre for Football Research 1989b). It is also worth noting that lower division clubs generate very few nuisances and the pressures for locational change may come more from the decaying fabric of the structures themselves than their locational characteristics. While it cannot be denied that some grounds are 'inner urban', a detailed locational classification (which has yet to be produced) of grounds would reveal that the intra-urban location of grounds lies within a spectrum ranging from inner city to peripheral. The same applies to countries elsewhere in Europe and in the USA.

Before considering specific site factors it will be worth noting that there are active 'pushes' from the traditional stadium locations, as well as peri-urban pulls which I will describe later. I will examine pushes from existing sites first and then explore the extent to which the logic of the pull factors will be able to operate.

Pushes from traditional sites

The major *external* pushes from the traditional homes of British football clubs have already been implied. The congestion, parking, and negative residential perception of the sport make existing sites unpopular. The often, but not invariably, cramped urban locations with incompatible land uses surrounding grounds make expansion to include lavish car-parking facilities plus other retail and recreational facilities virtually impossible. Other pushes, those of an *internal* kind, include the cost to clubs of installing additional seating following the recommendations of the Taylor Report. In many cases these would be only marginally less than selling up and building a new all-seater stadium with the revenue. What is more, it was argued in the mid-1970s that 'changing the location of a ground by up to 10 miles need not have any serious bad effect on attendance' (Rivett 1975), though virtually no empirical evidence exists to support this. What seems likely to happen is that initially attendances might even rise, given the novelty value of a new facility, but after a relatively short period crowds will return to their former numbers – or even fall if, as tends to be the case with new facilities, the ground capacity is reduced. In any case, attendance is increasingly less important to many clubs than revenue.

In addition to the negative reactions of residents and clubs, there are economic factors resulting from the nature of site use which encourage the removal of football and its replacement with other structures. From an economic perspective, more revenue can be obtained from multi-storey than from single-storey buildings. What is more, substantial revenue is only generated from football once every two weeks. A site given over to residential, office, or even car park development would certainly generate substantially more revenue than if it were used for football alone.

It is not quite as simple as this, however. First of all there is the not-to-be-ignored political activism of local fans who do not want to see their club move from its traditional site. As I have shown (see pp. 86–93) such activism can be remarkably successful in putting a brake on what are perceived (by fans) to be locational excesses. Furthermore, selling an existing site may not be particularly attractive if planning permission is not available for a land use which would generate a considerable profit for the new landowner. Land with planning permission for solely recreational use is of no real value to a supermarket chain which requires a change in the land-use regulations in favour of retail usage. What is more, planning permission for football would have to be available in the new site at the same time as permission for retailing was available at the old.

Some local residents' and community groups have, in the past, worked hard to ban football from their neighbourhood on the grounds that it generates unacceptably high levels of negative spillover effects, but none in modern times have actually succeeded in forcing a club to close down at its existing site and relocate. But the activism of local residents, pushed beyond the tolerable limits of nuisance consumption, cannot be ignored. While tolerating football, which has often been played in traditional locations longer than houses have been built there, the diversification of clubs' economies into other areas of the leisure industries generates more pressure for clubs to suburbanize than already exists. Those who attempt expansion and redevelopment *in situ* can face formidable opposition from local residents groups, as the experience of Aston Villa, discussed in Chapter 5, so clearly showed (see pp. 125–6).

Although a number of community groups have, over the years, opposed the actions of their local football club, most of them probably recognize that the club was there first and possesses 'user rights'. Successful opposition to football is more likely to occur, therefore, at sites where the sport is seen by fans as a promise but by others as a threat. The paradox is that these sites tend to be in the very areas where the scenarios for the brave new worlds of British football are being drawn up. It is to these that I now want to turn.

Exurban pulls

With a stadium located in open country, no local residents will exist to consume negative spillovers which will be 'internalized' in the surrounding landscape. The urban region of the twenty-first century, born of a car-owning meritocracy and an affluent, mobile middle class with a leisure lifestyle, has been viewed by geographer John W. Sommer (1975) as 'Hedonopolis'. A landscape manifestation of an increasingly ludic population, Hedonopolis will contain a broad girdle of land around it, termed by Sommer as a 'zone of repose', within which will be a variety of leisure facilities, including big stadium complexes. Just as in Chapter 2 I invoked an analogy with Foucault's description of the prison when describing the changes within the stadium, the banishing of stadiums beyond the urban edge is reminiscent of the establishment of strictly controlled containers for society's 'outsiders' (Foucault 1973, Philo 1986). Football and fun will have been isolated beyond the city limits. Disciplining people through the use of spatial organization is not confined to only the micro-spatial changes inside the football arena but also to the land-use changes within the broader scale of the urban arena. The outcome of such rational planning is sport's equivalent of a theme park, typified by the Munich Olympiapark in Germany. This is a vast area to the north of the city, essentially a milieu of achievement sport (to the extent of having the streets named after sporting heroes) which comes close to being a sporting Disneyworld. It is almost a city within (or more accurately, on the edge of) a city, futuristic in design with plastic and concrete dominating the environment (see Figure 6.3).

Whereas the traditional city football stadium is a single-purpose facility, a leisure complex is less of an economic risk to owners of capital since it spreads entrepreneurial risk among a variety of activities. A shopping mall, sports hall, massive car parking provision, and other possible facilities will characterize such sites, the modernistic stadium discussed towards the end of Chapter 2 being but part of a kind of futurescape of fun. I need to stress that in British terms this is a landscape of the future – some would say the very distant future – though as I will show, some blueprints have already been drawn up. Nevertheless, a suburban or exurban location seems to be broadly favoured by about half – but only about half – of the football clubs in England and Wales (Oliver 1986: 51).

In the early part of this chapter I stressed how the late-nineteenth-century clubs sought sites which tried to capitalize on access to population concentrations and transport facilities. At that time the point of minimum aggregate travel for residents throughout the city was close to the city centre. Radial train and bus routes, like the spokes of a wheel, brought the fans as close to the stadium as possible. The distribution of population within the city was also dominantly central and the drift to the suburbs had yet to occur. Although crowds were a nuisance to local residents, traffic and car parking were not since the ownership boom in

Figure 6.3 Olympiapark, Munich; a sporting analogue of Disneyworld – or perhaps EPCOT

private vehicles, essentially a post-1960s phenomenon, was a thing of the future.

Today, the major route arteries are motorways or ring roads. Inner cities tend to be congested and inaccessible and a large number of retail and recreational outlets have fled the city in favour of the suburbs. What is more, population movement in the post-war period has been from city centre to suburb, causing a shift in the balance of urban population. Indeed, with urban overspill plans, population has moved beyond the suburbs into new towns and new cities. Whereas in the early years of this century stadium locations matched the location of population and transport nodes, today they are out of touch with both. Between 1971 and 1981 the urban cores of Britain's major cities experienced population decreases of about 19 per cent, whereas the respective figures for the metropolitan rings and outer metropolitan rings were increases of around 10 and 15 per cent (Goddard 1984: 55). One example illustrates this general principle. In 1901 the population within 10 miles of Fratton Park, home of Portsmouth FC, was just under 42,000 whereas in 1971 it was over 430,000. However, the population of Portsea Island, on which Fratton Park is sited, fell from just under 190,000 to 140,000. Relocation of the ground less than 5 miles to the north would not only bring it nearer to the the focal point of local population distribution but also closer to the railway and excellent road connections with the town's hinterland (Ferrier 1976). About 50 acres of relatively flat land would be required for a modest complex requiring a landscaped stadium development, complete with practice pitches, additional sports facilities (for example, a sports hall), a superstore, and adequate parking. The purely hypothetical example of Portsmouth illustrates a general point which I will illustrate with actual examples later.

Access to population, open spaces and greenfield sites, motorway links or interchanges, plus proximity to a major railway line so that visiting fans can be channelled directly from train to stadium, are emerging as rational locational factors for a football stadium. In addition, the site would need to be sufficiently distanced from residences to allow negative externalities to be neutralized in a *cordon sanitaire* around the stadium.

In Britain several proposals had been made to shift clubs suburbanward, even before the Taylor Report's recommendations. Brighton and Hove Albion had planned a 25-mile move from the Goldstone Ground; Luton's flirtations with a greenfield site have already been noted (see pp. 89–91); and Oxford United have sought many suburban sites (see

Figure 6.2). Since Taylor's pronouncements, the proposals to suburbanize have mushroomed. But many such proposals have not got far beyond the drawing board. Surveys undertaken in 1990 by the Royal Town Planning Institute revealed that local planning authorities were aware that at least 42 of the 92 League clubs had at least proposed relocation whereas by 1991 only 34 fell into this category. Of the 42, six had already moved – though only two moves (three if the Scottish League is included) could be called permanent (Shepley 1990, Shepley and Barratt 1991). Relocation is clearly a far from simple undertaking. Clubs which dropped proposals to move between 1990 and 1991 did so because they found such relocations were not financially viable and/or decided to redevelop their existing sites. Many clubs were evidently facing great difficulty in implementing the recommendations of the Taylor report.

The first of the movers was the lowly Fourth Division club with one of England's most derogatory place names, Scunthorpe. This seemed an unlikely leader in the drive to suburbanize the British football industry. But in August 1988 that is what it did. The club's motives were certainly financial. Its existing site, The Old Showground, located among residences not far from the town centre, failed to meet the new safety standards imposed on football clubs following the Bradford fire disaster of 1986. But a football ground is only an attractive purchase if planning permission exists for something profitable to be sited on it when the club moves on. Retailing use is usually regarded as acceptable to developers and today The Old Showground site is an outlet of the Safeways supermarket chain. The Scunthorpe chairman was quoted in *Off the Ball* as follows:

> We had to move for financial reasons; we sold the ground for £3m and paid £2.5m for the new site, Glanford Park, one mile away. That left £500,000 which we needed to pay off our debts. We were in a major crisis and, without a move, would have folded.
>
> (Beauchampe 1989: 5)

Scunthorpe Council, while approving the supermarket development, could not offer an appropriate site for football – only one near the steelworks which would have symbolically forged a continuing link between football and nineteenth-century industry. The symbol for the twenty-first century, however, was found just outside the borough boundary in neighbouring Glanford where the council, anxious to get its name on the map, welcomed the club's presence, and planning permission for football was granted quickly. The new ground 'stands in open fields with a garden centre as its nearest neighbour' (Beauchampe 1989: 5). The new site seems to satisfy the new locational requirements noted earlier. It is peri-urban, accessible to motorway and dual carriageways, and distanced from the nearest residences. The nearby railway line provides the potential for a local halt from which fans can be disgorged, should Scunthorpe eventually generate such levels of support. The 800 car parking spaces contrast with the 50 at The Old Showground and a match-day bus service ferries in supporters from the town centre. It has been suggested that attendances have not declined, though only time will tell whether this is the result of the novelty of being in the first new English League ground for more than thirty years or the result of support for the club.

In Scotland a similar story is associated with the St Johnstone club which, in 1989, bade farewell to Muirton and occupied a new all-seater stadium at McDiarmid Park on the western edge of Perth. Located on a by-pass, it has a 16-acre site with spaces for 1,000 cars and 40 buses together with a floodlit plastic training pitch. Catering facilities and toilets are untypically plentiful. Praised by the Taylor Report, the new facility is not without its problems, however. As with the US suburban sports complex the more modest McDiarmid Park is located with the private-transport user in mind but, according to the Scottish fanzine *The Absolute Game*, 'it's fine for cars and supporters' buses [but] be warned that it's a good 25 minute walk from either the bus or rail stations' (Macgregor 1989: 6, see also Garven 1990). Others have noted the traffic congestion after matches and the new stadium has, in fact, developed a negative externality field more spacious in extent than that which formerly surrounded Muirton (Moncrieff 1991). Greater nuisance consumption by suburban residents seems to have resulted from the aforementioned traffic congestion, the larger car-borne crowds attracted by the novelty of the new stadium, and the fact that the stadium itself is not sufficiently distanced from the nearest residence. The presence of such negative spillovers illustrates the crucial significance of location *vis-à-vis* the urban edge and the necessity for new, suburban stadiums to be adequately insulated by a sufficient amount of non-residential land use for nuisances to be internalized.

The other example of late-twentieth-century relocation is that of Walsall which, at the start of the 1990/1 season took occupation of a new ground at Bescot Lane which is perhaps the best example in Britain of a futuristic site. It is located in what is planned as a 'retail park', itself surrounded in large part by light industry. There is substantial car parking provision, the stadium has its own railway station and excellent motorway access, close to the M5–M6 interchange. Although criticized for its lack of imagination in design (see pp. 48–9), the fact that the distance from the former ground at Fellows Park was minimal may have explained the almost non-existent opposition from fans to the move. Lack of opposition to relocation is also likely in cases where there is a need for a ground to meet certain standards, following the Taylor Report, in order to compete in the higher divisions. If it is not considered feasible for improvements to be made *in situ*, opposition to a move may be seen as obstructing the club's future success.

If clubs have to move, topophilia is most likely to be retained if it is over the shortest possible distance. In the mid-1970s it was suggested that if football is to relocate 'it will become essential to test rigorously the extent to which clubs are tied to their surroundings' (Bishop and Booth 1974). Such research is even more important now that talk of real change is in the air.

Scunthorpe and St Johnstone may be the two clubs that have succeeded in suburbanizing in recent years but the promise (or threat) of such relocation has been proposed by a large number of other clubs. Oxford United, for example, have explored twenty possible locations at the edge of the city during the last decade (see Figure 6.2), the greatest interest being shown in a site on the Oxford bypass with access to a railway line and space for substantial parking, retailing, and leisure facilities. Luton Town have, at different times, drawn up plans to locate beyond the town limits at the Bedfordshire village of Sundon Springs or to move even further afield to the new city of Milton Keynes, 20 miles to the north. Many other such plans have been mooted, only to have remained on the architects' drawing boards. Among the most speculative was a Merseyside proposal for a single stadium near Aintree racecourse which would house the two regional giants, Everton and Liverpool.

Given the rationality of such locations as those cited above, and the apparent precedents in the widespread growth of suburban sites in other areas of the leisure and retail industries, there is a need to consider the contrast between the theoretical attraction of suburban football and its limited applicability in practice to the British scene, which I do later in this chapter (see 'Resistance to change'). Before doing this, however, it is worth contrasting the static British situation with the locational dynamics of professional team sports in North America.

149

THE AMERICAN EXPERIENCE

In contrast to the locational stasis characteristic of most European football in recent decades, the professional sports team business in the United States has been characterized since 1950 by a state of locational flux. A recent article started with the assertion that 'stadium mania is sweeping the United States' as cities try to out-bid each other for new or relocated sports franchises (Baade and Dye 1990). In the last decade the football business has seen Oakland lose the Raiders to Los Angeles; the former Baltimore Colts bolted to Indianapolis; the New York Jets went to East Rutherford, New Jersey; the San Diego Clippers moved to Los Angeles; and the St Louis Cardinals flew to Phoenix. In baseball the post-war period has witnessed trans-continental migrations from rust-belt to sunbelt, mirroring the changing fortunes of the national economy. Such long-distance movement of franchises results, essentially, from the perceived profitability of new locations or from the unprofitability of the old. Frequently the desire to maximize television markets is a crucial factor in the relocation calculus. Such movements could, theoretically, occur in Europe if a continental-scale league was to develop.

Superimposed upon the considerable amount of trans-American (that is, long distance) movement of franchises is, on the one hand, the suburbanward shifts which have also been taking place and, on the other, the growth of new stadiums, or the refurbishing of existing ones, in downtown areas as anchors for urban regeneration schemes. Such latter developments have also taken place in a number of European countries though, as noted above, Britain is something of an exception.

Before 1960 none of the twenty-eight teams in the major North American baseball and football leagues played their regular season games outside a central city. By 1977 ten teams, or 19 per cent of the fifty-three pro football and baseball teams, played their home games in suburban sites. Of these eight moved from a central city to a suburban community (Rosentraub and Nunn 1977). I will consider one such move in slightly more detail.

In 1980 the Los Angeles Rams football outfit moved from the downtown, predominantly black area of Watts – home of the Los Angeles Coliseum where they had played – to Anaheim, home of Disneyland in glamorous Orange County. As Anaheim was within the 75-mile territorial limit of the market area of the team it was not officially registered as a move at all, just a switch of stadium within the statutory franchise area.

The way in which the relocation was orchestrated makes interesting

150

reading for those in Britain, where the repulsion of stadiums from suburban areas seems more likely to occur than the encouragement which seemed to exist in Los Angeles. In early 1978 the Los Angeles *Times* carried a full page advertisement, paid for by the 'Committee to Relocate the Rams to Orange County', encouraging the owner of the Los Angeles Rams, Carrol Rosenbloom, to move the football outfit to Anaheim (Ingham *et al.* 1987). The 'Committee' extolled the virtues of Anaheim − white, affluent, safe, comfortable and convenient, with 10 million people living within a 40-mile radius of the Anaheim stadium.

At the time of the advertisement Rosenbloom was having problems with the directors of the Coliseum. Seeking greater profitability, he wanted the playing area lowered and more seats added close to the edge of the pitch. Blocking such renovation was the fact that the City of Los Angeles had applied for the 1984 Summer Olympics and would need the running track around the field, at least until the summer of 1984. These issues were downplayed by Rosenbloom who stressed that the Rams did not want to be a burden on the local taxpayers who would have to subsidize any stadium renovations. If, on the other hand, the Rams moved across town, the taxpayers could be relieved and they could also continue to support the team. In other words, fan (enjoyment and convenience) and taxpayer (less cost to move, more cost to renovate) interests were invoked in justifying suburbanward migration.

But as Alan Ingham and his associates point out, private interests were masquerading as the public good. Anaheim had agreed to (a) expand its stadium facility to accommodate larger crowds; (b) install 108 luxury boxes in the renovated stadium; (c) provide executive offices and a practice field adjoining the stadium; and (d) work with Rosen-bloom in a $125 million shopping, hotel, and office complex in a prosperous white neighbourhood adjacent to the stadium. To an entrepreneur, Anaheim offered incentives that Watts could not; Anaheim's gain was Watts's loss (Ingham *et al.* 1987).

RESISTANCE TO CHANGE

There are several reasons why the apparently rational suggestion to suburbanize the British football industry is likely to meet with resistance which will inhibit the development of the locational pattern advocated by not only the Taylor Report but also by journals such *The Economist* (as noted at the start of this chapter) and by the voices of capital such as former club director of Luton, David Evans, MP (Conservative), who believe that the future picture of the sport is one of 'families going to

Luton Town, parking with ease, and enjoying fast food'.[4] Mr Evans elaborated on his vision of the future in a BBC TV series *Brass Tacks* in 1988:

> The vision at Luton is simple. It's going to be a whole day's entertainment, starting at 9 a.m. We are going to have a cinema, a night club, a drinking club for after the game. We're going to have a covered stadium and football is going to be 10 per cent of the usage of the ground. After all, of 365 days each year only 30 are used for playing football. For the other 335 days the ground will be a community centre dominated by the local authority, schools, youth clubs and any other interested parties.[5]

The first factor inhibiting suburban football growth is that planners seem reluctant to 'open up' green-belt land or countryside for the development of football grounds; second, there is the activism of local suburban (non-fan) residents who view football stadiums as noxious facilities to be repelled from their back yards; third, there is the opposition to suburban relocation by fans whose topophilic sentiments support existing, inner-urban locations; fourth, there are the cost factors; and fifth, possible ground sharing or club merger schemes could encourage the continuation of a reduced number of, but environmentally enhanced, existing stadiums to continue to be used. I will deal with each of these in turn.

Planners' perspectives

The Royal Town Planning Institute's (RTPI) message to the Taylor Report was that favourable consideration should be given to green-belt or open-area sites only if they were acceptable to fans on the one hand and did not create any significant amenity damage to local residents on the other. In addition, the Institute urged that existing grounds should be refurbished where possible (and include much greater community involvement than at present) since planning permission for anything other than open space or recreational use would likely be refused. It also argued that much greater municipal and government investment in football facilities was required.

Following the publication of the final Taylor report, a modest level of debate took place in the pages of *The Planner* following its editor's suggestion that decentralization of stadiums may be neither desirable nor feasible (Fyson 1990). Despite the fact that an entertainment facility attracting 40,000 people or more was often incongruously sited amid residential property and generated several negative spillovers, arguments for suburbanization were not convincing. This conclusion was based on the fact that 'countryside should no more be sacrificed to this cause than to that of the shopping centre' (Shepley 1990) with which the Taylor Report thought clubs should do deals to help finance stadium development. In addition, it was felt that 'the American pattern of out-of-town sports arenas, with their acres of car parking, could not be accommodated on this side of the Atlantic' (Shepley 1990). It was also argued that the local club was important as a community focus and that fans who traditionally walked to matches would be seriously disadvantaged by suburban locations. On balance it was therefore felt that the only alternative to suburbanization was a kind of *in situ* (re)development which should incorporate high standard but smaller sports stadiums as part of mixed recreational and commercial land use, not unlike that proposed by Charlton (see pp. 130–1). This view was broadly supported by the president of the RTPI who also argued that there was still a case for inner-city locations and that the importance of tradition and 'roots' should not be underemphasized, football grounds being seen as powerful urban symbols being accessible to young and car-less fans. It was also stressed that the post-Taylor explosion of proposals for peripherally sited football grounds were often thinly disguised attempts to push retail schemes through an otherwise inpenetrable planning system (Shepley 1990).

This view runs counter, therefore, to that of the Leicester sociologists who have suggested that 'the conditions and locations of many English football stadia are wholly unsuited to the staging of a spectator sport in a modern industrialized society' (Murphy *et al.* 1990). Few would deny that the conditions of many stadiums leave much to be desired, the rotting timber and rusty ironwork often in urgent need of replacement. Even grounds like Old Trafford have a dank and dusty aura between the turnstiles and the seats. That the locations of grounds are unsuited is more contentious however. Indeed, faced with outdated grounds and the possibility of relocation, some clubs have favoured considering moves, not to the suburbs but, almost literally, to a site next door. For example, Bournemouth, Millwall, and Chester have, at different times, each thought about relocating over minimal distances, hence maintaining a strong topophilic sport-place bond but at the same time taking occupancy of a modern facility. Walsall completed such a short distance move in time for the start of the 1990/1 season (see pp. 148–9).

Although planners stress that all countryside is not of high quality and that there are large tracts where development is no sacrifice, it was also stated that movement to the edge of towns for most First Division clubs was totally unrealistic (Shepley 1990). On balance, therefore, the planning profession appears to oppose the suburbanization of football stadiums, the evidence of Oxford United's inability to find a suburban location which satisfies the planning system providing graphic evidence of this (see Figure 6.2). Even when city councils may support a move, the local county council may oppose it, as in the case of Southampton's proposed move to a green-belt site.

Even in the United States where more relaxed attitudes exist towards development at the urban edge, the suburbanward drift of stadiums is far from inevitable. If pro sports find a good image in the suburbs then the inner city can improve its image with the continued presence of a stadium and an associated franchise. Professional sport is good for the image of the inner city. Indeed, riveting a stadium to the downtown area of the US city is seen as a potent source of urban regeneration and urban machismo. Just as place pride goes with a winning team, the revitalized inner city requires images of growth, dynamism and progress, images which are held to be more than physical structures alone. The spirit of the revitalized city manifests itself in, among other things, a winning sports team. For example, 'Pittsburgh became the "City of Champions" in the 'seventies as the Steelers [football] won four Superbowls and the Pirates [baseball] won two world series' (Holcomb and Beauregard 1981). An inner-city stadium serves to revitalize the inner city in an age when suburbanization of service industries has been the norm. Not only will inner-urban stadium development enhance the local tax base; it will, if hotel and convention facilities are integral, lead to an influx of tourists, especially as long-distance travel to a professional sports event is not uncommon.

The arguments used in the United States for the retention of inner-urban stadiums apply also to Europe. When the LA Rams moved to Anaheim (see p. 150) the Los Angeles Coliseum lost its major tenant and stood to lose $750,000 in rents. The incomes which Watts residents derived from the Coliseum were also lost, as was the 'psychic' income which the Rams brought to the local area. As Ingham *et al.* (1987) point out, the Rams' relocation materially and symbolically exacerbated the deformation of the Watts community.

The NIMBY effect

I have stressed in earlier chapters that for the average resident a football stadium is viewed as a noxious facility, to be repelled from sites near their residences. Plentiful evidence exists that articulate middle-class suburbanites have vigorously engaged in political activism to oppose proposals to locate football grounds at the urban edges of many British cities. This supports the well-known generalizations that (a) the middle classes tend to more vocal than low income groups in opposition to the existence of noxious facilities in their back yard, and (b) opposition tends to be greater before such facilities are built than in cases when they are already in existence. Such residents are, like the local activists described in previous chapters, classic examples of 'sporadic interventionists', being 'ordinary people', having had little, if any, prior involvement in politics and possessing a short-term interest in a single political event (Dowse and Hughes 1977).

The example of Oxford United's wish to locate a new stadium complex on the northern edge of the city elicited typically topophobic responses towards football grounds as the following letter to the *Oxford Mail* in 1985 makes clear:

> We are told that Oxford needs a new football stadium. Who is 'Oxford' in this context? What is the average number of spectators at a match? Ten thousand would be an over-estimate, and not all these would be city-dwellers. What about the views of the other hundred thousand city residents? I suggest that the vast majority of these would be against the proposal. ... There must be many who are silent but would be happy with no so-called 'first-class' football in Oxford at all.

Similar opposition came from residents of Milton Keynes at the time of Luton Town's proposal to locate there. Despite assurances from Luton supporters for the move that no visiting fans would be allowed, 'fear of violence and vandalism by football hooligans' by local councillors in Milton Keynes resulted in a unanimous rejection of the proposal (Williams *et al.* 1989a). Councillors in Christchurch, Dorset, similarly rejected a proposal for the re-siting of AFC Bournemouth at the village of Hurn (*Evening Echo* [Bournemouth], 10 May 1990: 3).

A more detailed examination can be made of the campaign by residents of the suburb of Mangotsfield, outside the Bristol city boundary and in the borough of Kingswood, to the proposal to site a new stadium for Bristol Rovers in their borough. Following the discontinuation of football at Rovers' former ground at Eastville, the club engaged in ground-sharing with the non-league club at Bath, 20 km away. A strong sense of city–club identity (and opposition from local residents living around the ground at Bath) led to pressure from fans and board to return the club to the city and the Mangotsfield site was proposed as the most appropriate location.

The response from local residents to the planned 11,000 all-seater stadium on green-belt land was predictable. The following extract from a letter to the local newspaper reveals a well developed – but exaggerated and at times simply incorrect – image of the stadium as a highly noxious facility, despite the counter-image projected by the club and architects of a sanitized, trouble-free football ground, insulated from the nearest housing by a dual carriageway and open land:

> Violence, vandalism and abuse of amenities are common in all localities which have soccer stadia. We do not want that in Kingswood – especially when people from outside the district try to foist it upon us. The infrastructure of the area (even with the completion of the ring road) will not support the influx of many thousands of people. There is no nearby railway station to cater for visiting supporters, and therefore all traffic will be confined to the roads. Parking will be random and affect a much wider area than the environs of the stadium ... We do not want our roads and streets clogged with hundreds of extra cars. The district is already jammed with traffic ... The noise level will be intolerable and unacceptable for those who live nearby.[6]

The growing activism of local residents can be illustrated by the sequence of stages through which the anti-stadium campaign progressed. Following letters to the Press, a pressure group, The Kingswood Residents Action Committee, was formed. The distribution of leaflets and the placing of over 100 placards on the site characterized the next stage of mobilizing support against the development. The commissioning of site surveys and environmental impact studies served to counter the views in the proposals submitted by the club. In mid-1990 the Borough Planning Committee turned the application down and Bristol Rovers started exploring the possibility of a site to the north of the city. Local residents had succeeded in distancing themselves from the stadium 'problem' and putting it in someone else's back yard.

In the USA where public funding of stadium development has been much more evident, middle-class resistance to new stadium developments has tended to focus upon the ethics of taxpayers subsidizing a private sports business. In recent years the general public has, in some cases, come to see through the commercial ideology of misguided stadium development in which massive public subsidies have benefited private organizations. The main beneficiaries of the municipal subsidies often provided for stadium development are the interests who develop the shops, hotels, and complexes in land adjacent to the stadium itself. Banks, architects, insurers, lawyers, and service companies connected to such developments also reap substantial benefits. The extent to which local people themselves benefit is more problematic. While hyped as a focal point for downtown renewal, the Busch Stadium in St Louis probably did more for the Anheuser Busch brewing company, the owners of the St Louis Cardinals, than for the people of St Louis. No slum housing was cleared in stadium construction and no new houses were built (Lipsitz 1984). In other cases, mega-stadium complexes come to be viewed as examples of urban monumentalism or as symbols of crass urban architecture. And in the most modern of American stadiums, as in much of the most technologically 'advanced' regions of the world, I am forced to return to the questions of containment and control which I raised in Chapters 2 and 3.

The examples of taxpayers actually voting *against* stadium development are growing in number. Three referendums in Miami failed to produce support for a new stadium, the result being that the owner of the Miami Dolphins was forced to build his own. Stadium operating deficits at the Silverdome (in Pontiac, Michigan) 'have galvanized taxpayer resistance across the country. For example, in Cleveland and in San Francisco taxpayers have voted down a number of proposals that would have cleared the way for public financial involvement' (Baade and Dye 1990).

Fans' feelings

Hard-core fans are not invariably opposed to relocation within their own town or city. Some have become resigned to it, given the the strictures of government policy about accommodation and safety. A survey of Northampton Town fans, for example, revealed that 99.4 per cent of those responding to a fanzine-distributed questionnaire would prefer the club to move from their ground which even hard-core fans described as 'a shambles'.[7] Having to share a ground with a county cricket club is somewhat exceptional, however; in Northampton's case it amounted to sharing a ground with another occupant from another sport – hardly conducive to a strong sense of propriety and hence of topophilia. Of respondents to the FSA survey (already alluded to several times), over 61 per cent disagreed that their club would benefit from a move to 'a newly built ground nearby' although over 90 per cent felt that they would still watch their club if it did so (Sir Norman Chester Centre for

Football Research 1989b). For many fans, however, as in the case of those who supported the survival of Fulham's Craven Cottage, the site comes first and survival in the urban area second. In the Northampton case cited above, opposition to a move may have been substantial if it had been to a site in another town.

A further factor which could possibly contribute to the continuation of traditional football locations is the strengthening of links with the local community by the football clubs themselves. In this way the club would be seen as a real community asset rather a source of annoyance, nuisance, or fear. The most well-documented example of a re-forging of community links is that of the London club, Millwall (see Chapter 7). For many years the club had a very bad reputation for hooliganism and violence but an impressive range of community schemes has changed the face of the club, including the forging of a sense of club involvement with the locality (Lightbown 1989). In the case of Halifax Town the community – in this case Calderdale Council – are the major shareholders in the club; in effect, the club is run on local taxes, the ground is owned by the local authority and the football club is viewed as a community asset in much the same way as it would subsidize an art gallery (see Chapter 7).

Fans' reactions to suburbanization would likely be economic as well as topophilic. Football's fandom is still mainly resident within the localities (however defined) within which stadiums are located – especially in the case of the typical clubs, if not for the Manchester Uniteds of this world (see Figure 4.3). For clubs where local support is still strong, relocaton over any significant distance would place an unfortunate financial burden upon many of the most supportive fans who would have to travel further to watch a home game.

Among a number of questions raised about the US sports relocation problem has been the ethical stance of owners who apparently just get up and leave when more profitable pastures beckon. The decision of the Oakland Raiders in 1982 to relocate, despite league objections and a history of community support, stimulated public debate over the rights of sports franchises to relocate at will (Ingham and Hardy 1984). A community which has supported a sports team for a long period of time appears to be unable to offer any resistence to club owners who wish to move. Charles Korr notes that when, in 1958, the Brooklyn Dodgers moved to LA 'the ultimate robbery took place, but the "crime" was legal' (Korr 1986: 18–19). The fans, who for decades had supported the Dodgers, had been robbed of something that had contributed greatly to their quality of life; but beyond that they had (literally) *supported* the team throughout its life in New York. It has been pointed out that 'representative' – in the sense of a football team 'representing' a community – 'presumes bonds of sentiment and loyalty' (Ingham and Hardy 1984), but such bonds appear to be all too frequently of secondary importance when community and the public interest is confronted with capital. It is usually capital which wins the day. Relocation in US team sports has led to cries for legislative proposals to restrict such movement or to penalize the league involved.

The cost of change

As was shown in Chapter 2, the cost of stadium mega-structures runs into hundreds of millions of pounds. For more modest stadium proposals some idea of the costs involved can be obtained by considering Table 6.1 which summarizes the costs of constructing a suburban stadium complex in Oxford. Figures presented in 1990 for the building

Table 6.1 Summary of building costs of a proposed stadium for Oxford United (1984 prices)

		£
1	Main grassed pitch including guard rails	95,000.00
2	PVC-piped low-temperature water underpitch heating	50,000.00
3	Floodlighting to meet colour television lighting levels	100,000.00
4	Stands to provide seating for 15,000 and standing room for 10,000. To include for changing rooms, offices, directors' suite, WCs, refreshment areas, club room	4,375,000.00
5	Stiles, entrance gates, box office	75,000.00
6	Two outdoor practice pitches	100,000.00
7	Floodlighting to practice pitches	30,000.00
8	Sports Hall including squash courts, 4 badminton courts and changing facilities	750,000.00
9	Gravel-finished car parking for 5,000 cars	1,250,000.00
10	Site services (electricity, gas, water)	100,000.00
11	Perimeter fencing to 70-acre site	100,000.00
12	Landscaping	100,000.00
	Estimated construction cost at December 1984 prices	7,125,000.00

Alternative costs			£
1	Synthetic playing area to main pitch	*add*	425,000.00
2	Electric cable heating to main pitch	*add*	50,000.00
3	Tarmac in lieu of gravel car parking	*add*	1,250,000.00

of a new stadium for Bournemouth, sited on council-owned ground near the club's existing site, amounted to £7 million. Details of the costs of US domed stadiums were cited in Chapter 2 (see pp. 164–6).

Following the publication of the Taylor Report the British government was adamant that no central government funds would be available from the ground improvements recommended by the Report. A new stadium, fit for the twenty-first century would therefore have to be one occupying prime, inner-urban land ripe for, and in possession of planning permission for, commercial development. To self-finance its environmental improvement the club is supposed to redevelop that site or sell it and relocate at a greenfield site. Cost could be further cut by ground sharing (see p. 35).

For a minority of clubs this might be a possibility, but even where such scenarios exist, I have already shown that difficulties, via protests of various kinds, are likely. For a substantial number of clubs, on the other hand, such scenarios simply do not apply. Humble, homely clubs like Forfar Athletic, for example, are typical of many throughout Britain. As Bert Moorhouse has commented

> the ground of Forfar Athletic was valued at £55,977 in its 1988 balance sheet. It sits on the edge of farmland in a small market town in the middle of nowhere. No one is likely to scramble to buy it for a leisure complex, science park or block of post-modern pads. Nor is any developer likely to go to the grounds of Albion Rovers, Alloa, East Fife or Stenhousmuir. There are very few yuppies in Cowdenbeath. Any number of the smaller clubs in Scotland face a bleak future in bleak places.
>
> (Moorhouse 1990: 11)

Moorhouse's comments apply equally to many English clubs.

A cost of stadium development which needs to be taken into account, especially if central or local governments are involved, is what economists term the 'opportunity cost' of such development. This can be calculated by identifying the expenditure which has been forgone on something else. Hence, the opportunity cost of a professional sports stadium may be a large number of smaller and less obvious recreational facilities which could be used by a wider range and larger number of people than those currently using the stadium.

Funding the modern stadium

As noted earlier, the prospect of the public funding of new football stadiums in Britain is gloomy. Indeed, following the publication of the

Taylor Report it became evident that the refurbishment of existing stadiums, let alone the construction of new ones, would not be financed through public funds. In contrast to the UK situation, many foreign stadiums are either publicly owned or have been constructed in whole or in part by public funds. In the United States, of the ninety-four stadiums used by professional sports teams since 1953, sixty-seven are publicly owned and the more recent the construction of new stadiums the greater the incidence of public ownership (Johnson 1986). In France and other European countries, clubs, as well as the stadiums they play in, are propped up with local municipal aid. In 1989 Olympique Marseilles, for example, received 14 million francs (£1.4 million) from its city authorities – more than the annual revenue generated by many British clubs. In the same year Bordeaux received 8.3 million and Nantes 10 million francs (Coggan et al. 1990).

Municipal aid to professional sports teams can, of course, assume a variety of forms. A basic categorization is between direct and indirect aid. Direct aid, which in the case of French soccer clubs in 1985 amounted to over 74 million francs for First Division clubs and nearly 42 million francs for Second Division clubs, amounts to over 50 francs per person in some municipalities. In some cities such direct subventions to professional football clubs may make up over one-quarter of total municipal aid to sport and culture (Chamont et al. 1989). Indirect aid assumes a number of forms and may involve the construction, maintenance, or refurbishment of a stadium which the club uses.

The attraction of stadiums (and hopefully sports franchises) for the cities that financially support them, lies in the fact that city officials from Florence to Florida believe that they are vital for the projection of a 'world class' image and that stadiums and successful teams provide tangible economic benefits for the cities in which they are found. Benjamin Okner has noted that

> many people think that the mere presence of a professional sports team in their city enhances a community's prestige. As one person put it, 'No place really can be considered a "big town" if it doesn't have a professional baseball or football team'. Since no community can attract such a team if it lacks adequate playing facilities, it follows that a big-league stadium is required to be a big town.
>
> (Okner 1974: 327)

A major reason why public subsidization takes place is that entrepreneurs prefer a public underwriting of the risk of stadium construction to committing their own funds to such a project. But in the United States proponents of public subsidies to sports stadiums have also argued that the economic revenues generated by stadiums exceed the costs, even though there has been considerable evidence to the contrary for many years. For example, studies by Benjamin Okner in the early 1970s revealed that of twenty publicly owned baseball and/or football stadiums, the average stadium covers only about 60 per cent of its costs when such things as taxes forgone and interest payments are included (Okner 1974). The escalation of initial cost estimates is a common phenomenon on the North American stadium construction stage. When originally mooted in 1985 the Toronto Skydome was expected to cost C$150 million; the final cost will be nearer C$600 million (Simon 1991). Revenues have fallen far short of the amount to fund the stadium debt – a not unfamiliar story. One of the mistakes made by those claiming a net gain to the city is that they forget that much expenditure in stadium events might have been made elsewhere in the city by city residents even if the stadium had not existed. It is also salutory to note that of twenty-two US franchise moves between 1970 and 1985 only two involved the abandonment of a privately owned stadiums (Baade and Dye 1988b). From a franchise owner's point of view, public funding does not provide much of a stake in the community.

If local tax payers are so involved in subsidizing sports stadium construction it is not surprising to find that several studies in the United States have explored the costs and benefits of new stadium attraction and development. A noteworthy example was an examination into the financial incentives used to attract the Washington Senators baseball outfit to Arlington, Texas, where they became the Texas Rangers. Thirty-year estimates of expenditures *made by the city council* with tax payers' money included over $8 million to purchase the broadcast rights, over $20 million on stadium construction and over $10 million on interest payments on stadium bonds. The total thirty-year expenditures exceeded $44 million. The revenues generated by the stadium and media network operation over the same period, however, totalled less than $22.5 million. According to Mark Rosentraub, author of the study, 'beginning in 1981, the residents of Arlington will be paying $8.41 per citizen each year for the financial commitments that brought the Rangers to Texas. These payments equal $36.18 per family' (Rosentraub 1977). Of course, a missing source of income which was not included in the analysis was that of a 'psychic' nature discussed in Chapter 4. If psychic income compensated for the shortfall between municipal expenditures and team revenues, then the attraction of the Rangers would have been worth it for the people of Arlington.

A hidden cost of suburban locations is argued by some to reflect the dependency of the motor car as a mode of transport. Assuming that suburbanization would increase car usage to football matches, some observers point to the fact that this would, in its own small way, simply fuel the energy crisis and reflect the anti-nature character of so much of the sports landscape. Deep ecologists would regard the suburban stadium as a triumph of concrete over nature.

From The Dell to Western Esplanade: a case study

The proposed relocation plans of Southampton FC illustrate in rather more detail the way in which logical locational assumptions can flounder in financial problems.[8] Southampton FC's ground is sited in a high-density residential area with little space for parking. The club has long been interested in moving to a new location, having been at The Dell in Archers Road since 1898. In the late 1970s the local council embarked on a project to transform 30 acres of semi-derelict land near the city centre called Western Esplanade. Various development plans alluded to the site's suitability for recreational uses, the South Hampshire Structure plan stating that it would be suitable for a football ground.

Given this background, the council invited applications to develop the area including a football stadium, mainly seated, with a capacity of 35,000, either for football alone or for football plus speedway and greyhound racing. The scheme was attractive from Southampton's point of view because it satisfied many of the locational requirements of a late-twentieth-century stadium. For a start it was directly adjacent to the railway station, providing easy control of visiting fans and the prospect of the containment of hooliganism. The bus station was already on the site making intra-urban access easy, and there were three feeder roads from a local motorway (the M27) which converged on the area. The potential for 3,000 car parking spaces existed on the site while the area around it was mainly commercial and industrial; negative externalities could be 'internalized' within relatively compatible land uses. A final point which was alleged to be in the site's favour was its centrality. This was viewed as an advantage because it would be highly visible to visitors to the city and provide a vibrant image of city pride.

The favoured plan for the site was that of an impressive, modern stadium. It was now that the scenario for relocation ran into problems. The club and the local council could not agree on how the stadium should be financed. Two proposals were made by the council to the club, the first being that the council should lease a plot of land to the club for 99 years with the club having to build the stadium itself, in return for The Dell being given to the council. This was unacceptable to the club and the council made a second offer in which it would give a 135-year lease of the plot and £3 million towards the building of the stadium. In return they wanted 5 per cent of all gate receipts, The Dell (free of charge), and free use of space under one of the stands. As the stadium would have cost £12 million to build, the club could not accept this offer either.

At this stage the club made two counter proposals. The first involved the council building the shell of the stadium with the club fitting it out, taking on a full repairing lease, and paying an annual rent based on gate receipts. The Dell would be sold for housing, the club keeping the receipts to finance the fitting out of the stadium, estimated at £1.5 million. The second proposal was that the council should sell a 15-acre site to the club at market value with permission to develop it. The club would then sell The Dell for housing and keep the receipts.

The council accepted neither proposal and the talks broke down. Southampton remain at The Dell, and though developments to increase the seating capacity have taken place there it remains a twentieth-century ground in nineteenth-century surroundings. Basically, the council had wanted the club to move to a better site but were unwilling, or unable, to finance it. From the club's point of view it was not prepared to give up its ground, a freehold possession which can be used as security against bank overdrafts. The club also felt that they were providing a service to the city and, as such, the city should have provided them with help. In 1991 the club was bidding to move to Stoneham on the outskirts of the city.

The above example is not entirely untypical from the perspective of finance. But it was an inner-urban site. More frequently talk is about suburban locations but the cost implications remain the same.

GROUND SHARING AND CLUB MERGERS

The idea that two Football League clubs should share the same stadium has been widely recommended by several reports into the game, including those by Sir Norman Chester (1965) and, of course, the Taylor Report. The sharing of grounds is a logical and rationally economic proposition, leading to significantly reduced costs. Ground sharing could occur at existing stadiums or in newly established, suburban sites.

The recent history of British football is littered with plans involving the sharing of grounds. In 1978 Arsenal and Tottenham Hotspur speculated about sharing a new ground at Alexandra Palace; in the same year Fulham and Wimbledon talked about sharing a ground at Wormwood Scrubs, while two years later Crystal Palace and Brighton similarly discussed a site near Gatwick Airport. Southampton and Portsmouth have discussed the possibility of ground sharing at a site between the two cities and close to the M27 motorway. These, and other proposals, were often highly speculative ideas and came to nought, opposition from fans being a significant factor; all the British evidence points to a reluctance of clubs to share football grounds, in contrast to the experience of Europe and the United States. In Italy, for example, Roma and Lazio share the Olympic Stadium in Rome, AC Milan and Internazionale share the San Siro Stadium, and Juventus and Torino share the Stadio Communale in Turin. In each case the stadium is owned by the respective municipality whereas in England and Wales the overwhelming majority of stadiums – about 80 per cent according to one survey (Oliver 1986) – are owned by the clubs themselves. Where the ground is not owned by the club it is not necessarily owned by the local authority but by companies of various kinds.

Obviously, ground sharing is not an option for many clubs in isolated locations, but in places such as Birmingham, Manchester, London, and Nottingham (and others) the geographical proximity of clubs makes ground sharing feasible. But given the strong topophilic sentiments discussed in Chapter 4 ground sharing seems unlikely in a UK context. Bristol Rovers, Chester, Maidstone, and Charlton – clubs which currently share with other football clubs – see such an arrangement as a temporary expedient and one survey (Oliver 1986) has shown that twice as many League clubs seem to be opposed to ground sharing as those in favour of it.

Such a statistic does indicate, however, that a sizeable minority of clubs would be prepared to share grounds with another club. One of the most ambitious of such schemes was that suggested for Merseyside. Located near Aintree Racecourse a mega-stadium would house both Liverpool and Everton, both clubs apparently being in favour of such a scheme before it was dropped on cost grounds. Respondents to the FSA survey were divided about ground sharing, nearly 49 per cent disagreeing with the idea with only 30.8 per cent supporting their club in sharing its present ground to cut costs (Sir Norman Chester Centre for Football Research 1989b). The feeling is nevertheless widespread that some clubs may have to share grounds eventually in order to survive.

A further rational development could be the merging of clubs. One of the most well known of such scenarios was that of entrepreneur Robert

Maxwell to merge Oxford United with Reading Town and establish the merged entity at the intermediate town of Didcot (under the mid-Atlantic name of 'Thames Valley Royals'). As noted earlier (see p. 91), fan reaction from both clubs brought this proposal to a hasty end. More recently, the chairman of Heart of Midlothian FC, Wallace Mercer, attempted a takeover of another Edinburgh club, Hibernian, the plan being to play at Heart's ground until a new, all-seater stadium was built (Cowan 1990). A tacit aim was to provide a 'giant' Edinburgh club to compete with the Glasgow clubs and eventually enter the inevitable Euro Super League. As with the Thames Valley Royals proposal, the 'Edinburgh United' idea floundered in the face of fierce fan opposition.

ECONOMIC IMPACTS OF NEW STADIUM DEVELOPMENTS

In contrast to the situation in Britain, a considerable number of American studies have explored the economic impact of professional team sports on the local economies in which they are found. Studies sponsored by sports outfits themselves, chambers of commerce, and professional economists, appear to provide impressive evidence of a substantial economic impact, amplified by local economic multipliers, which brings considerable wealth to cities across the nation. According to geographer David Harvey (1989a), stadium mania is 'the contemporary US version of that ancient cargo cult practice in Papua, New Guinea, of building an air strip in the hope of luring a jet liner to earth', and just as recent decades have witnessed what some term the 'mallification' of the United States, the current situation is almost one of 'stadiumization'. Not only are new stadiums seen by many civic worthies as symbols of urban machismo; they are also perceived as magnets to attract new economic development.

The desire to retain a stadium and a franchise is matched by the desire of other cities to attract one. In other words, stadium development is regarded as a magnet for local economic development. By this I do not simply mean enhanced sales for existing services but the attraction of new jobs and enhanced local incomes. But the hard evidence of such economic growth as a result of stadium development is difficult to find. For a start, many estimates of stadium-induced income or growth have been criticized on the grounds that they are often funded by those who stand to benefit from stadium development. As a result, stadium promoters tend to overestimate the benefits to the city or region and underestimate the risks and costs to local taxpayers through whom stadiums in the USA are often funded.

I have already noted that although professional team sports certainly generate a good deal of local spending, this may not compensate for the local taxes which residents have had to contribute if a new stadium is involved. It is now appropriate to consider the much-debated question about whether stadium development creates economic growth, the latter being interpreted as either new jobs or enhanced regional income. Studies undertaken by Robert Baade and Richard Dye (1990) reveal that 'the presence of a new or renovated stadium has an insignificant impact on area income for all but one of the metropolitan areas' which were studied while 'the impact of stadium construction or renovation on the metropolitan area's *share* of regional income is negative'. Such a finding appears to result from the fact that stadiums and pro sports tend to divert economic activity towards labour-intensive, relatively unskilled and low-wage activities, hence producing in a sports-minded area a falling share of regional income. Such findings are salutary in view of plans for stadium-based urban regeneration schemes in Britain.

Since the publication of the Taylor Report several observers have cast envious glances across both the English Channel and the Atlantic Ocean, contrasting the football stadiums of Britain with those of North America and much of mainland Europe. The differences between the old, rather decrepit UK grounds and those of Italy were highlighted during the 1990 World Cup while the nature of US stadiums are often transmitted to UK audiences in telecasts of gridiron football games. That Britain has much to learn from the experience of other countries is a commonly held view. For example, one of the most widely respected academic observers of the UK football scene has argued that the sport needs to abandon the economics of the corner shop and explore the possible multiplier effects of the 'national and other sports stadia which are the "homes" of teams that represent large collectivities [where] the probability of such multiplier effects will be substantial' (Dunning 1990). He cites the alleged multiplier effects of the New Orleans Superdome as a case in point. Likewise, the high priest of the post-modern sports stadium, Ron Labinski (1986), has stressed the way in which (his?) stadiums would bring economic gains to host communities in the UK.

What works in the USA, however, might not be applicable to the UK. The duplication of American sports situations in Britain, bred of a different national culture and ideology, will be far from automatic and may be extremely risky. Allan Roadburg (1980) has listed a number of differences between football in Britain and the United States which must raise questions about the possibility of the widespread replication of North American practices in Britain. For example, the operation of the local multiplier depends on a considerable amount of new money coming into a city which would not otherwise be spent there. Such spending in the North American context is usually associated with visitors who are of different socio-economic status from those in the UK, possessing greater spending power and hence being able to stay overnight and spend considerable sums in hotels and restaurants (see Figure 4.8, for example) – not something that is at present typical of football in Britain. In order to exploit the economic multiplier effects to the full, British football clubs would have to enhance further the allegiance of fans living at a sufficient distance from their stadiums to justify overnight accommodation or a full weekend visit. A European super-league could provide this, but it is doubtful if a league constituted solely within the UK could.

Other recommendations for the North American scene would not be applicable to the UK. For example, Baade and Dye (1988a) have urged that for a sports facility to be economically successful it requires regular use and that for every $1 million of debt that the stadium developer incurs, there should be two occasions throughout the year of large crowd (that is, capacity) stadium use. A $100 million stadium would hence require 200 days of such use each year. This would require the accommodation of non-footballing activities, including rock concerts and other such events which, in a UK context, is difficult to envisage with the reversion to grass surfaces on the one hand and the inner-urban location of many stadiums on the other.

Another recommendation from North America is that because massive car parking space would 'minimize the chance of ancillary development' since parking space minimizes consumers' exposure to other commercial activities, fans should be channelled 'through carefully planned commercial corridors' (Baade and Dye 1990) in order to help maximize local spending. Given the nature of the policing and surveillance of British football crowds on the one hand, and the social class and gender composition of most such crowds on the other, such a model seems of dubious value in the British context where the traditional working-class supporter is likely to prefer the pre-match ambience of a pub to that of a boutique.

These observations suggest that what may work in North America, with professional sports' more middle-class clientele, may not work in Britain. The prospect of converting British football into a middle-class

168

recreational activity overnight is a doubtful one. Although signs of *embourgeoisment* have been occurring, the widespread changes of football culture associated with such proposals as those outlined above are unlikely. At the very least, as I have shown, they will be contested by the fans.

CONCLUSION

The Leicester sociologists summarize the deep cultural conservatism of the British football fan by stating that 'arguably more than in any other sport in any other modern, industrialized country, English football fans display a proprietorial attachment to the football ground ... in which their favoured team plays' (The Sir Norman Chester Centre for Football Research 1989b). At the same time, the inter-war inertia on the part of football's administrators, in contrast to that of their late-nineteenth and early-twentieth-century predecessors, has also contributed to the situation in which British football currently finds itself. But these factors need supplementing with others if the full story of the future map of the UK football industry is to be understood. The sport has obtained a negative image, an image which has been amplified in the minds of suburban residents who view new football grounds as noxious facilities rather than recreational resources. The success of NIMBY-style activism, plus the prevailing attitudes of planners to green-belt land has also contributed to the fossilized face of British football.

By the end of the 1990/1 football season the Royal Town Planning Institute felt that three broad messages had emerged as a result of their surveys into the state of the British game. The first was that clubs should strengthen their links with local communities and local authorities; the second was that local authorities needed to assist clubs where possible, recognizing their role in the community; and third, and perhaps most important, central government needed to monitor the financial situation and consider additional public funding to provide the prescribed facilities for the future (Shepley and Barratt 1991).

What do the developments described in this chapter mean? And what does the future hold for football in the country which gave it to the world? I move towards answers to these questions in the final chapter.

7

INTERPRETATIONS AND PROSPECTS

In the preceding chapters I have described the changing geographical patterns of football at the intra-stadium (Chapters 2 and 3) and intra-urban (Chapters 4 to 6) scales. Each of these changing patterns is a result of attempts to *improve* the sport's environment – for players, for spectators, and for those who own the clubs. Although a recent book, *Football on Trial*, alluded to Britain's football grounds as 'reflections of residual resistance to processes of modernization' (Murphy *et al.* 1990), I would argue that the current spatial and environmental organization of football, both at the scale of the stands and the terraces and within the urban area itself, does, in fact, represent a 'modernizing' – perhaps not a full modernization but certainly a 'civilizing' – of the former unenclosed and socially integrated space of early organized football. I use the word 'civilizing' here in the sense used by Norbert Elias (Elias and Dunning 1989), and subsequently by Eric Dunning *et al.* (1989). As summarized by Dunning and Sheard (1979) the 'civilising process' has been characterized by:

1 an elaboration and refinement of social standards;
2 an increase in the social pressure on people to exercise self-control; and
3 the growth of more subtle and all-pervasive forms of external restraint, with the use of direct force being much less obvious than previously.

The application of each of these to the football environment in particular and to sport in general should be obvious from what I have written in the previous chapters, and mirrors the ideas – applied in different contexts – of a number of other scholars to whom reference has already been made.

The more 'civilized' and rationalized environment in which football is today played is indeed safer for spectators in a number of respects. It is probably safer to sit down to watch football just as it is safer for all supporters to be exposed to discrete surveillance operations. It is safer for fans to be herded from railway station to ground and it will be safer if new grounds are built at suburban sites. It may also be more comfortable to sit than to stand (though this is far from universally accepted by fans) and more comfortable to occupy a new suburban stadium than a dank inner-urban ground. Although many grounds in Britain may continue to be in Victorian locations and appear ramshackle by the standards of North American and many European stadiums (see Figure 7.1), modernizing (and 'civilizing') tendencies, of which the territorialization and rationalization (that is, the modernization) of football have been central features, have certainly seemed to be going on over the past century. Indeed, it can be argued that 'sports as theatrical representations, with a clear differentiation in space between different types of players (the ground, seating and stand) are undoubtedly a creation of modernity'.[1] In this chapter I first ask what interpretations might be placed on such modernization and territorialization, and then explore further the paradoxes of rationalism and of modern sportscapes. I apply to the football environment ideas developed from the work of Sack (1986), Relph (1976, 1981, 1987, 1989b), and Eichberg (1991a), respectively.

Figure 7.1 Bramhall Lane, home of Sheffield United, typifies the appearance of the English football ground

171

I will also explore what I tentatively call 'post-modern' tendencies in football's environment, fully recognizing that 'post-modernism' is a current buzz word; yet given recent developments in the football environment I find such an application difficult to resist. I am happy to adopt a definition which views post-modernism as an 'approach' which opposes the rationality of modernism,[2] mainly in a landscape context, reacting against the boredom and monotony of the modern world and accepting the validity of 'other people's' points of view. The landscapes of football are increasingly tending to defy neat and tidy categorization, at both intra-stadium and intra-urban scales, and I believe that there have been recent changes in the sport which *do* appear to be different from what went before in some ways. The question is how these changes should be interpreted. But first I want to look at the ways in which we can interpret one of the most characteristic tendencies of 'modernism' – that is, territorialization, one of the basic themes of this book.

INTERPRETING THE TERRITORIALIZATION OF FOOTBALL

The spatial confinement of the world's most popular sport has assumed a number of forms as the previous chapters have shown. The parcelling of the space in which games are played, the confinement of spectators in the stands, the route-marching of fans under police surveillance, and the location of stadiums in suburban 'pleasure zones' all exemplify the neat and tidy world resulting from the imposition of acts of territoriality with a place for everything and everything in its place.

In the words of Robert Sack, 'modern abstract emptiable space and impersonal relations may in themselves appear neither to be benign nor malevolent. But have they been used overall to one or the other effect?' (Sack 1986: 196). This is the question, applied to the football environment, that I want to explore, but as Sack goes on to say, 'we cannot hope to *prove* that they have or have not; we can only present arguments favoring one interpretation or the other' (Sack 1986: 196–7).

The increased efficiency view

The first interpretation (which in Sack's terms is a kind of neo-Smithian perspective) is that the various forms of territorialization in football help increase efficiency and 'productivity' and are for the benefit of all concerned. In a football context the compartmentalization of the stadium, the close surveillance of urban crowds, and the suburbanized, sanitized stadiums located away from residential areas, makes the management of the urban environment more efficient for the benefit of police, spectators, and public. The productivity of football can be increased by other rational developments such as the introduction of plastic pitches which produce more games and avoid the inconvenience of cancellations resulting from adverse weather conditions, and the sharing of grounds which increases the productivity of particular football spaces. The development of domed stadiums would further neutralize the effects of weather and other physical variables. The stadium as part of a leisure or retail complex can produce economies of agglomeration and contribute to the generation of *family* outings on Saturday (and Sunday) afternoons, breaking down the traditional gender-bound division of weekend time and replacing the masculine pre-match ritual of drinking in the local pub with Americanesque, car-park based 'tailgate parties' or whatever equivalent could be adapted to the European climate. In this way representational sports serve to assist the recomposition of community spirit and civic pride without the aberration of 'hooliganism'.

Club–community initiatives of various kinds also serve to further enhance a pride in place and a sense of community cohesion. Such initiatives are exemplified by that at Halifax where the ground is basically owned by the local authority. In this case Calderdale Council baled the club out of chronic financial difficulties, owns the ground, and is the majority share holder (Williams 1989). The football club's activities are monitored by an advisory panel made up of local councillors, club representatives, and supporters. As owners of the stadium at Halifax the council hires out the ground to the club for its matches, just as it would to any other user who wished to use it. The local authority subsidizes football in much the same way as it would subsidize the high cultural forms such as ballet, opera and art, for example, arguing that over the last century the commercial model of football has failed. Of 434 Halifax supporters questioned about such community involvement 47 per cent approved, with a substantial proportion (34 per cent) unsure and only a small number (18 per cent) disapproving (Sir Norman Chester Centre for Football Research 1990). The number of those disapproving among *non-fans* would likely be much larger. In the Halifax case, 70 per cent of fans felt that since the community had become involved with the club facilities for spectators had improved.

The Halifax case typifies intensive local authority involvement with the local football club and lies at one end of a spectrum which includes a

173

very varied degree of community–club interrelations. The Millwall case is one near to the Halifax end of the spectrum. The south-east London club has established strong links with the local community, not as a result of being owned by it but by intensifying (and, some would argue, resurrecting) its sense of identity with the local area. The club's attempt to redress the popular feeling of antagonism towards it involved bringing the club and local community into much greater contact than previously. Club facilities were opened up, not just to the young but also to the 'Over-50s Club' which meets weekly in the executive lounge; the club runs week-long soccer schools in local parks during school holiday periods; the club was the first to open a crèche; it initiated work-experience schemes for local youngsters; club staff take coaching sessions at a local school for students with severe learning difficulties; the club helped subsidize a local basketball team; the Millwall Lionesses use the club facilities and have become one of the major women's teams in the country; the club has a community development officer who is responsible for developing links with the community. The other side of the coin is provided by Lewisham Council which provides various forms of sponsorship (Lightbown 1989).

Other clubs have established some of these initiatives and a large number of community–school–club linkages have been developed. These include coaching of local schoolchildren, supervised match-day visits, social evenings, and old-age-pensioners tea parties.[3] Interpreted in these ways, the tendencies which have been described in previous pages are for the benefit of all parties concerned with the world of football.

The Marxist view

The second interpretation, which is more of a neo-Marxist perspective, would stress that territoriality in football cannot be properly understood unless it is couched within the context of capitalism on the one hand and class conflict on the other. Marxist geographer David Harvey emphasizes that

> capital seeks to discipline labor ... because it is only in terms of an all-embracing domination of labor, *in every facet of its life*, that the 'work ethic' and 'bourgeois values' necessarily demanded by the capitalist work process can be created and secured (emphasis added).
>
> (Harvey 1985: 57)

Improvements in football's environment would therefore be seen as 'illusions' which provide 'a sense of satisfaction and contentment which would lead to spontaneous cooperation and efficiency in the work place' (Harvey 1985: 56). In this interpretation, improvements in football are, like football itself, part of the 'bread and circus' ideology which keeps the work-force happy. Indeed, the neo-Marxist, Bero Rigauer (1981), argues that the standardized spatial and temporal confines of the field of 'play' *mirror* the standardized confines and restrictions of the workplace; and the spatial organization of sport space could be used as a model for the broader society. Territorialization also serves to subtly control people through its ultimate form of confinement to an individual space and through the various, but unobtrusive, forms of surveillance; the parallels with the factory will again be obvious.

As I noted in Chapter 2, representational sport tends to replace class conflict with place conflict. According to this interpretation, modern team sports serve to recompose communities which had been decomposed with the onslaught of the *Gesellschaft* society during the industrial revolution. In this way, as Hargreaves has noted, 'groups of similarly placed, deprived and exploited working class youth from different localities strive to defend the communities symbolized by the teams they support' (Hargreaves 1986: 44). The support for a *place* serves to obfuscate support for a social *class* and this interpretation, therefore, also views football ideologically. Different club affiliations in different stadiums in the same town serve to further divide the working class on the basis of place. From this perspective, as Alan Ingham and his associates cleverly point out, the contradiction

is between the *Gemeinschaft* of the mind and the objective relations of *Gesellschaft*. Via sport as a serialized civic ritual, those who would make our interpretations *for* us attempt to coopt the interpretations made *by* us in an assertion that the interests of the dominant are the dominant interests.

(Ingham *et al.* 1987: 460)

Taking the argument a stage further, the function of football (or in other countries other sports) in bonding the community together can also be interpreted as illusion. In fact, it can be argued that it serves a quite opposite function. My discussion of football's negative spillovers in Chapter 5 described such externalities in terms of physical impacts on the environment around the stadium resulting in local political activism or what US observers call 'turf politics' (an appropriate turn of phrase in the context of football). According to Kevin Cox (1984), the emergence of turf politics (or, perhaps, 'astroturf politics') results from the idea that the community is a kind of commodity – something from which certain kinds of people can be excluded. So while football claims to make a positive contribution towards community cohesion it can, at the same time, be interpreted as contributing towards intra-community conflict involving those who support and those who oppose football in urban (or suburban) stadiums.

THE LAST FOOTBALL LANDSCAPE?

I now want to examine the modernization of the football environment from a somewhat different perspective. As Edward Relph (1981) has put it, the western world has experienced 'powerful rationalistic techniques for manipulating environments and communities regardless of the values and qualities which might be displaced in the process'. I illustrated the paradoxical nature of the modern football landscape in Chapter 3 in which I showed how 'obvious gains and subtle losses ... are conjoined' (Relph 1981). I cannot describe the modern football milieu better than by including a lengthy further quote from *Rational Landscapes and Humanistic Geography*:

> The landscapes of scientific humanism are monumental achievements, huge and often spectacular in both their scale and design. But they are also frequently awful, dwarfing people, lacking detail, allowing no involvement ... They are a manifestation of rationalism pushed to its limits and already turning against itself, becoming restrictive rather than enlightening. In such modern landscapes humanism in any sense is already disappearing. The future to which they point is one with a landscape of efficient order, with occasional loud and glossy parts ... for a population too sated with material luxuries to notice or to care about the loss of values and of freedom. The means of control will have become invisible ...
>
> (Relph 1981: 211)

The application of these ideas to both the football stadium itself and the broader urban presence of the football industry should be obvious. But in view of the fact that territoriality of some kind or other will probably be employed in the years ahead what will football's future look like?

Whether it is at the intra-stadium or urban scale, most people would prefer good football landscapes to bad ones. This would apply to fans and non-fans, those actively and those passively involved in the sport, and those who love it and those who hate it. Relph's notion of good and bad landscapes can be applied to the world of sport in general and football in particular. Good football landscapes are, among other things, those which display evidence of local involvement (including that of local residents), possess elements which do not simply serve utilitarian ends but also give small pleasures, are imperfect in small ways (that is, 'human'), show responsibility for what has been inherited, and result from mutual aid. Bad football landscapes are the opposites of these. They are hard-edged, straight-lined and result from greed. There are plenty of examples of good and bad at both stadium and city levels of scale. Ultimately, what we get will depend on the planners and architects but we are not helpless puppets adopting knee-jerk responses to the decisions of a power-elite. I have tried to show that there has been a long history of active involvement from various actors on the football stage – fans, local residents, and community groups. And in any changes which may (or may not) be occurring in the map of British football it should be remembered that resistance to the sport-modernizing tendencies have, for different reasons, come from various muted and almost marginal (fan) groups within the urban arena and that the experience of the sport is a fractured one. Movements to resist organization of intra-stadium space or the removal of a club from a traditional site are established by the fans, expressing through their political actions the power of topophilia. Movements to resist the construction of new stadiums in suburban sites, on the other hand, come from middle-class suburban residents for whom football generates a sense of topophobia. Such residents will seek protection against the perceived devaluation of their capital and the ravages of 'development' at the city's edge. To paraphrase Relph, change in the football landscape should be resisted whenever it threatens the freedom of being able to take responsibility for one's environment and 'whenever it demonstrates manipulation through detached expertise' (Relph 1989b: 286).

In the mid-1930s J. B. Priestley commented that despite football being characterized by 'absurd publicity', 'monstrous partisanship' and widespread gambling, 'the fact remains that it is not yet spoiled' (Priestley 1984). Sixty years later I too ask whether the game has now been spoiled.

Since most British stadiums of today are, more or less, the same ones that Priestley was talking about, their fabric, geography and crowds are, basically, very similar to what they were like in the 1930s. Some changes, described in the early chapters of this book, have, of course, taken place, but their 'development' has not yet reached the stage of those in the American professional team sports industries with dominantly home crowds in continental-scale super-leagues and sanitized all-seater stadiums, or simply minor elements of larger service-industry complexes insulated from local residents by substantial parking lots or other forms of non-residential space, be they in city centre or suburban sites.

In conceptualizing the various forms football has taken, and which it could theoretically take in the future, I am drawn to Henning Eichberg's 'trialectic' of body- or movement-cultural configurations. This can be used to indicate the landscape implications of different kinds of movement cultures and, as applied to football, is shown as Figure 7.2.

At the present time football is mainly played in two of the forms shown in Figure 7.2 – as a serious professional sport where the essential aim is to win, and as a physical activity where the aim is to obtain exercise and enjoyment (that is, as part of Physical Education on the one hand and recreation on the other). Even at the level of the primary school the general tendency is for students to be pressured into the *leistungssport* (achievement sport) or disciplinary (PE) moulds. As Eichberg is at pains to point out, however, each of these forms of football is time- and space-bound (Eichberg 1985, 1990a, 1991a). They are contained within the straight lines of the pitch and the limits of the stop-

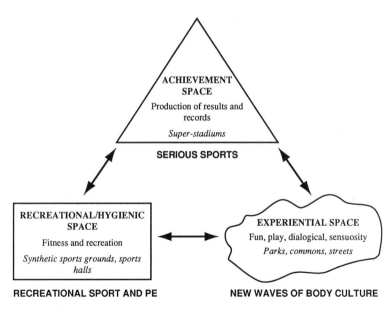

Figure 7.2 A sport landscape trialectic. (After Eichberg 1991a)

watch, adopting the geometrical and temporal traditions of space–time confinement. These characteristics of modernity define what are unquestionably the dominant modes within which the sport is practised but they are also the modes (especially that of serious professionalism) which are most likely to lead to bad football landscapes. So, first of all, how might achievement-football 'develop'?

In the future the mega-clubs will stage dramatic spectacles on a continental sporting stage. These clubs will be the inheritors of achievement space, an environment which has emerged as a result of enclosure, artifice, segregation, and confinement over a period of a century or more. The achievement space of sport mirrors that of society with its motorways, supersonic airline networks, concrete tower blocks, and shopping malls – straight-lined and efficient but often bland and boring. Such landscapes of achievement will be a response to the dictates of sport as business and, at the same time, its associated concerns with the *citius, altius, fortius* ethos and the safety and comfort of spectators. But as in other modern landscapes they will make people feel less like persons and more like things (Gregory 1989: 370). These landscapes of spectacle will attract the discriminating consumer rather than the committed fan, their stadium complexes covering substantial tracts and their fandoms covering vast geographic areas, international in scale. Because of their vast fandoms such clubs may be able to relocate without the locational constraints imposed by traditional hard-core fans who support the club first and the quality of football second. Such fans may 'support you evermore', but only within limited spatial margins. The super clubs will provide spectacles which may symbolize community – but they will only *symbolize* it. At this level at least, and in David Harvey's words, 'place and community' will have given way to 'space and capital' (Harvey 1989a: 17).[4]

Recreational football will grow while the lower divisional clubs will increasingly adopt a semi-professional outlook and develop closer links with their communities, with the sharing of their facilities and the possible reinstallation of multi-use surfaces. In some cases these clubs will be perceived by local governments in the same way as they view libraries or theatres. They will continue to face potential problems with the nuisances which they generate since most will be unable to find new locations in residence-free parts of the city. Football at the lower divisional levels will continue to reflect *local* pride in place. Already, such topophilic sentiments are cited by far more people as a reason for supporting a lower division club than the numbers mentioning it as a reason for supporting one of the mega-clubs (see Figure 7.3).

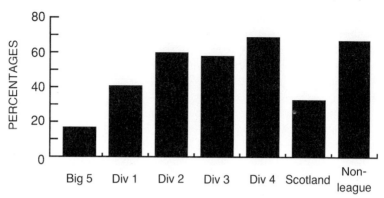

Figure 7.3 The varying percentages of respondents citing local pride as a factor influencing support for a team. The 'big 5' are Arsenal, Everton, Liverpool, Manchester United, and Tottenham
Source: Curren and Redmond (1991: 10).

Let me now return to Figure 7.2 and the third form of football – that which tends towards pure play and reflects the sport's folk-game traditions. This hardly exists any more except in its museumized forms at places like Ashbourne, Eton, and Florence where, because of its museumization it can hardly be called authentic, though some very limited evidence does exist of a renewed interest in less serious and less rational forms of football. The reassertion of football as pure play or frolic with a de-emphasis on achievement and victory would not require special spaces and would simply take place where room for play existed. Rigid rules would not exist, it would not be taken seriously, and it would espouse the dictum that if a thing's worth doing it's worth doing badly. Such a form of football may have existed, to some extent, in Maoist China and in the kind of games which were observed being played in the parks of Paris in the 'flower power' era of the late 1960s and early 1970s. Such latter games were typified by spontaneity; rules were liberally interpreted; they were games between teams, not clubs; they were not played in designated 'football spaces' and no touch lines existed, the ground often being as wide as it was long. The teams were composed of players of mixed age and gender and the number of players increased as more arrived. This was one part in a catalogue of new body cultures – alternative football or 'groovy soccer' (Bourdieu 1986: 222). A reduction in the seriousness of sports has also been typified by 'co-operative' games. Terry Orlick, something of a guru of the alternative games movement, has suggested various alternative forms of football including cases where goal scorers would change sides after scoring and for a team to win every player should have scored a goal (Orlick 1978, 1979). These kinds of activities, while having significantly different landscapes and environments from achievement-oriented football, are highly unlikely to replace football's other forms, though as I have shown, elements of play *have* reasserted themselves on the terraces.

The 'sports trialectic' is not static, the arrows between each mode of football (see Figure 7.2) showing shifts of emphasis and, indeed, there may be a hint of a breakdown in the territorialization of the English stadium, as described in earlier chapters. Eichberg (1991a) has argued that 'the configuration of sporting modernity *is* in question' and he hints at several tendencies already present in the game which demonstrate the equivocal nature of 'modernity' and its contradictory character. In other words the dichotomy between modern and post-modern football is itself equivocal. But how might *post-modern* football actually look? Is the sport being injected with more fun and laughter and less seriousness? Do the game's post-modern tendencies point, to some extent, towards the promise of some of Relph's 'good landscapes'? If so, I believe that they are most evident in five particular areas – each of which will be dealt with in turn before the 'concluding comments'.

The fences come down

In architecture it is widely regarded that the symbolic end of modernism occurred in 1972 when the Pruitt-Igoe apartment blocks in St Louis, constructed in the mid-1950s, were dynamited and demolished. The housing development had become uninhabitable. In British football 1990 might be flagged as the beginning of the post-modern stadium when the metal fences surrounding the pitches at many grounds were taken down and scrapped. As Hillsborough had demonstrated, the enclosed terraces (like Pruitt-Igoe) had become uninhabitable. The old suddenly seemed to be new again. This tendency towards a slightly reduced rigidity and a slightly increased permeability of the boundaries between players and spectators may mark the start of a blurring of inter-place divisions and reflect the increased permeability which some observers feel to be a feature of other areas of society (Meyrowitz 1985: 314). In a sense, therefore, stadium space is a macrocosm of the field of play with its spatial order and specialization of roles. But while the *overall* tendency on the field has been for the 'kick and rush' style to be replaced by a greater division of labour among players, from time to time a post-modern style has surfaced, best typified, perhaps, by the

181

'total football' of the Dutch teams of the late 1970s and early 1980s. And stadium space is also a microcosm of the broader urban space where exactly the same tensions exist – from growing order on the one hand to a tendency towards spatial disorder on the other (see pp. 184–5).

Also, the ambivalent plastic pitch (see Figure 7.4) meant that some football grounds became, for a few years in the late 1980s, 'shared spaces' which football used alongside other activities, an isotropic plane becoming a site for heterotopic play. Whether technology produces further improvements in playing surfaces which satisfy all participants in football, inducing a return to plastic, remains to be seen.

Football as carnival

The second post-modern trend is the way in which certain carnivalistic traits have appeared in the football environment in recent years, despite the confining tendencies described in Chapter 2. Just as in the 1960s and 1970s the terrace songs represented a 'musicalization' of football, so in the late 1980s there were attempts to enliven the increasingly and depressingly confined intra-stadium spaces with exuberance and colour. Although the colour of the banners and the flags which characterize terrace iconography in parts of Mediterranean Europe have not (yet?) appeared in Britain to nearly the extent found in Italy (see Figure 7.5), a counter-revolution which brought the fanzines, the inflatable icons, and increased use of face paints and zany fancy dress styles, has provided a post-modern and carnivalesque atmosphere to counter the pressures for zombie-like passivity. The hint of a shift in emphasis in England in 1991 was from the aggravation of the 'English hooligan' to the celebration of the 'Danish roligan' (*rolig* is Danish for 'peaceful') (Eichberg 1990b, Taylor 1991a),[5] but carnivals have always tended to be interpreted as a form of mild subversion and such developments in football can there-fore also be viewed as a subversive response to the bourgeoisification of the game for consumption by 'polite' society. I should note, however, that any relaxation in the attitudes of the authorities to terrace behav-iour can be interpreted as an attempt to *ritualize* such behaviour – that is, part of the 'football as safety valve' theory. The argument is that the carnivalization of football fan behaviour – like other forms of carnival – 'is a relatively harmless and ritualized way for subordinate groups to express their sense of injustice' (Jackson 1989: 80) – or, in a football context, their frustration.

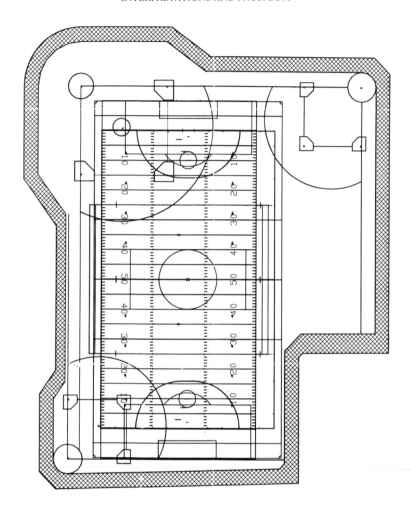

Figure 7.4 The ambiguity of a modern sports landscape. The Astroturf surface at the Demske Athletic Complex, Canisius College, Buffalo, New York, permits a wide range of body cultural events from baseball, softball, lacrosse, hockey, various kinds of football to carnival. While obviously 'modern' the playing surface permits a 'post-modern' use of sport-space; it is no longer a form of sport monoculture

Source: Astroturf Industries Inc.

Figure 7.5 Football, its iconography, and the atmosphere of carnival in the
Italian football stadium
Source: Bromberger (1988: 152).

Sports architecture and spatial planning

In recent years there has been growing criticism of 'container architecture' which, in the football context, is typified by the concrete bowl and
the football fortifications discussed in Chapters 2–4. There has also
been criticism of suburban stadium growth based on ecological (often
'deep ecological') criteria in that such developments become more
dependent than ever on the use of the motor car, the burning of more
oil, and the use of more concrete, implicitly demonstrating the dominance of achievement sport and its own 'achievement space' over nature
(Galtung 1984, Eichberg 1988). And I must re-emphasize the large
number of examples provided in previous pages of the active criticism
by football fans of many of the tendencies broadly described as 'modern'. The history of such resistance goes back to the traditions of folk-
football of course, and continues to the present day in the form of the
love affair that many fans have with their stadium, supporters' associations, and the associated political activism. Yet future stadiums need
not necessarily assume the bland containerized forms found in so many
new facilities (see pp. 48–9). Consider, for example, the Stade Louis

II in Monaco which Simon Inglis describes as a stadium 'only for want of a better word'. He notes that:

> the first thing that confounds most visitors when they arrive at the stadium's main entrance, is that there should be a football ground at all behind the facade; it is, apparently, no more than a collection of shops and offices, albeit ranged attractively in blocks of varying heights with modern, post-modern and traditional forms happily commingling. Inside the main entrance, so pristine are the chrome turnstiles, escalators and ticket booths that one still doubts that a stadium, rather than say, a hotel or conference centre, could lie within.
>
> (Inglis 1990: 110–11)

What is more, the complex contains four storeys of car parking space, an Olympic-sized swimming complex, a bistro, residential accommodation for young footballers, and a multi-purpose sports centre. It is a classic example of 'heterotopia' – a place made up of fragmentary and incongruous juxtapositionings. It would be extravagant to suggest that such design features were emerging in British football but the previously noted non-League Dorchester Town's ground (see Figure 7.6a) is certainly different from the quintessentially English ramshackle structures (see Figure 7.1) on the one hand, and the container architecture of high-modernism (see Figure 3.2) on the other. And the Don Valley stadium in Sheffield (see Figure 7.6b), built for the staging of the World Student Games in 1991 but potentially the shared home of the two Sheffield clubs, gives the impression of the 'inside-out' style of the Pompidou Centre or of Lloyds building in London.

Some sports environments have moved away from the straight lines and geometric traditions of record-oriented and competitive sports, the best example being in the architecture of water sports where the geometric pool has given way to milieux of fun and bodily experiences rather than competition and training.[6] It is doubtful whether the football environment will break out of its geometric confines in this way but it could be argued that football (and other team sports) has never become fully 'modern' in the sense that the ultimate modern sports event – the 100-metre sprint – has (Eichberg 1991b).[7] With its straight track, its synthetic surface, the runners' scientific starting practices, the aerodynamic clothing, the timing to one-thousandth of a second, the lack of time for competitors to make the slightest mistake, and the total absence of the opportunity to engage in banter or laughter, the 100 metres is the quintessence of the purest of modern sportifications. Foot-

185

A

B

Figure 7.6 Defying the stereotype: post-modern styles of design in British football. (a) A return to south of England vernacular at non-League Dorchester Town, and (b) the tubular exterior of the Don Valley stadium in Sheffield

ball, on the other hand, is still able to accommodate an element of play (as the antics of Gascoigne-style players show), even on the field. It certainly exists on the terraces. And in one respect its playing area has not become fully modern either; the sizes of grounds have never been standardized and despite an upper limit on length and breadth (see p. 10), considerable variation remains in the surfaces, slopes and sizes of pitches among British clubs (see Table 7.1).

Intra-urban location patterns

A fourth area of interest in any consideration of modernist/post-modern sports landscapes lies in the location patterns of football in urban space. The modern city is characterized by the suburbanward shift of a large number of traditionally central land uses – residences, retailing and industry, together with the presence of neat and tidy urban zonation. The football stadium should, according to rationalistic tendencies, also move to the suburbs and occupy 'sports complexes' or 'sports parks'. In earlier chapters I noted that pressures for such movement currently exist and that in both mainland Europe and the USA the suburbanization of sport has already begun. In the case of the UK such movement has been extremely limited (see pp. 146–9) and a wholesale flight to the suburbs has simply not happened; no *general model* of stadium location can be drawn up (the opposite of what modern urban theory would suggest) and football space is unevenly patterned in Britain's urban areas. In Britain's football space everything remains out of place. In the United States the inner-city stadium is viewed as a focus for downtown

Table 7.1 Extremes of pitch sizes in the UK football leagues

	Largest		Smallest	
Club	Pitch size (sq. yds)	Club		Pitch size (sq. yds)
Manchester City	9,401	Brechin City		7,370
Manchester Utd	9,164	Raith Rovers		7,571
Carlisle Utd	9,126	Cowdenbeath		7,632
Queen of the South	9,000	Clyde		7,632
Nottingham Forest	8,970	Halifax Town		7,700
Aldershot	8,816	St Johnstone		8,066

Source: *Rothman's Football Yearbook, 1987–88*, London, St Annes Press, 1988.

regeneration while in Britain the planning profession tends to favour the continuation of inner-city football, though in refurbished stadiums.

From internationalism to regionalism

A final focus for post-modern football may lie in its return to a more regionally based series of leagues, rather than the proposed internationalized Euro-League and the national-oriented English and Scottish Leagues. The reintroduction of regional leagues for the lower divisions has been advocated for several decades. In the 1930s and 1940s the Third Divisions were regionalized on the basis of North and South. Whether even smaller regional divisions will emerge, with clubs playing on a semi-professional basis in modest but safe grounds remains to be seen but regionalism and even localism could reassert themselves at the same time as the mega-clubs are developing the inevitable Continental-scale 'super league'. Such a development would parallel the growing interest in small-scale sports festivals and the revival of local games and sports (Eichberg 1991a).

The question remains, however, about how to interpret football's post-modern tendencies. Are they, as Marxists would suggest, simply part and parcel of the latest stage in the evolution of capitalism (Harvey 1989b), or are some of the tendencies which I have described a real drive towards a new view of sports landscapes, movement culture, and bodily experience?

CONCLUDING COMMENTS

This book started by considering the changing geography of the stadium and responses to such changes by those who occupy it. I was able to demonstrate that, at a certain level, resistance had taken place to the changes which had occurred, reflecting the love of place which fans had for their ground. But in subsequent chapters I also stressed that for other groups the stadium provided a source of nuisance and annoyance and that such groups could also resist the presence of football in existing and potential locations. The redrawing of the map of British football, both at the intra-stadium and intra-urban scales is, therefore, likely to be a process of *contestation* involving a variety of actors on the urban stage. Whether such resistance is an illusion and simply a safety valve can only be a matter of opinion. But within the broad structures of British society football does exemplify a context where rationalistic trends have been challenged. Partly as a result, the football landscapes of modern Britain are not quite what we might expect.

NOTES

1 INTRODUCTION: SPORT, FOOTBALL, AND THE CITY

1 For example, Critcher (1979); Ingham (1978); Marsh et al. (1978); Redhead (1986, 1991a). The coffee table end of the market is well catered for by Morris (1981).

2 Much of this is reviewed in Canter et al. (1989).

3 Although they tend to be set in a North American context, Guttmann's books are valuable aids to an understanding of modern sport per se. See Guttmann (1979, 1986, 1988).

4 A bibliography of Eichberg's writings on sport would fill many pages; several of his papers and books are cited in the bibliography to this volume. A good example of his provocative and stimulating writing is Eichberg (1988). Korsgaard's work is less prolific; good examples are Korsgaard (1982, 1989, 1990). Interesting fieldwork studies of football in selected French and Italian cities are found in Bromberger (1988, 1989a and 1989b).

5 A serious history of fanzines has yet to be written but until it is see Shaw (1989), Duke (1991), Redhead (1991a) and Jary et al. (1991). I should stress that in recent years fanzines have also emerged in sports such as cricket and rugby (both codes).

6 For an early, but brief, geographical view of football see Bale (1979).

7 The geography of sport has been approached from several perspectives. For representative examples see Rooney (1974), Rösch (1986), Mathieu and Praicheux (1987), Bale (1989a) and Errais et al. (1991). As in many other areas of the subject, some of the best 'geographical' work on sports has been written by non-geographers; see, for example, Eichberg (1988); Bromberger (1989a, 1989b).

2 THE CHANGING SHAPE OF THE STADIUM

1 For a discussion of the spatial bases of sport see Wagner (1981); note also Bale (1989a: 10–14).

2 Recent geographical writing has claimed Foucault as a 'post modern

geographer' given his concern with space and confinement; see, for example, Philo (1986); Soja (1989); Lowman (1989); Cloke *et al.* (1991: 194–6). In Foucault's own writings the 'geography' tends to be implicit. His most explicit comments are in Foucault (1980). The relevance of Foucault's work has also been noted in sports studies, though usually *en passant*; see Brohm (1978), Eichberg (1988: 27), Penz (1990), Giulianotti (1991), but note Harvey and Sparks (1991). I need to stress that I am using Foucault's description as an analogy.

3 There is some debate about the first use of the word 'record' as a noun; see Krüger and Ito (1977). The debate has, in fact, assumed the dimensions of a book: that of Carter and Krüger (1990).

4 It should be stressed that my concern is with British football. It has been suggested that in late sixteenth-century Florence a form of football (*calcio*) did possess precisely expressed and specific dimensions of the playing space based on measurements of the Piazza Santa Croce (see McClelland (1990: 55, 62n.)) but other sports historians dispute this claim (Pierre Lanfranchi, in conversation, August 1991).

5 Almost exactly the same point is made by Foucault (1980: 68): 'Territory is no doubt a geographical notion, but it's first of all a juridico-political one: the area controlled by a certain kind of power.'

6 Note also that 'by its very nature a spatial activity, sport naturally lent itself to geometrical quantification' (McClelland 1990: 61), though it should be pointed out that there is nothing natural about sport.

7 Similar spatial laws were applied to American football in the same period. In 1882, for example, the minimum yardage gain rule was introduced (see Reisman and Denny 1971).

8 Quoted in Soja (1989: 49–50). Note similar comments in Whitsun (1987: 245), showing how students of geography and sports each arrive at applications of Lefebvre's (1991) ideas.

9 The distinction between play and display was drawn by Stone (1971).

10 It is possible, of course, that little crowd trouble existed inside grounds because relatively few fans travelled to support away teams. I am unaware of any information which describes the ratio between 'home' and 'away' fans in the history of British football crowds.

11 For an example from Italy, see Bromberger (1991).

12 On surveillance see Dandeker (1990).

13 Quoted in Baade and Dye (1990).

14 Quoted in 'Football: a ritual of violence?', unpublished English version of Archetti (1992). I am grateful to Pierre Lanfranchi for a copy of this.

3 THE PARADOX OF MODERN STADIUM LANDSCAPES

1 Quoted in Wimmer (1975: 210).

2 Quoted in Wimmer (1975: 215).

3 Quoted in *Avon Calling*, no. 4, 1990.

4 Quoted in Keating (1990).

5 Quoted in Keating (1990).

6 'The stadium issue', *What a Load of Cobblers* 2 (6), 1990.

7 *The Lion Roars* 18, 1990, p. 20.

8 A survey of over 1,000 readers of *When Saturday Comes* revealed that '80% of terrace fans were against all seater stadiums'; see *When Saturday Comes* 51, 1991, p. 22. The overall evidence of these surveys suggests that 'the populist defence of terrace culture' *is* represented by fans and is *not* just the 'fantastic' representation of the 'well educated ... independent entrepreneurs producing the fanzines' (Taylor 1991b: 15).

4 FOOTBALL, THE STADIUM, AND A SENSE OF PLACE

1 Note also Lever (1983: 111).

2 The social control function of sport is a much debated subject. Examples where football was clearly used in such a way are found (for the case of Russia) in Walvin (1975) and (for the Witwatersrand) in Badenhorst and Rogerson (1985). Note also the neo-Marxist view of Brohm (1978).

3 Similar estimates were reached by Ferrier (1976).

4 Quoted in *Voice of The Valley*, no. 23, 1990.

5 For a comparison of distances travelled from home to ground when fans started supporting a club with that currently travelled see Curren and Redmond (1991: 20–1).

6 Chester City FC match programme 1989. I have been unable to identify the precise date of issue of the programme from which this extract comes. I am grateful to Rich Callaway for drawing my attention to it.

7 Note also Bromberger *et al.* (1991: 26–31) who list a large number of 'ingredients' of, at least Christian, religious practice in football. For example, each possesses the 'faithful', various 'brotherhoods', a theatricalization of social relations, the expectation of sacrifice and, as Charlotte Wilhelmsen (in conversation, October 1991) reminded me, the overwhelming dominance of men in organization and officiating.

8 For rituals associated with mourning in Liverpool following the Hillsborough disaster, see Walter (1991: 608–20).

9 Some parts of the stadium may, on the other hand, become derogatory places – even small landscapes of fear. Following the horror of Hillsborough, the Leppings Lane end of the ground was closed and for some time became a space for which no use could be found.

10 Bromberger *et al.* (1991: 29) refer to this as a form of 'fetishistic vigilance'.

11 But for an alternative view, applied to Fulham's Craven Cottage, see Magenis (1990).

12 Quoted in 'The Derby County Story', BBC Radio Derby, 1984. I am indebted to Andy Ward for providing me with a transcription of part of this recording. On olfactory environments, see Porteous (1985).

13 These are reviewed in Bale (1989a: 29–33).

14 Here, Malmberg is using 'territoriality' in a Lorenzian, not a Sackian, sense.

15 'Charlton's Vale of Tears', *The Guardian*, 9 September 1985.

16 Quoted in Hill (1990).

17 This subject is dealt with in many introductory texts. Two excellent examples (each of which just happen to include case studies from football) are Kirby (1982: Ch. 2) and Pinch (1985: Ch. 3).

18 Such comments are not restricted to football fanzines; similar views are expressed in those of other sports. Threatened in 1990 with having to leave their famous Odsal Stadium, fans of Bradford Northern Rugby League club mounted a campaign in *The Steam Pig*, the club fanzine. I am grateful to David Schofield for this information, and for a sample issue of 'the Pig'.

19 Details of the election results are in *Voice of The Valley*, no. 21, 1990.

5 WHEN SATURDAY COMES: FOOTBALL AS NUISANCE

1 The phrase 'landscapes of fear' is used by Tuan (1979) but his examples are mainly from historical contexts which is frustrating in view of the many modern landscapes which are extremely frightening for many people.

2 Liverpool City Council, 'Football in the Community', in Sir Norman Chester Centre for Football Research (1987b).

3 The basic conclusions of this study are summarized in Saunders (1972).

4 The ban was lifted in time for the 1991/2 season.

5 BBC TV, *Brass Tacks* showing of 'The English Disease', May 1988.

6 Their 'Up the City' is an unpublished English version of this paper.

7 The next few paragraphs are drawn from the unpublished English version of Goodey *et al.* 1986.

8 Solicitor's statement to the General Purposes Committee, Birmingham City Council, 13 April 1989 (emphasis added). I am very grateful to Iris Broadbent for much information on the conflict between Aston Villa and local residents' associations over this issue.

9 Letter to *Cambridge Evening News*, 10 July 1981. I am grateful to Gary Phillips for this reference.

10 Quoted in *Voice of The Valley*, no. 19, 1990, p. 53.

11 I am grateful to John Williams and Paul Weston for information concerning the National Federation of Stadium Communities.

6 QUESTIONS OF LOCATION AND RELOCATION

1 Quoted in Whitsun (1987: 242).

2 'The game that died', *The Economist*, 22 April 1989, p. 13.

3 Note also Waylen and Snook (1990).

4 Quoted in Williams *et al.* (1989a).

5 Quoted in BBC TV's *Brass Tacks* showing of 'The English Disease', May 1988.

6 Letter to the *Evening Post* (Bristol), 27 February 1989.

7 Noted in *What a Load of Cobblers* 2 (6), 1990.

8 This section is derived from Oliver (1986).

7 INTERPRETATIONS AND PROSPECTS

1   Quoted in the unpublished English version of Archetti (1992).
2   This is admittedly a crude definition of something which, almost by its nature, makes definition something of a contradiction. See, for example (among geographers), Gregory (1989), Harvey (1989b), Cooke (1990), Dear (1988), Relph (1991). A very good introduction is in Cloke *et al.* (1991: Ch. 6).
3   A survey undertaken in 1991 showed that 82 per cent of Football League clubs surveyed were running coaching courses in local primary schools (Eardley 1991).
4   The triumph of space over place is illustrated by the fact that almost 50 per cent of a sample of supporters of one of the super-clubs, Liverpool, agreed with the idea of the club occupying a new shared stadium in suburban Aintree. The proposed stadium was aborted because of its cost.
5   Note also Giulianotti (1991).
6   See, for example, Hess (1989) and Fache (1990).
7   The 100-metre straight lines on their isotropic plane bring to mind Le Corbusier, on the one hand, and Walter Christaller, on the other. The link between these two, modernist architect and positivist geographer, is illustrated by Ley (1989: 242).

BIBLIOGRAPHY

Ahrens, W. (1980) 'Playing with aggression' in J. Cherfas and R. Lewin (eds), *Not Work Alone*, London: Temple Smith.

Archetti, E. (1992) 'Il calcio: un rituale della violenza?', in P. Lanfranchi (ed.), *Il Calcio e suo Publico*, Naples: Edizione Scientifiche Italiane.

Allen, D. (1968) *British Tastes*, London: Hutchinson.

Baade, R. and Dye, R. (1988a) 'An analysis of the rationale for public subsidization of sports stadiums', *Annals of Regional Science* 22 (2), 37–47.

——, —— (1988b) 'Sports stadiums and area development: a critical review', *Economic Development Quarterly* 2 (3), 265–75.

——, —— (1990) 'The impact of stadiums and professional sports on metropolitan development', *Growth and Change* 21 (2), 1–14.

Badenhorst, C. and Rogerson, C. (1985) '"Teach the native to play"; social control and organized black sport on the Witwatersrand, 1920–1939', *GeoJournal* 12 (2), 197–202.

Bakhtin, M. (1968) *Rabelais and His World*, Cambridge, Mass.: MIT Press.

Bale, J. (1978) 'Geographical diffusion and the adoption of professionalism in football in England and Wales', *Geography* 63 (3), 188–97.

—— (1979) 'The development of soccer as a participant and spectator sport; geographical aspects', *State of the Art Review*, no. 20, London: Sports Council/SSRC.

—— (1988) 'Rational and rustic landscapes of cricket', *Sport Place* 2 (2), 5–16.

—— (1989a) *Sports Geography*, London: Spon.

—— (1989b) 'Football and topophilia; the public and the stadium', *Colloquium Papers*, 232/89, Florence: Centre for European Culture Research, European University Institute.

—— (1990) 'In the shadow of the stadium: Football grounds as urban nuisances', *Geography* 75 (4), 325–34.

Baumeister, R. and Steinhilber, A. (1984) 'Some paradoxical effects of supportive audiences on performance under pressure: the home field disadvantage in sports championships', *Journal of Personality and Social Psychology* 47 (1), 85–93.

Beauchampe, S. (1986) 'Family fodder', *Off the Ball*, November.

—— (1989) 'Scunthorpe living on the edge', *Off the Ball*, no. 16, 5–6.

Bennett, J. (1988) 'One man's Valley', *Voice of The Valley*, no. 1.

194

Berry, B. *et al.* (1974) *Land Use, Urban Form and Environmental Quality*, Research Paper 155, Chicago: Department of Geography, University of Chicago.

Bird, P. (1982) 'The demand for league football', *Applied Economics* 14 (6), 637–49.

Bishop, J. and Booth, R. (1974) 'People's images of Chelsea Football Club', Working Paper 10, Architectural Psychology Research Unit, Kingston Polytechnic.

Boal, F. (1970) 'Social space in the Belfast urban area', in N. Stephens and N. Glasscock (eds), *Irish Geographical Essays in Honour of E. Estyn Evans*, Belfast: Queens University.

Bourdieu, P. (1986) *Distinction: A Social Critique of the Judgement of Taste*, London: Routledge.

Bowen, M. (1974) 'Outdoor recreation around large cities', in J. Johnson (ed.), *Suburban Growth*, Chichester: Wiley.

Brohm, J-M. (1978) *Sport: A Prison of Measured Time*, London: Ink Links.

Bromberger, C. (1988) 'Sur les gradins, on rit . . . aussi parfors', *Le Monde Alpin et Rhodanien*, no 3/4, 137–56.

—— (1989a) 'Le stade de football: une carte de la ville en réduction', *Mappemonde*, no. 2, 37–40.

—— (1989b) 'Les dieux et L'Ohème', *Autrement*, February, 1–12.

—— (1991) 'Fireworks and the ass', Working Paper, Unit for Law and Popular Culture, Manchester Polytechnic.

——, Hayot, A. and Mariottini, J-M. (1987) 'Allez L'O.M! Forza Juve!', *Terrain*, no. 8, 8–41.

——, ——, —— (1991) 'Allez L'O.M! Forza Juve! The passion for football in Marseilles and Turin', Working Paper, Unit for Law and Popular Culture, Manchester Polytechnic.

Burgess, E. (1925) 'The growth of the city', in R. Park (ed.), *The City*, Chicago: University of Chicago Press.

Bushnell, J. (1990) *Moscow Graffiti: Language and Subculture*, Boston: Unwin Hyman.

Canter, D., Comber, M. and Uzzell, D. (1989) *Football in its Place*, London: Routledge.

Carter, J. and Krüger, A. (eds) (1990) *Ritual and Record: Sports Records and Quantification in the Pre-Modern Societies*, New York: Greenwood Press.

Cashmore, E. (1990) *Making Sense of Sport*, London: Routledge.

Centre for Leisure Research (1984) *Crowd Behaviour at Football Matches: A Study in Scotland*, Dunfermline: Centre for Leisure Research, Dunfermline College of PE.

Chamont, D., le Samedy, G. and Quantin, J. (1989) 'Les grandes villes et les clubs professionel de football', *Les Geographes et le Tiers Temps*, Cahier de Géographie 30, University of Besançon, 147–76.

Chester, N. (1965) *Report of the Committee on Football* (The 'Chester Report'), London: Her Majesty's Stationery Office.

Clarke, J. (1978) 'Football and working class fans; tradition and change', in R. Ingham (ed.), *Football Hooliganism: The Wider Context*, London: Inter-Action Inprint.

Clay, G. (1988) 'Run it down the field again, fellows', *Sport Place* 2 (2), 23–5.

Cloke P., Philo, C and Sadler, D. (1991) *Approaching Human Geography*, London: Paul Chapman.

Coakley, J. (1987) *Sport and Society*, St Louis: Mosby.

Coggan, P., Dawkins, W. and Wyles, J. (1990) 'Business pitches in', *Financial Times*, 25 September, p. 20.

Cohen, S. (1987) *Folk Devils and Moral Panics* (2nd edn), Oxford: Blackwell.

Coleman, J. (1961) 'Athletics in high school', *Annals of the American Academy of Political and Social Science*, no. 338, 33–43.

Coles, R. (1975) 'Football as a "surrogate" religion', in R. Hill (ed.), *A Sociological Yearbook of Religion in Britain*, no. 8, London: SCM Press.

Cooke, P. (1990) 'Modern urban theory in question', *Transactions of the Institute of British Geographers* (New Series) 15 (3), 331–42.

Cooper, S. (1990) 'Primary Schools, Football and the Community', Unpublished MA Dissertation, Keele University.

Cowan, M. (1990) 'Hearts in the right place', *When Saturday Comes*, no. 42, p. 6.

Cox, K. (1984) 'Social change, turf politics and concepts of turf politics', in A. Kirby, P. Knox and S. Pinch (eds), *Public Service Provision and Urban Development*, Beckenham: Croom Helm.

Critcher, C. (1979) 'Football since the war', in J. Clarke, C. Critcher and R. Johnson (eds), *Working Class Culture*, London: Hutchinson.

Curren, M. and Redmond, R. (1991) 'We'll support you evermore? Football club allegiance – a survey of *When Saturday Comes* readers', IT Working Paper, Sir Norman Chester Centre for Football Research, Leicester University.

Dandeker, C. (1990) *Surveillance, Power and Modernity*, Cambridge: Polity Press.

Dear, M. (1988) 'The postmodern challenge: reconstructing human geography', *Transactions of the Institute of British Geographers* (New Series) 13 (3), 262–75.

—— and Long, J. (1978) 'Community strategies in locational conflict', in K. Cox (ed.), *Urbanization and Conflict in Market Societies*, London: Macmillan.

Derrick, E. and McRory, J. (1973) 'Cup in hand; Sunderland's self-image after the Cup', Working Paper 8, Centre for Urban and Regional Studies, University of Birmingham.

Douglas, B. (1987) 'Fans rate major league baseball parks', *Sport Place* 1 (2), 36.

Dowse, R. and Hughes, J. (1977) 'Sporadic interventionism', *Political Studies* 25 (1), 84–92.

Duke, V. (1991) 'The sociology of football: a research agenda for the 1990s', *The Sociological Review* 39 (3), 627–45.

Dunning, E. (1990) *Soccer as a Political Football: The Game in Britain Now and in the Future*, Colloquium Paper 70/90, Florence: European Culture Research Centre, European University Institute.

—— and Sheard, K. (1979) *Barbarians, Gentlemen and Players*, Oxford: Martin Robertson.

——, Murphy, P. and Williams, J. (1989) *The Roots of Football Hooliganism*, London: Routledge.

Eardley, P. (1991) 'The football in the community project and its influence on primary schools' sport', Unpublished MA Dissertation, Keele University.

Edgell, S. and Jary, D. (1973) 'Football; a sociological eulogy', in M. Smith, S. Parker and C. Smith (eds), *Leisure and Society in Britain*, London: Allen Lane.

Ehrenberg, A. (1980) 'Aimez-vous les stades? Architecture du mass et mobilisation', *Recherches*, no. 43, 25–54.

Eichberg, H. (1982) 'Stopwatch, horizontal bar, gymnasium; the technologizing of sport in the eighteenth and early nineteenth centuries', *Journal of the Philosophy of Sport* 9 (1), 43–59.

—— (1985) 'De rette og de krumme linier', *Centring* 6 (2), 110–30.

—— (1986) 'The enclosure of the body – on the historical relativity of "health", "nature" and the environment of sport', *Journal of Contemporary History* 21 (2), 99–121.

—— (1988) *Leistungsräume: Sport als Umweltproblem*, Münster: Lit Verlag.

—— (1989a) 'The labyrinth – the earliest Nordic "sports ground"?', *Scandinavian Journal of Sports Sciences* 11 (1), 43–57.

—— (1989b) 'Body culture as paradigm: the Danish sociology of sport', *International Journal for the Sociology of Sport* 19 (1), 43–63.

—— (1990a) *Crisis and Grace: Football in Denmark*, Colloquium Paper 66/90, Florence: European Culture Research Centre, European University Institute.

—— (1990b) 'Forward race and the laughter of pygmies; on Olympic sport', in M. Teich and R. Porter (eds), *Fin de Siècle and its Legacy*, Cambridge: Cambridge University Press.

—— (1990c) 'Stronger, funnier, deadlier; track and field on the way to the ritual of the record', in J. Carter and A. Krüger (eds), *Ritual and Record*, New York: Greenwood Press.

—— (1991a) 'A revolution of body culture? Traditional games on the way from modernisation to "post-modernity"', in J-J. Barreau and G. Jaoueu (eds), *Eclipse et Renaissance des Jeux Populaires aux Regions des Europe*, Rennes: Institut Culturel de Bretagne.

—— (1991b) 'Race track and labyrinth: the space of physical culture in Berlin', *Journal of Sport History* 17 (2), 245–60.

—— (1993) 'New spatial configurations of sport? Experiences from Danish alternative planning', *International Review of the Sociology of Sport* 27, forthcoming.

Elias, N. and Dunning, E. (1986) *Quest for Excitement*, Oxford: Blackwell.

Errais, B., Mathieu, D. and Praicheux, J. (eds) (1991) *Géopolitique du Sport*, Besançon: Laboratoire de Géographie Humaine, Université de Franche-Commte.

Everitt, R. (1989) 'Battle for the Valley', *Voice of The Valley* no. 11, 18–22.

—— (1990) 'Political football', *When Saturday Comes* no. 41, p. 7.

Eyles, J. (1985) *Senses of Place*, Warrington: Silverbrook.

—— (1989) 'The geography of everyday life', in D. Gregory and R. Walford (eds), *Horizons in Human Geography*, London: Macmillan, 102–17.

Farnsworth, K. (1982) *Wednesday!*, Sheffield: Sheffield City Libraries.

Fache, W. (1990) 'Innovative water leisure centres in temperate countries', *Leisure and Society* 12 (2), 341–60.

Ferrier, A. (1976) 'Some traffic effects of spectator oriented sports events',

Unpublished MA Thesis, University of Manchester.

Fishwick, N. (1989) *English Football and Society 1910–1950*, Manchester: Manchester University Press.

Football Trust (1988) *Digest of Football Statistics*, London: The Football Trust.

Foucault, M. (1967) *Madness and Civilization*, London: Tavistock.

—— (1973) *Madness and Civilization*, New York: Random House.

—— (1979) *Discipline and Punish*, Harmondsworth: Penguin.

—— (1980) 'Questions on geography', in C. Gordon (ed.), *Power/Knowledge; Selected Interviews and Other Writings 1972–1977*, Brighton: Harvester Press.

—— (1982) 'Afterword', in H. Dreyfus and P. Rabinow *Michel Foucault: Beyond Structuralism and Hermeneutics*, Brighton: Harvester Press, 208–26.

Fyson, T. (1990) 'Should football decentralize?', *The Planner* 76 (5), 3.

GMA (1989) *Bristol Rovers New Football Stadium: Environmental Statement*, London: GMA.

Galtung, J. (1984) 'Sport and international understanding: sport as a carrier of deep culture and structure', in M. Ilmarinen (ed.), *Sport and International Understanding*, New York: Springer-Verlag.

Garven, R. (1990) 'Patron saint', *When Saturday Comes*, no. 46, p. 17.

Giulianotti, R. (1991) 'Scotland's tartan army in Italy: the case for the carnival-esque', *The Sociological Review* 39 (3), 503–27.

Goddard, J. (1984) 'Changes in the urban system', in J. Short and A. Kirby (eds), *The Human Geography of Contemporary Britain*, London: Macmillan.

Goldlust, J. (1987) *Playing for Keeps*, Melbourne: Longman Cheshire.

Goodey, B., Guttridge, I. and Smales, L. (1986) 'Indicao da tensao espacial', *Arquitetuia Urbanismo* 2 (6), 78–83.

Grayson, M. (1971) 'Travel generated by a football stadium', Unpublished M.Sc. Thesis, University of London.

Gregory, D. (1989) 'The crisis in modernity? Human geography and critical social theory', in R. Peet and N. Thrift (eds), *New Models in Geography* (vol. 2), London: Unwin Hyman.

Guttmann, A. (1979) *From Ritual to Record*, New York: Columbia University Press.

—— (1986) *Sports Spectators*, New York: Columbia University Press.

—— (1988) *A Whole New Ball Game*, Chapel Hill: University of North Carolina Press.

Hall, C. (1989) 'The politics of hallmark events', in G. Symes, B. Shaw, M. Fenton and W. Mueller (eds), *The Planning and Evaluation of Hallmark Events*, Aldershot: Avebury.

Halsall, M. (1991) 'Middlesbrough taps football and fission in its tourism drive', *The Guardian*, 3 January.

Hard, G., Gerdes, W. and Ebenham, D. (1984) 'Graffiti in Osnabruck: eine geographie spurrusicherung in einer kleinen Grosstadt', *Urbs et Regio*, no. 32, 265–331.

Hargreaves, J. (1986) *Sport, Power and Culture*, Cambridge: Polity Press.

—— (1987) 'The body, sport and power relations', in J. Horne, D. Jary and A. Tomlinson (eds), *Sport, Leisure and Social Relations*, Sociological Review Monograph no. 33, London: Routledge.

Harrington, J. (1968) *Soccer Hooliganism*, Bristol: Wright.

Harrison, M. (1988) 'Symbolism, "ritualism" and the location of crowds in early nineteenth century English towns', in D. Cosgrove and S. Daniels (eds), *The Iconography of Landscape*, Cambridge: Cambridge University Press.

Harrop, K. (1973) 'Nuisances and their externality fields', Seminar Paper no. 23, University of Newcastle-upon-Tyne.

Harvey, D. (1985) *Consciousness and the Urban Experience*, Oxford: Blackwell.

—— (1989a) 'From managerialism to entrepreneurialism: the transformation of urban governance in late capitalism', *Geografiska Annaler* 71B (1), 3–17.

—— (1989b) *The Condition of Postmodernity*, Oxford: Blackwell.

Harvey, J. and Sparks, R. (1991) 'The politics of the body in the context of modernity', *Quest* 43 (2), 164–89.

Hay, R. (1981) 'Soccer and social control in Scotland, 1873–1978', in R. Cashman and R. McKernan (eds), *Sport, Money, Morality and the Media*, Sydney: New South Wales University Press.

Hess, I. (1989) 'Bade-Landschaften', in H. Eichberg and J. Hansen (eds), *Körperkulturen und Identität*, Münster: Lit Verlag.

Hewitt, M. (1983) 'Bio-politics and social policy: Foucault's account of welfare', *Theory, Culture and Society* 1 (2), 67–84.

Hill, B. (1961) *Football*, Oxford: Basil Blackwell and Mott.

Hill, D. (1989) *Out of His Skin*, London: Faber.

Hill, R. (1990) 'The Power of Place in Professional Soccer', Unpublished Undergraduate Dissertation, Loughborough University.

Hoare, A. (1983) *The Location of Industry in Britain*, Cambridge: Cambridge University Press.

Holcomb, B. and Beauregard, R. (1981) *Revitalizing Cities*, Washington, DC: Association of American Geographers.

Holmes, C. (1985) 'Drainers and fenmen: the problem of popular political consciousness in the seventeenth century', in A. Fletcher and J. Stevenson (eds), *Order and Disorder in Early Modern England*, Cambridge: Cambridge University Press.

Holt, R. (1989) *Sport and the British*, Oxford: Oxford University Press.

Hopcraft, A. (1968) *The Football Man*, London: Collins.

Humphrys, D., Mason, C. and Pinch, S. (1983) 'The externality fields of football grounds; a case study of The Dell, Southampton', *Geoforum* 14 (4), 401–11.

IPC (1975) *Leisure*, London: IPC Marketing Services.

Ingham, A. and Hardy, S. (1984) 'Sport, structuration, subjugation and hegemony', *Theory, Culture and Society* 2 (2), 85–103.

——, Howell, J. and Schilperoort, T. (1987) 'Professional sports and community; a review and exegesis', *Exercise and Sports Sciences Reviews*, no. 15, 427–65.

Ingham, R. (ed.) (1978) *Football Hooliganism: A Wider Context*, London: Interaction Inprint.

Inglis, S. (1987) *The Football Grounds of Great Britain*, London: Collins.

—— (1990) *The Football Grounds of Europe*, London: Collins.

Institute for Advanced Studies (1987) *The Future of Football; Children's Opinions*, Manchester: Department of Law, Manchester Polytechnic.

Jackson, J. (1984) *Discovering the Vernacular Landscape*, New Haven: Yale University Press.

Jackson, P. (1989) *Maps of Meaning*, London: Unwin Hyman.

Jakle, J. (1987) *The Visual Elements of Landscape*, Amherst: University of Massachusetts Press.

Jary, D., Horne, J. and Bucke, T. (1991) 'Football "fanzines" and football culture: a case of successful cultural contestation', *The Sociological Review* 39 (3), 581–97.

Johnson, A. (1985) 'The sports franchise relocation issue and public policy responses', in A. Johnson and J. Frey (eds), *Government and Sport: The Public Policy Issues*, Totowa, N.Y.: Rowman & Allenheld.

—— (1986) 'Economic and policy implications of hosting sports franchises: lessons from Baltimore', *Urban Affairs Quarterly* 21 (3), 411–33.

Karp, D. and Yoels, W. (1990) 'Sport and urban life', *Journal of Sport and Social Issues* 14 (2), 77–102.

Keating, F. (1990) 'Ground for approval as Dorchester build a ground fit for a prince', *The Guardian*, 18 August, p. 14.

Keaton, G. (1972) *The Football Revolution*, Newton Abbott: David & Charles.

Kirby, A. (1982) *The Politics of Location*, London: Methuen.

Kircher, R. (1928) *The Games of Merrie England*, London: Collins.

Korr, C. (1986) *West Ham United*, Urbana: University of Illinois Press.

Korsgaard, O. (1982) *Kampen om Kroppen*, Copenhagen: Gyldendal.

—— (1989) 'Fighting for life; from Ling and Gruntvig to Nordic visions of body culture', *Scandinavian Journal of Sports Sciences* 19 (1), 3–8.

—— (1990) 'Sport as a practice of religion: the record as ritual', in J. Carter and A. Krüger (eds), *Ritual and Record*, New York: Greenwood Press.

Krüger, A. and Ito, A. (1977) 'On the limitations of Eichberg's and Mandell's theory of sports and their quantification in view of *Chikariaishi*, *Stadion* 3 (2), 244–56.

Labinski, R. (1986) 'The way forward', in Sports Council, *Football, the Club and the Community*, London: Sports Council.

Lang, J. (1969) *Report of the Working Party on Crowd Behaviour at Football Matches*, London: HMSO.

Lefebvre, H. (1991) *The Production of Space*, Oxford: Blackwell.

Lever, J. (1973) 'Soccer in Brazil', in J. Talimini and C. Page (eds), *Sport and Society; an Anthology*, Boston: Little, Brown & Co.

—— (1983) *Soccer Madness*, Chicago: University of Chicago Press.

Levi-Strauss, C. (1966) *The Savage Mind*, Chicago: University of Chicago Press.

Ley, D. (1989) 'Fragmentation, coherence, and limits to theory in human geography', in A. Kobayashi and S. Mackenzie (eds), *Remaking Human Geography*, Boston: Unwin Hyman.

—— and Cybriwsky, R. (1974) 'Urban graffiti as territorial markers', *Annals of the Association of American Geographers*, no. 64, 491–505.

—— and Olds, K. (1988) 'Landscape as spectacle: world's fairs and the culture of heroic consumption', *Society and Space* 6 (6), 191–212.

Lightbown, C. (1989) *Millwall*, London: Millwall FC.

Lipsitz, G. (1984) 'Sports stadia and urban development; a tale of three cities', *Journal of Sport and Social Issues* 8 (2), 1–18.

Lorenz, K. (1967) *On Aggression*, London: Methuen.

Lowman, J. (1989) 'The geography of social control: some clarifying themes', in D. Evans and D. Herbert (eds), *The Geography of Crime*, London: Routledge.

Lyngsgård, H. (1990) *Idraetens Rum*, Copenhagen: Borgen.

Maaløe, E. (1973) 'The aesthetic joy and repetition of the ever unpredictable', in R. Kuller (ed.), *Architectural Psychology*, Lund: Studentlitteratur, 135–47.

MacAloon, J. (1984) 'Olympic Games and the theory of spectacle in modern societies', in J. MacAloon (ed.), *Rite, Drama, Festival, Spectacle*, Philadelphia: Institute for the Study of Human Issues.

McClelland, J. (1990) 'The numbers of reason; luck, logic and art in Renaissance conceptions of sport', in J. Carter and A. Krüger (eds), *Ritual and Record*, New York: Greenwood Press.

Macfarlane, N. (1986) *Sport and Politics*, London: Collins.

Macgregor, A. (1989) 'I have seen the future', *The Absolute Game*, October/November, pp. 6–7.

Magenis, M. (1990) 'Craven image', *When Saturday Comes*, no. 38, p. 11.

Malcolmson, R. (1979) *Popular Recreations in English Society, 1700–1850*, Cambridge: Cambridge University Press.

Malmberg, T. (1980) *Human Territoriality*, The Hague: Mouton.

Markovits, A. (1988) 'The other American "exceptionalism" – why there is no soccer in the United States', *Praxis International* 8 (2), 125–50.

Marples, M. (1954) *A History of Football*, London: Secker & Warburg.

Marsh, P. (1977) 'Football hooliganism: fact or fiction?', *British Journal of Law and Society* 4 (2), 256–9.

——, Rosser, E. and Harre, R. (1978) *The Rules of Disorder*, London: Routledge.

Mason, C. and Robins, R. (1991) 'The spatial externality fields of football stadiums: the effects of football and non-football uses at Kenilworth Road, Luton', *Applied Geography* 11 (4), 251–66.

Mason, T. (1980) *Association Football and English Society, 1863–1915*, Brighton: Harvester.

Mathieu, D. and Praicheux, J. (1987) *Sports en France*, Paris: Fayard/Reclus.

Mehrabian, A. (1970) *Public Places and Private Spaces*, New York: Basic Books.

Meyrowitz, J. (1985) *No Sense of Place; the Impact of Electronic Media on Social Behavior*, New York: Oxford University Press.

Michener, J. (1976) *Sports in America*, Greenwich, Conn.: Fawcett.

Miller, H. and Jackson, R. (1988) 'The impact of the professional football strike on the Chicago land area', *Illinois Business Review* 45 (1), 3–7.

Moncrieff, A. (1991) 'The effect of relocation on the externality effects of football grounds: the case of St Johnstone Football Club', Unpublished Undergraduate Dissertation, Southampton University.

Moorhouse, H. (1984) 'Professional football and working class culture; English theories and Scottish evidence', *Sociological Review* 32 (2), 285–315.

—— (1990) *On the Periphery; Europe Viewed from East Stirlingshire, Forfar Athletic and Queen of the South*, Colloquium Paper 64/90, Florence: European Culture Research Centre, European University Institute.

Morris, D. (1981) *The Soccer Tribe*, London: Cape.

Murphy, P., Williams, J. and Dunning, E. (1990) *Football on Trial*, London: Routledge.

Murray, B. (1984) *The Old Firm*, Edinburgh: John Donald.

Mützelberg, D. and Eichberg, H. (eds) (1984) *Sport, Bewegung und Ökologie*, Bremen: Studienganges Sportwissenschaft der Universität Bremen.

Nagbøl, S. (1991) 'De levende og døde skygger', *Forskningsoverslgt*, Danish State Institute of Physical Education.

Neilson, B. (1986) 'Dialogue with the city; the evolution of the baseball park', *Landscape* 29 (1), 39–47.

Noll, R. (1974) 'The US team sports industry; an introduction', in R. Noll (ed.), *Government and the Sports Business*, Washington, DC: The Brookings Institute.

—— (1982) 'Major league sports', in W. Adams (ed.), *The Structure of American Industry*, New York: Macmillan.

Nys, J-F. (1990) *L'Economie du football en France*, Colloquium Paper 103/90, Florence: European Culture Research Centre, European University Institute.

Okner, B. (1974) 'Subsidies of stadiums and arenas', in R. Noll (ed.), *Government and the Sports Business*, Washington, DC: The Brookings Institution.

Oliver, G. (1986) 'The location and relocation of football clubs in England and Wales', Unpublished Undergraduate Dissertation, Southampton University.

Oriard, M. (1976) 'Sport and space', *Landscape* 21 (1), 32–40.

—— (1981) 'Professional football as cultural myth', *Journal of American Culture* 4 (3), 27–41.

Orlick, T. (1978) *Winning through Cooperation*, Washington, DC: Hawkins & Associates.

—— (1979) *The Cooperative Sports and Games Book*, London: Writers & Readers Publishing Co.

Osgerby, B. (1988) ' "We'll support you evermore": conflict and meaning in the history of a professional football club', *British Society of Sports History Bulletin*, no. 8.

Parkes, D. and Thrift, N. (1980) *Times, Spaces and Places*, Chichester: Wiley.

Peabody, R. (1988) 'When Saturday comes; football's imprint on the urban landscape', Unpublished Undergraduate Dissertation, Cambridge University.

Penz, O. (1990) 'Sport and speed', *International Review for Sport Sociology* 25 (2), 158–67.

Philo, C. (1986) ' "The same and the other": on geographies, madness and outsiders', Occasional Paper no. 11, Loughborough: Department of Geography, Loughborough University.

—— (1989) ' "Enough to drive one mad"; the organization of space in 19th. century lunatic asylums', in J. Wolch and M. Dear (eds), *The Power of Geography*, London: Unwin Hyman.

Pinch, S. (1985) *Cities and Services*, London: Routledge.

Pollard, R. (1987) 'The home advantage in soccer; a retrospective analysis', *Journal of Sports Sciences* 4 (3), 237–48.

Polsky, N. (1985) *Hustlers, Beats and Others*, Chicago: University of Chicago Press.

Porteous, D. (1985) 'Smellscape', *Progress in Human Geography* 9 (3), 356–78.

Pratt, J. and Salter, M. (1984) 'A fresh look at football hooliganism', *Leisure Studies* 3 (3), 201–30.

Priestley, J.B. (1984) *English Journey* (Jubilee edition), London: Heinemann.

Raitz, K. (1987) 'Perception of sports landscapes and gratification in the sports experience', *Sport Place* 1 (1), 4–19.

—— (1988) 'Place, space and environment in America's leisure landscapes',

Journal of Cultural Geography 8 (1), 5–16.

Redhead, S. (1986) *Sing When You're Winning*, London: Pluto.

—— (1991a) *Football with Attitude*, Manchester: Wordsmith.

—— (1991b) 'Some reflections on discourses on football hooliganism', *The Sociological Review* 39 (3), 479–86.

Reisman, D. and Denny, R. (1971) 'Football in America: a study in cultural diffusion', in E. Dunning (ed.), *The Sociology of Sport*, London: Cass.

Reiss, S. (1978) 'The geography and history of professional ball parks 1871–1930', *Proceedings of the American Society of Sports History*, 35–6.

Relph, E. (1976) *Place and Placelessness*, London: Pion.

—— (1981) *Rational Landscapes and Humanistic Geography*, London: Croom Helm.

—— (1987) *The Modern Urban Landscape*, London: Croom Helm.

—— (1989a) 'Responsive methods, geographical imagination and the study of landscapes', in A. Kobayashi and A. Mackenzie (eds), *Remaking Human Geography*, London: Unwin Hyman.

—— (1989b) 'A curiously unbalanced condition of the powers of mind: realism and the ecology of environmental experience', in D. Livingstone and F. Boal (eds), *The Behavioural Environment*, London: Routledge.

—— (1991) 'Postmodern geography', *The Canadian Geographer* 35 (1), 98–105.

Rigauer, B. (1981) *Sport and Work* (trans. A. Guttmann), New York: Columbia University Press.

Rivett, P. (1975) 'The structure of League Football', *Operational Research Quarterly*, no. 26, 801–12.

Roadburg, A. (1980) 'Factors precipitating fan violence', *British Journal of Sociology* 31 (2), 265–76.

Robins, D. and Cohen, P. (1978) *Knuckle Sandwich*, Penguin, Harmondsworth.

Robson, B. (1982) 'The Bodley barricade: social space and social conflict', in K. Cox and R. Johnston (eds), *Conflict, Politics and the Urban Scene*, London: Longman.

Rooney, J. (1974) *A Geography of American Sport; from Cabin Creek to Anaheim*, Reading, Mass.: Addison-Wesley.

Rösch, H-E. (1986) *Sport und Geographie*, Düsseldorfer Sportwissenschaftliche Studien, no. 1, University of Düsseldorf.

Rosentraub, M. (1977) 'Financial incentives, locational decision-making and professional sports; the case of the Texas Ranger baseball network and the city of Arlington, Texas', in M. Rosentraub (ed.), *Financing Local Government; New Approaches to Old Problems*, Fort Collins: Western Social Science Association.

—— and Nunn, S. (1977) 'Suburban city investment in professional sports; estimating the fiscal returns of the Dallas Cowboys and Texas Rangers to investor communities', *American Behavioral Scientist* 21 (3), 393–414.

Sack, R. (1986) *Human Territoriality*, Cambridge: Cambridge University Press.

Saunders, L. (1972) 'The characteristics and impact of travel generated by Chelsea Football Club', Research Memorandum no. 344, London: GLC Department of Planning and Transportation.

Schaffer, W. and Davidson, L. (1985) *Economic Impact of the Falcons on Atlanta: 1984*, Suwanee, Ga.: Atlanta Falcons.

Scottish Education Department (1977) *Report of the Working Group on Football Crowd Behaviour*, Edinburgh: HMSO.

Seamon, D. (1979) *A Geography of the Lifeworld*, London: Croom Helm.

Shaw, P. (1989) *Whose Game is it Anyway?*, Hemel Hempstead: Argus Books.

Shepherd, J. (1990) 'Violent crime in Bristol', *British Journal of Criminology* 30 (3), 287–305.

Shepley, C. (1990) 'Planning and Football League grounds', *The Planner* 76 (38), 15–17.

—— and Barratt, A. (1991) 'Football League grounds – update', *The Planner* 77 (17), 8–9.

Shields, R. (1991) *Places on the Margin*, London: Routledge.

Short, J. (1986) *The Humane City*, Oxford: Blackwell.

Sibley, D. (1981) *Outsiders in Urban Societies*, Oxford: Blackwell.

Simon, B. (1991) 'The roof starts to fall in on Toronto's SkyDome', *Financial Times*, 2 February.

Sir Norman Chester Centre for Football Research (1987a) *Football and Football Hooliganism in Liverpool*, Leicester: Department of Sociology, Leicester University.

—— (1987b) *Young People's Images of Attending Football*, Leicester, Department of Sociology, Leicester University.

—— (1989a) *Crowd Control and Membership at Football*, Leicester: Department of Sociology, Leicester University.

—— (1989b) *Football and Football Spectators after Hillsborough: A National Survey of Members of the Football Supporters Association*, Leicester: Department of Sociology, Leicester University.

—— (1990) *Halifax Town Survey*, Leicester: Department of Sociology, Leicester University.

Sloane, P. (1971) 'The economics of professional football; the football club as a utility maximiser', *Scottish Journal of Political Economy* 18 (2), 121–46.

—— (1980) *Sport in the Market?*, Hobart Paper no. 85, London: Institute of Economic Affairs.

Smith, M. and Keller, M. (1986) 'Managed growth and the politics of uneven development in New Orleans', in S. Fainstein, N. Fainstein, R. Hill, D. Judd and M. Smith (eds), *Restructuring the City*, New York: Longman.

Smith, P. (1979) *Architecture and the Human Dimension*, Westfield, N.J.: Eastview Editions.

Soja, E. (1989) *Postmodern Geographies*, London: Verso.

Sommer, J. (1975) 'Fat city and Hedonopolis: the American urban future?', in R. Abler, D. Janelle, A. Philbrick and J. Sommer (eds), *Human Geography in a Shrinking World*, North Scituate, Mass.: Duxbury Press.

Sports Council (1986) *Football, the Club and the Community*, (Workshop Report), London: The Sports Council.

—— (1991) *A Stadium for the Nineties*, London: The Sports Council.

Stone, G. (1971) 'American sports; play and display', in E. Dunning (ed.), *The Sociology of Sport*, London: Cass.

Taylor, I. (1971a) 'Football mad; a speculative sociology of football hooliganism', in E. Dunning (ed.), *The Sociology of Sport*, London: Cass.

—— (1971b) 'Soccer consciousness and soccer hooliganism', in S. Cohen (ed.), *Images of Deviance*, Harmondsworth: Penguin.

—— (1989) 'Hillsborough, 15 April 1989: some personal contemplations', *New Left Review*, no. 177, 89–110.

—— (1991a) 'From aggravation to celebration', *The Independent*, 21 April, p. 31.

—— (1991b) 'English football in the 1990s: taking Hillsborough seriously?', in J. Williams and S. Wagg (eds), *British Football and Social Change*, Leicester: Leicester University Press.

Taylor, Lord Justice (1990) *The Hillsborough Stadium Disaster; Final Report*, London: HMSO.

Thorpe, M. (1989) 'Scottish arrests point up card contradiction', *The Guardian*, 17 January, p. 14.

Thrift, N. (1981) 'Owners' time and own time: the making of a capitalist time-consciousness, 1300–1880', in A. Pred (ed.), *Space and Time in Geography*, Lund: Gleerup.

Tipp, G. and Watson, V. (1982) *Polymeric Surfaces for Sports and Recreation*, London: Applied Science Publications.

Tischler, S. (1981) *Footballers and Businessmen*, New York: Holmes & Meyer.

Trivizas, E. (1980) 'Offences and offenders in football crowd disorders', *British Journal of Criminology* 20 (3), 281–3.

Tuan, Y-F. (1974) *Topophilia*, Englewood Cliffs: Prentice-Hall.

—— (1975) 'Geopeity; a theme in man's attachment to nature and to place', in D. Lowenthal and M. Bowden (eds), *Geographies of the Mind*, New York: Oxford University Press.

—— (1977) *Space and Place*, London: Arnold.

—— (1979) *Landscapes of Fear*, Oxford: Blackwell.

—— (1984) *Dominance and Affection: the Making of Pets*, New Haven: Yale University Press.

Vamplew, W. (1989) *Pay up and Play the Game*, Cambridge: Cambridge University Press.

Von Kortzfleisch, S. (1970) 'Religious Olympism', *Social Research* 37 (2), 231–6.

Wadmore, J. (1988) 'No end of trouble', *When Saturday Comes*, no. 15, 16–17.

Wagg, S. (1984) *The Football World*, Brighton: Harvester.

Wagner, P. (1981) 'Sport: culture and geography', in A. Pred (ed.), *Space and Time in Geography*, Lund: Gleerup.

Walter, T. (1991) 'The mourning after Hillsborough', *The Sociological Review* 39 (3), 599–625.

Walvin, J. (1975) *The People's Game*, London: Allen Lane.

—— (1986) *Football and the Decline of Britain*, London: Macmillan.

Waylen, P. and Snook, A. (1990) 'Patterns of regional success in the Football League, 1921 to 1987', *Area* 22 (4), 353–67.

Webber, M. (1963) 'Order in diversity; community without propinquity', in L. Wingo (ed.), *Cities and Space*, Baltimore, Md.: Johns Hopkins University Press.

Wesson, A. (1987) 'The Luton Experiment; a home win', *Justice of the Peace*, 31 January, p. 72.

Whitsun, D. (1987) 'Leisure, the state and collective consumption', in J. Horne, D. Jary and A. Tomlinson (eds), *Sport, Leisure and Social Relations*, Sociological Review Monograph no. 33, London: Routledge.

Williams, J., Dunning, E. and Murphy, P. (1989a) *The Luton Town Members Scheme; Final Report*, Leicester: Department of Sociology, Leicester University.

——, ——, —— (1989b) *Crowd Control and Membership at Football*, Leicester: Department of Sociology, Leicester University.

——, ——, —— (1989c) *Hooligans Abroad* (2nd edn), London: Routledge.

Williams, J. and Wagg, S. (eds) (1991) *British Football and Social Change*, Leicester: Leicester University Press.

Williams, R. (1989) 'Shay business', *When Saturday Comes*, no. 32, 8–9.

Wimmer, M. (1975) *Olympic Buildings*, Leipzig: Editions Leipzig.

Zeller, R. and Jurkovac, T. (1989) 'A dome stadium; does it help the home team in the National Football League', *Sport Place* 3 (3), 36–9.

INDEX

207